SAP PRESS e-books

Print or e-book, Kindle or iPad, workplace or airplane: Choose where and how to read your SAP PRESS books! You can now get all our titles as e-books, too:

- By download and online access
- For all popular devices
- And, of course, DRM-free

Convinced? Then go to www.sap-press.com and get your e-book today.

 PRESS

SAP PRESS is a joint initiative of SAP and Rheinwerk Publishing. The know-how offered by SAP specialists combined with the expertise of Rheinwerk Publishing offers the reader expert books in the field. SAP PRESS features first-hand information and expert advice, and provides useful skills for professional decision-making.

SAP PRESS offers a variety of books on technical and business-related topics for the SAP user. For further information, please visit our website: *www.sap-press.com*.

Merz, Hügens, Blum
Implementing SAP BW on SAP HANA
2015, 467 pages, hardcover and e-book
www.sap-press.com/3609

Brogden, Sinkwitz, Marks, Orthous
SAP BussinessObjects Web Intelligence (3rd Edition)
2014, 691 pages, hardcover and e-book
www.sap-press.com/3673

Silvia, Frye, Berg
SAP HANA: An Introduction (4th Edition)
2017, 549 pages, hardcover and e-book
www.sap-press.com/4160

Baumgartl, Chaadaev, Choi, Dudgeon, Lahiri, Meijerink, Worsley-Tonks
SAP S/4HANA: An Introduction
2017, 449 pages, hardcover and e-book
www.sap-press.com/4153

SAP BW/4HANA®

Jesper Christensen, Joe Darlak, Riley Harrington,
Li Kong, Marcos Poles, Christian Savelli

SAP BW/4HANA®

An Introduction

Rheinwerk
Publishing

Editor Meagan White
Acquisitions Editor Hareem Shafi
Copyeditor Melinda Rankin
Cover Design Graham Geary
Photo Credit Shutterstock.com/374577103/© Lagarto Film
Layout Design Vera Brauner
Production Marissa Fritz
Typesetting III-satz, Husby (Germany)
Printed and bound in the United States of America, on paper from sustainable sources

ISBN 978-1-4932-1531-7
© 2017 by Rheinwerk Publishing, Inc., Boston (MA)
1st edition 2017

Library of Congress Cataloging-in-Publication Data
Names: Christensen, Jesper, author.
Title: SAP BW/4HANA : an introduction / Jesper Christensen, Joe Darlak, Riley
  Harrington, Kong Li, Christian Savelli, Marcos Poles.
Description: 1st edition. | Bonn ; Boston : Rheinwerk Publishing, 2017. |
  Includes index.
Identifiers: LCCN 2017011723 | ISBN 9781493215317 (alk. paper)
Subjects: LCSH: SAP Business information warehouse. | Database management. |
  Data warehousing. | Business intelligence--Data processing. | Management
  information systems.
Classification: LCC HF5548.4.B875 C468 2017 | DDC 005.7--dc23 LC record available at https://lccn.loc.gov/2017011723

Contents at a Glance

Dear Reader,

For years, SAP HANA has been the talk of the town, as the database and platform revolutionizing IT environments. But it can't do everything on its own. To integrate, manage, and store data, you need a robust data warehouse like SAP BW. Put these two all-star solutions together and you have a powerful product that allows you to leverage huge amounts of business data in real time.

Between these pages, you'll find everything you need to get started with SAP BW/4HANA. Expert authors Jesper Christensen, Joe Darlak, Riley Harrington, Li Kong, Marcos Poles, and Christian Savelli have provided you with the latest on what this solution offers. From the simplified data models to new ways of handling data lifecycle management, you'll see what SAP BW/4HANA can do for you!

As always, your comments and suggestions are the most useful tools to help us make our books the best they can be. Let us know what you thought about *SAP BW/4HANA: An Introduction*! Please feel free to contact me and share any praise or criticism you may have.

Thank you for purchasing a book from SAP PRESS!

Meagan White
Editor, SAP PRESS

meaganw@rheinwerk-publishing.com
www.sap-press.com
Rheinwerk Publishing · Boston, MA

Contents

3 Installation and Setup

4 SAP BW/4HANA in the Cloud

5   Data Modeling   101

8   Integrating External Data   251

11 Security

12   The Future of SAP BW/4HANA   397

Preface

Welcome to the first book on SAP BW/4HANA. SAP Business Warehouse (SAP BW) has been in the market for many years, but the release of SAP BW/4HANA has changed the landscape. SAP BW/4HANA is an entirely new application with new features—not part of the legacy SAP BW.

Who This Book Is For

This book is for anyone interested in learning about SAP BW/4HANA and its key components. While prior knowledge of SAP BW is not required, we will cover the differences between SAP BW/4HANA and SAP BW powered by SAP HANA for those who are already familiar with the current solutions. Customers, partners, consultants, business leaders, and process owners planning to evaluate or implement SAP BW/4HANA will find this book a good starting point.

How This Book Is Organized

We have organized this book into technical and functional chapters covering the capabilities of SAP BW/4HANA. Each chapter covers the following:

- **Chapter 1**
  This chapter introduces SAP BW/4HANA, discusses how it is different from SAP BW and SAP BW powered by SAP HANA, and briefly discusses the benefits and capabilities of SAP BW/4HANA.
- **Chapter 2**
  This chapter provides you with an introduction to SAP HANA. It discusses deployment options, hardware options, and the different ways in which SAP HANA can be used.
- **Chapter 3**
  This chapter provides you with instructions for installing and setting up SAP BW/4HANA.
- **Chapter 4**
  This chapter discusses SAP BW/4HANA in the cloud, with a close look at the cloud providers and some criteria for choosing the correct cloud provider for your company.

- **Chapter 5**

  This chapter covers data modeling with SAP BW/4HANA. It discusses the new, simplified data models in SAP BW/4HANA, as well as the process of data modeling.

- **Chapter 6**

  This chapter covers data acquisition, including the different source systems and data sources supported for loading data into SAP BW/4HANA.

- **Chapter 7**

  This chapter provides you with information regarding reporting and analytics in SAP BW/4HANA. It has information covering topics from SAP BW/4HANA queries to SAP BusinessObjects and third-party tools.

- **Chapter 8**

  This chapter covers integrating external data into SAP BW/4HANA. It discusses SAP HANA smart data access and SAP HANA smart data integration, among other tools.

- **Chapter 9**

  This chapter cover data lifecycle management in SAP BW/4HANA. The chapter includes information on hot storage, warm storage, and cold storage, as well as near-line storage.

- **Chapter 10**

  This chapter cover administrative tasks for SAP BW/4HANA. It divides tasks by frequency, from those that must be performed every day, to those that are monthly, quarterly, or even annual.

- **Chapter 11**

  This chapter cover SAP BW/4HANA security, including roles, authorizations, privileges, and handling secure access to data in SAP BW/4HANA.

- **Chapter 12**

  This chapter cover the SAP BW/4HANA roadmap and future outlook.

We recommend reading this book sequentially from Chapter 1 onward; however, if you prefer, you can directly go to any chapter and start reading about that topic.

Acknowledgments

As mentioned previously, a book such as this one, which provides an overview of the SAP BW/4HANA solution is a true team effort. First, the book would not exist if the management team at Comerit did not believe in the project and provide their enthusiastic support. We would also like to thank Hareem Shafi and Meagan White at Rheinwerk Publishing.

Conclusion

Reading this book will provide you with a comprehensive overview of SAP BW/4HANA solution and empower you to engage confidently in any SAP BW/4HANA evaluation and implementation conversation. This book will serve as your foundational knowledge source for the SAP BW/4HANA product, and you can build on your knowledge with SAP BW/4HANA training and additional resources that are available from. Let's get started and proceed to Chapter 1 with an overview of SAP BW and SAP BW/4HANA.

Chapter 1
Introduction to SAP BW/4HANA

In this chapter, we'll look at how SAP BW has evolved until now and what makes SAP BW/4HANA different. We'll also provide a high-level overview of SAP BW/4HANA's capabilities.

SAP Business Warehouse (SAP BW) as an application has been around since 1998 and has evolved tremendously over the years. With SAP BW/4HANA, SAP is taking a step toward discontinuing the legacy SAP BW application and replacing it with a more modern and agile application that should help improve the time to information for companies. This chapter will look at the history of SAP BW, then give a brief overview of SAP BW/4HANA and the implementation approach options available for SAP BW/4HANA.

1.1 History of SAP BW

SAP BW was developed as a product for offloading the reporting workload from SAP R/3 systems to avoid performance issues caused by reporting and improve analytical capabilities with online analytical processing (OLAP) "slice and dice" analysis, allowing for easily interchanging measures and characteristics at runtime. In this section, we'll cover some of the main SAP BW releases and what capabilities they offered to help illustrate how SAP BW became what it is today.

Figure 1.1 shows the SAP BW releases timeline, starting in 1998 and running to 2016 and the release of SAP BW/4HANA.

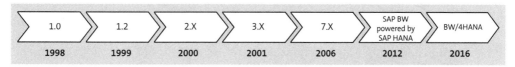

Figure 1.1 SAP BW Release Timeline

1.1.1   SAP BW Release 1.0

The first release of SAP BW wasn't generally available. A few select customers agreed to be part of a pilot program and started their implementations with SAP BW 1.0, but most customers went live with release 1.2 in the following year.

The initial SAP BW release 1.0 was based on Ralph Kimball's data mart principles, described in his book, *The Data Warehouse Lifecycle Toolkit*.

The InfoCube was the only InfoProvider type that could be used for reporting. What set SAP BW apart from other tools was that SAP included standard data models and extraction programs for a few reporting areas with SAP BW, which gave customers quick implementation of elements such as sales reporting compared to building custom data marts.

The frontend for release 1.0 was Excel-based and had slice and dice capabilities. This was a great improvement over some of the list reports available in SAP R/3. The frontend tool was based on SAP's Open Information Warehouse Excel frontend for SAP R/3 and was further developed for SAP BW.

1.1.2   SAP BW Release 1.2

SAP BW 1.2A was released in 1998; release 1.2B in 1999 was the official release, with general availability for customers to implement SAP BW for production use.

SAP BW release 1.2 provided a small set of data-modeling options structured around the following elements:

- **Standard extractors**
  Standard extractors were available for many more SAP R/3 modules, and flat file loading was available to load external data into SAP BW.

- **Transfer and update rules**
  Transfer and update rules were used to apply transformations to the data in SAP BW. The rules allowed for full use of the ABAP Workbench and programming language, which made them very flexible.

- **InfoObject**
  InfoObjects were the building blocks of SAP BW and provided the capability to build both simple and complex data entities with master data, language-dependent texts, and hierarchies.

- **InfoCube**
  InfoCubes were the multidimensional data marts used for reporting; all queries were developed on InfoCubes. The extended star schema made it possible to build

models that reused InfoObjects across subject areas, but data integration required all fact data to be in one InfoCube.

- **MultiProvider**
  MultiProviders introduced the capability to union data from multiple InfoProviders for use in reporting. This opened the option to separate data in InfoProviders by data type and combine it for reporting.

- **SAP Business Explorer frontend tools**
  The frontend tool was SAP Business Explorer (SAP BEx) analyzer, embedded as an add-in in Excel; this new tool had new features compared to the Open Information Warehouse tool. The query development tool was accessed from within Excel, and the result grid was rendered in Excel. In addition, SAP provided an open interface option based on Microsoft OLE DB for OLAP. This allowed for tools like Cognos and SAP BusinessObjects to consume data from SAP BW.

1.1.3 SAP BW Release 2.0 and 2.1

SAP BW 2.0 was released in 2000 and introduced several new capabilities that had been lacking in release 1.2, allowing for better data modeling and consumption of reporting. SAP BW 2.x was a significant extension from the data mart architecture and included some of Bill Inmon's information factory concepts, such as the operational DataStore (ODS) object.

Some of the most notable features introduced include the following:

- **Operational DataStore**
  The ODS object allowed for flat modeling of objects rather than the start schema modeling offered with InfoCubes. It also allowed for delta calculation when a record was loaded multiple times, thus allowing for just changes to be loaded to InfoCubes.

- **Web reporting**
  The initial release of web reporting in SAP BW was quite crude and required many workarounds, so many customers didn't make use of the web reporting until later releases. SAP BEx in Excel was still the main tool.

1.1.4 SAP BW Release 3.x

Late 2001 saw the release of SAP BW 3.0A, which introduced new tools that some customers had requested. However, the major 3.x release came in 2004 with SAP BW 3.5, which offered enhancements such as the following:

- **InfoSpokes**

  The 3.x SAP BW releases included InfoSpokes as a first method for SAP to address a concern of many customers, centering on getting data out of SAP BW and loading that data into other tools or data marts.

- **SAP BW InfoSet**

  The SAP BW InfoSet object was introduced to allow for joins between tables and for reporting on the joined objects. InfoSets had been available with SAP R/3 for years and were modified slightly to fit in as an object type in SAP BW. They still had performance issues, however, like those experienced in SAP R/3.

- **Virtual providers**

  Virtual providers were introduced to allow for real-time reporting of data in SAP R/3 and for combining it with data in SAP BW. This solution worked well for small datasets but had severe performance issues with larger datasets.

- **Analysis Process Designer**

  The analysis processes were introduced to allow for modeling of data processing inside SAP BW and were very useful for calculating top customers for customer segmentation and other such information.

- **SAP BEx frontend tools**

  The major new feature was in new set of frontend tools that provided great improvements in capabilities and better integration with both Excel and web-based reporting. The SAP BEx browser was replaced with the SAP Enterprise Portal. The Excel add-in was improved, and the web reporting was completely revamped and included more Excel add-in features.

The SAP BW 3.x releases provided a robust data warehousing solution for enterprises and were the starting point for a lot of implementations of SAP BW.

1.1.5   SAP BW Release 7.0 to 7.3

SAP made a lot of changes again with the release of SAP BW 7.0, also called SAP NetWeaver 2004s when released. This release was also the base for all development up until today's version of SAP BW.

The SAP BW 7.0 to 7.31 release time frame stretched from 2005 to 2012; there was development but were no major changes aside from the SAP BusinessObjects integration, which started when SAP acquired BusinessObjects in 2008. The features that had the biggest impact were as follows:

- **Write-optimized DataStore objects**

  The write-optimized DataStore objects (DSOs) were introduced to allow for the implementation of Layered Scaleable Architecture (LSA), which uses several persistent layers of data during the transformation.

- **OpenHub destination**

  SAP replaced the InfoSpoke object with OpenHub, which also introduced separate licensing for OpenHub to allow for distribution of SAP BW data to other applications with non-SAP named users.

- **Transformation**

  The transfer and update rule "double" transformation logic was replaced with a single object called transformation. Transformations allowed for both start and end routines and expert routines.

- **Data transfer processes**

  The info package loading process was partially replaced by data transfer processes (DTPs).

- **Composite provider**

  The first versions of CompositeProviders were introduced in SAP BW 7.3 to replace InfoSets, but they had severe performance issues with large data volumes.

- **New frontend tools**

  The SAP BEx analyzer as we know it today was introduced in SAP BW 7.0; it's undergone some enhancements but is still very much the same tool used now in SAP BW 7.5. The web applications and web templates have also not evolved much since the initial release of SAP BW 7.0.

- **Integration with SAP BusinessObjects**

  The reason for the lack of development of the SAP BW frontend tools was that SAP acquired BusinessObjects in 2008; hence, most frontend development effort centered on integrating the SAP BusinessObjects tools to consume SAP BW data. The integration took effort away from most legacy SAP BEx tools, except maybe the query designer, which is still used heavily with both SAP BusinessObjects Web Intelligence and SAP Lumira Designer.

1.1.6 SAP BW 7.4 and 7.5 Powered by SAP HANA

In late 2013, SAP BW 7.4 was released, the first version of SAP BW developed to take advantage of the SAP HANA platform. It included some new features specifically optimized for use on SAP HANA, as follows:

- **Advanced DSO**

  The Advanced DSO was introduced in SAP BW 7.4 SP 08 and was built to replace all other DSO types, as well as InfoCubes. It required a lot of SAP Notes to get the functionality working as expected; hence it was recommended to be on SAP BW 7.4 SP 12 before using Advanced DSOs.

- **SAP HANA CompositeProviders**

  The SAP HANA CompositeProviders were also made available in SAP BW 7.4 SP 08, but also required a lot of SAP Notes. On SAP BW 7.4 SP 10 with some additional SAP Notes, they were usable.

- **Open ODS views**

  The Open ODS views were more stable and provided a great way to expose an SAP HANA table to the SAP BW OLAP engine without having to load the data into an SAP BW object first. The functionality is also possible to achieve with SAP HANA CompositeProviders, so Open ODS views weren't used much.

- **SAP HANA analysis process**

  The SAP HANA analysis process was introduced to replace the Analysis Process Designer; it opened a new world of features from the SAP HANA platform, such as integration with the Predictive Analysis Library (PAL) and database procedures.

- **BW modeling tool**

  The BW modeling tool provided a new, modern frontend option for development integrated into the SAP HANA Studio Eclipse tool. The SAP GUI tool could still be used for most old development tasks, but new object types had to be developed in the BW modeling tool in Eclipse.

- **Data flow modeling**

  Data flow modeling was a new way to build data models in the BW modeling tool, providing a more graphical depiction of the data model and flow of data.

- **SAP HANA views**

  As part of the integration with the SAP HANA platform, SAP HANA view modeling was available. All SAP BW objects could generate an SAP HANA view that could then be used for additional modeling in SAP HANA. The views could also be accessed directly by SAP HANA database users from tools like SAP BusinessObjects Web Intelligence, SAP Lumira Designer, SAP Lumira, and a variety of third-party tools.

SAP BW Object Inflation

The enhancement and development of SAP BW over the past 20 years has caused an inflation in the number of objects available for modeling the enterprise data warehouse. A lot of object types were developed for very specific niche use cases and caused a lot of additional logic to be built into the OLAP engine in SAP BW. Figure 1.2 illustrates the inflation in object types over the years and the complexity that SAP BW developers and support staff had to manage.

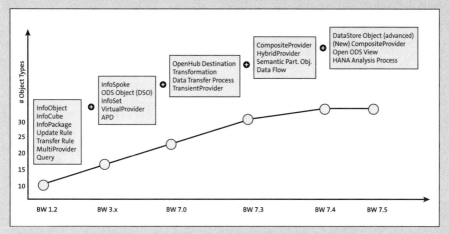

Figure 1.2 SAP BW Innovation and Increase of Object Types

1.2   SAP BW/4HANA Overview

SAP BW/4HANA is a new product that includes both some features from the legacy SAP BW application and some completely new features. SAP has redeveloped quite a bit of functionality, using new design principles and removing functionality that was no longer needed.

1.2.1   SAP BW/4HANA Design Principles

The SAP BW/4HANA design principles applied in the development of the software include the following:

- Simplicity: Make it simple to use and build in SAP BW/4HANA, get up and running sooner and keep running at lower costs, and reduce development efforts.

- Openness: Manage all kinds of data and integration with all systems, whether you're in an SAP application or SQL system, and be able to access all models through an open SQL interface.

- Modern interfaces: Ensure simple access to data through easy-to-use tools with the new UI in Eclipse.

- High performance: Use the power of SAP HANA to leverage large amounts of data in real time.

With these design principles applied, it's been necessary to remove object types from SAP BW and simplify the OLAP engine, slimming down the programming required for an SAP BW application that supported many different database platforms.

1.2.2   Simplified Data Model

One of the main differences between SAP BW and SAP BW/4HANA is that SAP BW/4HANA only allows for a few object types for data modeling. Old legacy objects that have been part of SAP BW since its inception, such as InfoCubes and classic DSOs, have been replaced and aren't allowed in SAP BW/4HANA. Figure 1.3 shows the simplified data model objects, which include only CompositeProviders, Open ODS views, and Advanced DSOs for modeling transaction data or facts. InfoObjects can be used still but are no longer required. This simplifies the design and build process and makes support easier for both SAP and customers.

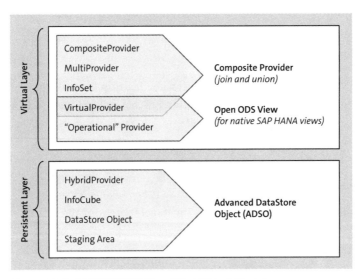

Figure 1.3 SAP BW/4HANA Simplified Object Model

SAP BW/4HANA has also removed other legacy SAP BW functionality. The SAP BEx query designer is no longer supported; you must use the SAP BW query designer in the BW modeling tool in Eclipse. Modeling in SAP GUI also isn't supported; all modeling should be performed in the BW modeling tool in Eclipse.

The SAP BusinessObjects BI content packages are being replaced by SAP BW/4HANA content packages, but the latter don't yet cover all the areas that the SAP BI content packages supported. SAP has published a list detailing functions that aren't supported in SAP BW/4HANA and whether there are tools to help convert legacy objects (see Table 1.1).

SAP BW	Conversion Method	SAP BW/4HANA
SAP BEx analyzer, SAP BEx web templates, SAP BEx tools	Manual	SAP BusinessObjects Cloud and enterprise client and tools
BW query, SAP BEx query designer	Tool-based	BW query (BW modeling tools query designer)
Classic object types (InfoCube, DSO, MultiProvider, InfoSet	Tool-based	New object model: DataStore object (adv.) and CompositeProvider
SAP GUI modeling and workbench	Tool-based	SAP HANA studio-based BW modeling tools
Source system types DB Connect, Extractor (S-API), SAP BW	Tool-based	Consolidation to new SAP HANA source system and ODP
Source system types UD connect, data services, partner ETL	Manual	Consolidation to new SAP HANA source system
BI content packages	Semi-automated	New SAP-HANA optimized SAP BW/4HANA content packages
PSA/InfoPackages	Tool-based	Operational delta queue, field-based DataStore Object (adv.)
Easy query	Manual	OData query

Table 1.1 SAP BW/4HANA Removed Legacy Functionality

SAP BW	Conversion Method	SAP BW/4HANA
Analysis Process Designer	Manual	SAP HANA analysis process, new data flow
Virtual InfoProvider	Manual	SAP HANA calculation views, Open ODS view
Near-line storage partner solutions	Manual	New SAP HANA-based data temperature management with SAP IQ and Hadoop

Table 1.1 SAP BW/4HANA Removed Legacy Functionality (Cont.)

There have been a lot of changes from the old SAP BW application to SAP BW/4HANA, so it's important to be trained on the changes.

> **Tip**
>
> There's a good openSAP class for SAP BW/4HANA. Check it out at *https://open.sap.com/courses/bw4h1*.

1.2.3   Openness

Openness has always been an issue in SAP BW, so it's great to see that openness is one of the design principles in SAP BW/4HANA. Openness to Hadoop specifically is one element that many customers requested over the past three to four years as the implementation of data lakes and big data platforms based on Hadoop has become more prevalent.

The integration between SAP BW/4HANA and the SAP HANA platform also allows for direct SQL consumption of SAP BW/4HANA data via generated SQL views, as shown in Figure 1.4.

In addition to openness of consumption of data, there's also more openness to integrating data from all types of sources, including integration with Hadoop, all databases, and social media, as seen in Figure 1.5.

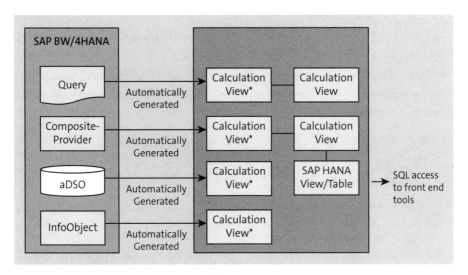

Figure 1.4 SQL Consumption of SAP BW/4HANA Data

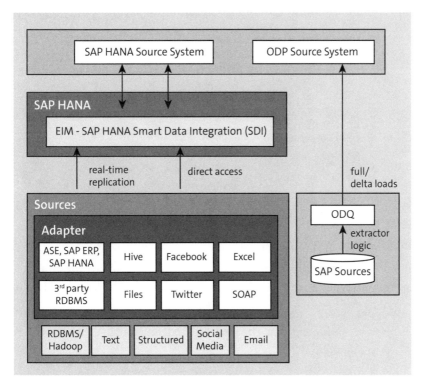

Figure 1.5 SAP BW/4HANA Data Integration Options

One of the areas in which SAP has improved openness in SAP BW/4HANA is data lifecycle management, for which Hadoop can be used for cold data store with standard SAP near-line storage tools. The data lifecycle management approach in SAP BW/4HANA allows for detailed management of data—from hot in memory to warm on disk to cold in other storage media—with the tools provided in SAP BW/4HANA and the SAP HANA platform (see Table 1.2).

SAP HANA	SAP HANA Dynamic Tiering	SAP IQ Near-Line Storage and Retention Management	SAP Vora, HADOOP
Hot data	**Warm data**	**Cold or frozen data**	**Candidate data**
■ Modern in-memory platform ■ Real-time transaction and analysis ■ Native predictive, text, and spatial algorithms	■ New: in-memory dynamic tiering option ■ Disk-based, dynamic tiering option using smart columns ■ High performance and efficient compression ■ Excels at queries on structured data, from terabyte to petabyte scale ■ No data duplication	■ Data persistence optimized in system landscape through relocation of infrequently accessed data to SAP IQ ■ Less frequently accessed data archived in time partitions ■ Near-line storage data resides in a highly compressed state in cost-efficient storage with fewer backups to reduce operational costs	■ Acceleration with SAP Vora ■ SAP HANA smart data access technology capability for Hive- and Spark-type scenarios

Table 1.2 SAP BW/4HANA Data Temperatures and Types

1.2.4 Modern Interfaces

As the SAP BW application has aged, so have the UIs, both for modeling and support and for end users consuming the data. The new BW modeling tool in Eclipse provides a fresh new look to the tools.

In addition, SAP BusinessObjects tools, such as SAP Lumira Designer, SAP Lumira, SAP BusinessObjects Analysis for Office, and SAP BusinessObjects Cloud, also provide a new, more modern UI for the SAP BW/4HANA application compared to the legacy SAP BW BEx.

1.2.5   High Performance

The high-performance design principle makes use of the power of the SAP HANA platform and the capabilities that the platform provides.

With SAP BW/4HANA, further optimization of the application logic and push down to SAP HANA will take place from within the OLAP engine, data management, and planning functions, as shown in Figure 1.6. This has already been done to some extent in SAP BW 7.5 powered by SAP HANA, but in SAP BW/4HANA the old logic can be removed, because only the SAP HANA platform is supported, slimming down the application logic dramatically.

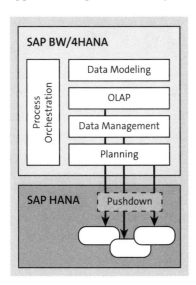

Figure 1.6 SAP BW/4HANA Pushdown of Application Logic to SAP HANA

An additional area in which logic in the SAP HANA platform can be used is in the SAP HANA analysis processes that allow for database procedures to be used that can tap into the Application Function Library (AFL), PAL, and other libraries installed on the SAP HANA platform (see Figure 1.7).

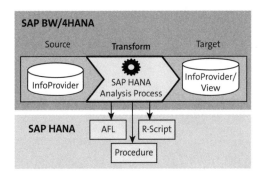

Figure 1.7 SAP HANA Analysis Processes Using SAP HANA DB Procedures

This has proven to be powerful for predictive and statistical analysis.

1.3   Implementing SAP BW/4HANA

SAP BW/4HANA can be implemented in one of the following three ways:

- New installation of SAP BW/4HANA
- System conversion of an existing SAP BW system
- Landscape consolidation of more than one SAP BW system into one SAP BW/4HANA

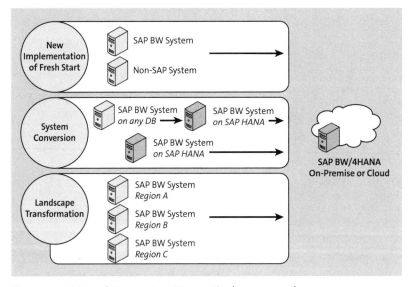

Figure 1.8 SAP BW/4HANA Transition Paths (Source: SAP)

The three transition paths are illustrated in Figure 1.8. We'll discuss these options in the next subsections.

1.3.1   New Installation of SAP BW/4HANA

Installing a new SAP BW/4HANA system is currently the most common way to implement SAP BW/4HANA. This approach is referred to as *greenfield* because it involves a clean installation of SAP BW/4HANA, with no customizations, objects, or legacy programs that need conversion. The new installation option will be covered in detail in Chapter 3.

Some companies decide to install a new SAP BW/4HANA system even when they have a legacy SAP BW system for a fresh start and to move only the customizations that they want to retain to the SAP BW/4HANA system. This approach can be costly, as these companies end up with two systems running in parallel over a significant period, which results in increased support costs. In addition, we've seen that this approach also has significant development costs, as each development is evaluated and optimized for SAP BW/4HANA.

1.3.2   System Conversion of Existing SAP BW System

SAP BW/4HANA is a new product, as noted previously. This means that moving to SAP BW/4HANA doesn't just upgrade an existing SAP BW system. The move to SAP BW/4HANA from an existing SAP BW system therefore requires a few steps.

The first step is to migrate the system to SAP BW powered by SAP HANA 7.5 and then convert all objects to SAP HANA-supported objects, such as Advanced DSOs and CompositeProviders. SAP provides an interim release called SAP BW powered by SAP HANA with SAP BW/4HANA starter add-on or SAP BW, edition for SAP HANA, which allows for prechecks and conversions to take the place of legacy objects using SAP-delivered tools.

One transfer tool that allows for a complete dataflow transfer can be executed with Transaction RSB4HTRF (see Figure 1.9).

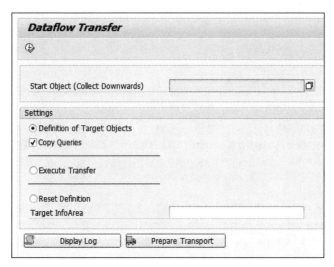

Figure 1.9 Transaction RSB4HTRF: Dataflow Transfer Tool to SAP BW/4HANA

This tool will create a new dataflow with SAP BW/4HANA-compatible objects but will not transfer the data. The tool currently supports conversion of the object types listed in Table 1.3.

Old Object Type	New Object Type
DSO	Advanced DSO
InfoCube	Advanced DSO
MultiProvider	SAP HANA CompositeProvider
CompositeProvider (object type COPR)	CompositeProvider (see also SAP Note 2080851)
HybridProvider (InfoCube plus DSO)	Advanced DSO

Table 1.3 Object Conversions Supported in Transaction RSB4HTRF

Process chains and other objects aren't converted or copied.

Note

See more details in SAP Note 2238220 (BW on HANA: Transfer Enhancements).

Another tool available is program RSO_CONVERT_IPRO_TO_HCPR, which converts SAP BW InfoProviders to CompositeProviders. This tool allows for conversion of an existing InfoProvider, including its queries, into an SAP HANA CompositeProvider, with options to simulate and create a backup of the old InfoProvider and move or copy the queries (see Figure 1.10).

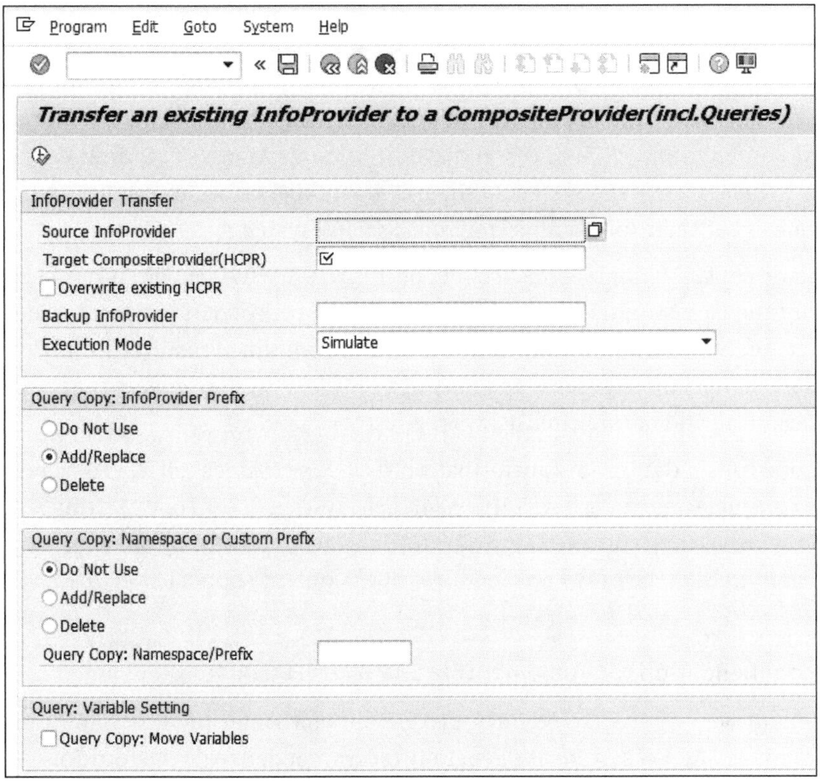

Figure 1.10 RSO_CONVERT_IPRO_TO_HCPR Program Selection Screen

A conversion tool for Advanced DSOs, including data conversion, is still in development, but the conversion tools are evolving quickly. SAP's development roadmap for SAP BW/4HANA predicts the tools being completely delivered in 2017.

However, the process of converting an existing SAP BW system to SAP BW/4HANA currently has quite a few limitations, as add-on components like SAP BPC "classic" is not supported.

> **Note**
>
> SAP Note 2383530 (Conversion to BW/4HANA—Step-by-Step Description) contains the detailed steps required to perform a conversion from SAP BW 7.5 to SAP BW/4HANA.

1.3.3   Landscape Consolidation

Companies with multiple SAP BW systems sometimes target consolidating their systems into one SAP BW/4HANA system going forward. This process requires a lot of analysis of configuration differences and data harmonization. SAP is innovating some tools to help, such as the System Comparison Workbench, which can be used to find differences between, for example, regional SAP BW systems.

The landscape consolidation approach isn't specific to SAP BW/4HANA; it has been applied over the past 18 years in other SAP BW system consolidations. Most issues that arise generally center on master data harmonization, which requires setting up a master data management process and maybe an MDM system to ensure that master data stays clean and harmonized across regions.

The landscape consolidation, or transformation, as it's sometimes called, can be performed by consolidating into a new SAP BW/4HANA system or into one existing SAP BW system, which is then converted to SAP BW/4HANA. Which option to choose normally depends on the type of system and how much content should be retained.

1.3.4   Recommendation for Implementing SAP BW/4HANA

The implementation of SAP BW/4HANA can be difficult when there is significant investment in the SAP BW system. It's generally recommended to go the route of system conversion, especially when a majority of the content in the legacy SAP BW system is still required in the SAP BW/4HANA system. The benefits that companies have gleaned with just the technical migration of their legacy SAP BW systems to SAP BW powered by SAP HANA can provide fast and real success as part of the longer road of moving to SAP BW/4HANA. Table 1.4 shows guidelines for choosing a path. The clear option if you have an SAP BW system powered by SAP HANA is to move forward with conversion to SAP BW/4HANA. A new installation and rebuild of the SAP BW/4HANA system is possible for all scenarios, but should be considered against the cost and effort of having two systems running for a significant amount of time.

Starting Point	Path 1: New Install	Path 2: System Conversion	Path 3: Landscape Transformation
One or more legacy systems	Possible alternative path	Not supported	Possible alternative path
SAP BW on any DB	Possible alternative path	Possible alternative path	Possible alternative path
SAP BW powered by SAP HANA	Possible alternative path	Recommended path	Possible alternative path
SAP BW, edition for SAP HANA	Possible alternative path	Highly recommended path	Possible alternative path
Multiple SAP BW systems	Possible alternative path	Not supported	Highly recommended path

Table 1.4 Paths to SAP BW/4HANA

1.4 Summary

SAP BW/4HANA is new software, not just a continuation of the SAP BW software. To move to SAP BW/4HANA will require more work than just a system upgrade, as a lot of legacy SAP BW functionality is no longer available in SAP BW/4HANA. It's also important to note that the legacy SAP BW software is still supported on databases other than SAP HANA, whereas SAP BW/4HANA is only supported on the SAP HANA platform.

Chapter 2
Introduction to SAP HANA

If you're new to SAP HANA, this is the place to start. In this chapter, we'll explain the ins and outs of SAP HANA and the different deployment options currently available.

When SAP HANA was first introduced to the business world, it was an in-memory database principally for SAP BusinessObjects Business Intelligence (SAP BusinessObjects BI). Since then, SAP HANA has evolved from just a database to the data platform at the center of SAP's development of current and future products. SAP BW/4HANA is a fitting example of how SAP is optimizing its products around SAP HANA.

Organizations that have deployed an SAP HANA platform have the tools at hand to tackle problems that were once thought impossible. An insurance company is leveraging satellite data, geospatial microservices, and spatial processing, all powered by SAP HANA to better assess and manage risk; freight and airline companies are using SAP HANA for route optimization; retailers are identifying fraud and price-fixing with their suppliers; and all the information is available in real time. Monthly status reports can become a thing of the past with SAP HANA providing real-time data at your fingertips.

In this chapter, we'll provide an overview of SAP HANA, including SAP HANA as an application platform, SAP HANA as a database for SAP applications, SAP HANA's many deployment options, and virtualization of SAP HANA.

The goal of this chapter is to give you a comprehensive understanding of SAP HANA and hopefully make you comfortable with some of its associated key words and tricky phrases.

2.1 What Is SAP HANA?

To put it simply, SAP HANA is one of the fastest data platforms on the market. It's an in-memory, column-oriented, relational database, a technology and a platform that gives companies the ability to perform real-time analytics and develop and deploy real-time applications. We'll start by explaining the difference between traditional and in-memory databases, then we'll get into the basics of SAP HANA.

2.1.1   Traditional Database versus In-Memory Database

In a traditional relational database management system, data is stored on disk. When the database has a request for data, it must be loaded into random-access memory (RAM) before being consumed by the central processing unit (CPU). That means the choke point in the supply chain of data is the speed of the disk. Because the average price of RAM per gigabyte has dropped significantly—from $189 in 2005 to $4.37 in 2015—an in-memory database is now an affordable option.

The term *in-memory database* means that all data is stored in RAM. With the data residing in-memory, the time-consuming task of data being pulled from disk to RAM is now removed. The increased speed provided by storing data in RAM is further accelerated using multisocket, multicore CPUs. The basic concept of an in-memory database is illustrated in Figure 2.1.

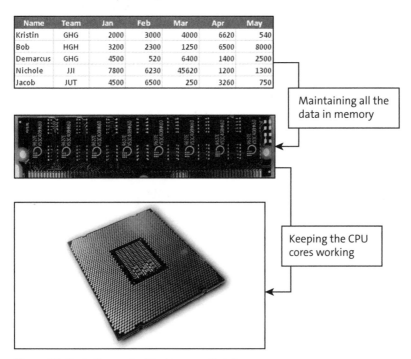

Name	Team	Jan	Feb	Mar	Apr	May
Kristin	GHG	2000	3000	4000	6620	540
Bob	HGH	3200	2300	1250	6500	8000
Demarcus	GHG	4500	520	6400	1400	2500
Nichole	JJI	7800	6230	45620	1200	1300
Jacob	JUT	4500	6500	250	3260	750

Maintaining all the data in memory

Keeping the CPU cores working

Figure 2.1 Basic Concept of In-Memory Database

It's important to understand that there's a difference between an in-memory database and a database with caching. A database with caching still uses the disk as the main data store and will create memory snapshots to speed up processing. Any changes or updates to the data can only be processed directly on the disk. Therefore, the only speed gain from caching occurs when accessing the same data with no changes. A database with caching provides improved performance over a traditional database, but it can't provide the speed that a real in-memory database can.

2.1.2   SAP HANA

SAP HANA is a true in-memory data platform that still provides data protection by maintaining data on disk as a persistence layer. With SAP HANA, every action is written to logs called *redo logs* on disk. These redo logs are used like instant replays for the database in case of power outages and provide point-in-time database recoveries. Data from memory is pushed to disk at regular intervals, but is designed so that it doesn't affect performance. Therefore, if there is a large workload on the database, this action will wait until there is sufficient server capacity so as not to impact performance. When nonvolatile RAM (NVRAM) becomes commercially available, the necessity for maintaining data on disk as persistence will disappear, because NVRAM doesn't lose data when power is lost.

SAP HANA consists of multiple communicating services, as shown in Figure 2.2. The main component of an SAP HANA database is known as the *index server*. The index server contains the data stores and engines that process the data from incoming SQL or MDX statements. These statements are generated from authenticated sessions and transactions.

The persistence layer, as noted earlier, is responsible for the durability and atomicity of transactions. It ensures that the database can be restored to the most recent state after a restart.

SQLScript is SAP HANA's own database scripting language. It addresses the problems from classical applications that tend to copy data repetitively to and from the database and those from programs that iterate over large data loops. SQLScript operates on tables using SQL queries for set processing, allowing for parallelization over multiple processors. Specialized and optimized functional libraries, such as BFL and PAL, can also be installed and integrated with different data engines of the index server. SQLScript can be used to call directly from these libraries.

The preprocessor is used by the index server for analyzing text data and extracting the information on which text search capabilities are based. The name server holds information about the topology of the SAP HANA system. In a distributed system, the name server keeps track of where data is located and what components are running on each server.

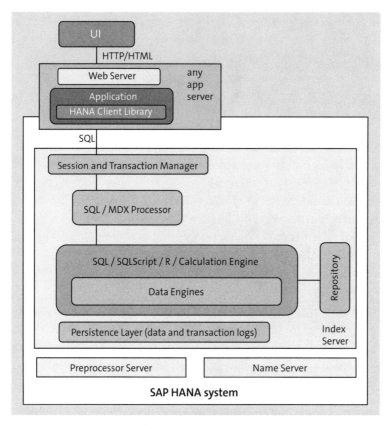

Figure 2.2 SAP HANA Database High-Level Architecture

SAP HANA creates a symphony of hardware and software working together to use the full potential of technology. Deployable in the cloud or on-premise, SAP HANA accelerates business processes and simplifies an IT environment by providing the foundation for all data needs. Companies are now working with enormous data sets, asking complex and interactive questions, and have an increasing need for the data to be recent or, better yet, in real time. SAP HANA can address all of those needs at lightning speed.

Now that you have a basic understanding of SAP HANA, let's discuss some of the different implementations that SAP has to offer.

Further Reading

For a more in-depth look at SAP HANA, check out *SAP HANA: An Introduction*, available at *https://www.sap-press.com/4160*.

2.2   SAP HANA as an Application Platform

At its core, SAP HANA is a database that can support any type of application—not only SAP software. SAP has been working passionately to provide an application platform that's flexible and powerful enough to meet the ever-changing needs of the business landscape.

With the advent of SAP HANA SPS 5, SAP released SAP HANA extended application services, classic model (SAP HANA XS). Prior to this release, to connect an application or a web page to your data in SAP HANA, you needed to follow the traditional approach for creating applications, which involves using a separate application server to connect to the database (see Figure 2.3). For example, SAP NetWeaver ABAP or JAVA can connect to the SAP HANA system and use an Open Database Connectivity (ODBC) or Java Database Connectivity (JDBC) connection to pass SQL statements. Now with SAP HANA XS, the application server, web server, and development environment are built into SAP HANA, allowing developers to create applications with direct access to the SAP HANA database through the XS engine.

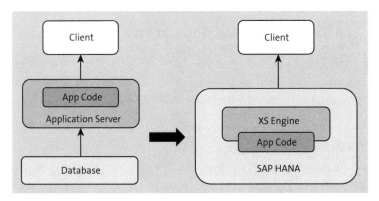

Figure 2.3 Traditional Application Development versus Development with SAP HANA XS

SAP enhanced SAP HANA XS with the release of SAP HANA extended application services, advanced model (SAP HANA XSA), which builds on the foundation of SAP

HANA XS by adding support for JavaScript, Node.js, and Java, GitHub, and Maven. Now, you can create applications with components written in different programming languages all on the same SAP HANA server. SAP HANA XSA uses the microservices approach, in which applications are broken into their own specific program runtime environments, meaning you can apply a patch to one component without having to take down the entire application.

SAP HANA XSA also introduced a new runtime controller based on Cloud Foundry, which added build packs in the SAP HANA development environment. These build packs include a set of compilers and utilities used in application design with the following languages:

- SAP HANA XS JavaScript (XSJS)
- Node.js
- Java on Apache TomEE 1.7.3
- Java on Apache Tomcat 8.0.32

The runtimes in SAP HANA XSA are separated from the database in SAP HANA, which allows for flexible scaling during peak demand. New servers or nodes can be added and removed as needed to meet your business needs.

In short, SAP HANA XSA has completed the transformation of SAP HANA from a specialized application server and high-speed database to a fully developed application platform.

2.3   SAP HANA as a Database for SAP Applications

SAP HANA was created to be SAP's core database for all its future application developments. In this section, we'll walk through the history of SAP ERP to the creation of SAP S/4HANA, and we'll briefly discuss the evolution of SAP BW.

2.3.1   SAP Enterprise Resource Planning

Since the 1970s, SAP has been improving and evolving its enterprise software. As shown in Figure 2.4, SAP has come a long way from the days of SAP R/1 to SAP S/4HANA. SAP is moving away from designing its enterprise software to run on software from other companies, transitioning customers to a faster, flexible, and all-SAP landscape.

There's a lot of confusion around SAP R/3, SAP ERP, and SAP ECC. SAP R/3 was developed and released in the early 1990s; starting in 2003, SAP began using the term SAP ERP, which was later changed to SAP ECC, and then switched back to SAP ERP. SAP ERP is the main component of the SAP Business Suite.

SAP Business Suite supports processes for manufacturing, finance, procurement, IT management, human resources, product development, marketing, sales, and supply chain management and services. It's comprised of a set of fully integrated applications such as SAP ERP, SAP Customer Relationship Management, SAP Supply Chain Management, and SAP Supplier Relationship Management that empower businesses to run their core operations more efficiently.

Deciding whether to move directly from SAP Business Suite to SAP S/4HANA or to SAP Business Suite powered by SAP HANA can be a difficult task for customers. We'll break down the differences between these options in the following sections.

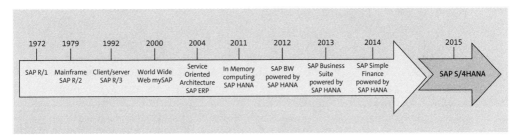

Figure 2.4 History of SAP Enterprise Resource Planning

SAP Business Suite on SAP HANA

The first implementation option for SAP HANA is SAP Business Suite on SAP HANA. When a migration to SAP HANA is performed without changing the frontend, it transforms SAP ERP to SAP Business Suite on SAP HANA. This means that SAP HANA is used as the underlying database for the SAP Business Suite applications, but SAP HANA is only used as a database. Doing so allows businesses to benefit from the power of SAP HANA without restructuring the application layer; users don't have to become accustomed to a new system.

The migration to SAP HANA doesn't change any code or optimize any transactions in your system. It only moves your existing data to memory. In the next section, we'll discuss transitioning to SAP S/4HANA, which will implement optimized transactions designed for SAP HANA.

Choosing SAP Business Suite allows for a simple migration to SAP HANA with two options:

1. A full migration, in which the entire SAP Business Suite is moved to SAP HANA.

2. A sidecar implementation, in which an additional instance of SAP Business Suite is created on the SAP HANA database and hardware. This approach allows businesses to become accustomed to SAP HANA and can optimize specific processes in a test environment.

Implementing SAP HANA requires minimum software versions and components: SAP NetWeaver 7.3, SAP ERP 6.0 EHP 6, and ABAP AS 7.4. If your current software doesn't meet the required minimum versions, you'll be able to upgrade to the required version with a service pack.

In short, in a migration to SAP HANA without changing the frontend, SAP ERP becomes SAP Business Suite on SAP HANA, allowing businesses to benefit from SAP HANA without changing the application layer.

SAP S/4HANA

SAP S/4HANA is the evolution of SAP ERP software. It isn't just a release or a service pack; SAP S/4HANA was designed and optimized for SAP HANA and moves away from the SAP R/3 or SAP ERP architecture. SAP changed the core code and rewrote models one by one with one thought in mind: SAP HANA. The simplified, fourth generation of SAP Business Suite on SAP HANA becomes SAP S/4HANA when new business functions are activated.

Although many of the features and functions of SAP S/4HANA are similar to those of SAP ERP, the traditional modular concepts for Financials (FI) and Controlling (CO), Sales and Distribution (SD), Materials Management (MM), Warehouse Management (WM), and the like are gone. These ideas were rethought and reorganized to fit the way that business is organized, by processes: procure-to-pay, plan-to-produce, order-to-cash, request-to-service, human resources, human capital management, and finance. This structure was designed to emulate better than the modular concept how new systems or functionalities would be implemented.

One of the major benefits of SAP S/4HANA over SAP Business Suite on SAP HANA lies in financial management and accounting. SAP S/4HANA covers a range of tasks that includes planning, accounting, analysis, compliance, and risk management. This allows you to quickly build models, real-time cost and revenue analysis, and cash flow optimization. Compliance and monitoring financials become easier and quicker, because SAP S/4HANA centralizes data and eliminates redundant data.

SAP Fiori is leveraged by SAP S/4HANA to prove a new user experience (UX), maximize the speed and power of SAP HANA, and introduce the possibility of a single database for both online transaction processing (OLTP) and online analytical processing (OLAP). The digital core of SAP S/4HANA is illustrated in Figure 2.5.

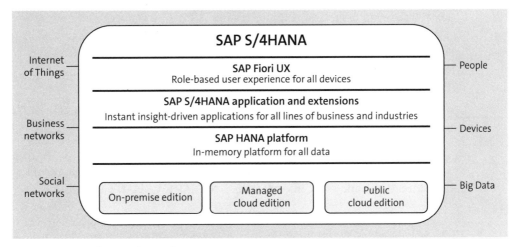

Figure 2.5 Digital Core of SAP S/4HANA

When it comes to transitioning your landscape to SAP S/4HANA, there are several options. Each option depends on your deployment model (on-premise, cloud, or hybrid), your business needs, and what the digital future of your company looks like.

The three main options are as follows:

1. *New implementation*, also referred to as a *greenfield deployment*. This option is mainly for customers who are migrating from a non-SAP system or for existing SAP ECC customers who want to implement a fresh system. After the installation of SAP S/4HANA, transaction and master data are migrated from the legacy system. *Deployment:* on-premise or cloud.

2. *System conversion*, commonly known as a *lift and shift*. Existing customers on SAP ECC or SAP Business Suite on SAP HANA undergo a complete system conversion. If the existing system is SAP ECC, it will be transitioned to SAP Business Suite on SAP HANA and then converted to SAP S/4HANA. *Deployment:* on-premise or cloud.

3. *Landscape transformation*. This scenario allows customers to either consolidate current SAP systems or separate selected entities—for example, if a company

wants to create one global SAP S/4HANA system or deploy it as a hybrid solution. *Deployment:* on-premise, cloud, or hybrid.

> **Note**
>
> All databases and tables will be converted into a columnar structure and obsolete aggregated tables and indices removed. Any applications or modifications created by the customer will need to be evaluated for such modifications to work properly going forward.

Deployable on-premise, in the cloud, or in a hybrid solution, SAP S/4HANA is SAP's replacement for SAP ERP. Although customers aren't forced to make the switch, all future advancements will be centered on SAP S/4HANA.

Now that we've covered SAP's enterprise software, let's explore the deployment options for SAP BW and some information on the SAP BW/4HANA add-on.

2.3.2   SAP Business Warehouse

As with most data warehouses, SAP BW is a combination of databases and database management tools used to help make decisions. Providing more than infrastructure, SAP BW also provides preconfigured data extractors, business process models, and analysis and report tools. It can transform and consolidate data from a variety of sources. SAP has been continually optimizing SAP BW to use SAP HANA—not just as a database, but to transform itself into a next-generation data warehouse.

In this section, we'll be covering the differences between SAP BW powered by SAP HANA and SAP BW, compatibility mode, formally known as SAP BW 7.5, edition for SAP HANA.

SAP BW Powered by SAP HANA

SAP BW powered by SAP HANA was first introduced with SAP BW 7.3 SP 5 as one of the first steps toward enhancing SAP's products on SAP HANA, much like transitioning SAP ERP to SAP Business Suite on SAP HANA. Using SAP BW powered by SAP HANA means that no other database is required. With the introduction of SAP BW 7.4 powered by SAP HANA, activities such as activations for DSOs and other transformations perform the same way, but the processing has been moved to SAP HANA. This reduces the amount of data moved during each process, thus executing the processes with much greater speed.

Making the switch to SAP BW powered by SAP HANA is a lift-and-shift operation, in which the data in the database is migrated to SAP HANA. This again is just like migrating from SAP ERP to SAP Business Suite on SAP HANA, in that the application layer of SAP BW stays the same but capitalizes on the power that SAP HANA can provide. For example, you can still modify and create InfoCubes, DSOs, MultiProviders, InfoSources, and DataSources, just as before.

SAP BW, Compatibility Mode

SAP BW, compatibility mode is SAP BW powered by SAP HANA with the SAP BW/4HANA add-on installed. The SAP BW/4HANA add-on allows for using new object types, such as Advanced DSOs, CompositeProviders, and Open ODS views. Although this option allows for supporting the existing object types, they can't be modified or created. The new object types, which we we'll discuss further in Chapter 5, optimize SAP BW to take advantage of SAP HANA.

Now that we've looked at SAP HANA as a database for SAP applications, let's move on to examine the deployment options for SAP HANA.

2.4 SAP HANA Deployment

In this section, we'll discuss deploying on-premise, hardware options, and scale-out versus scale-up. There are five dimensions of deploying SAP HANA that can be combined for each of the deployment methods, as illustrated in Figure 2.6.

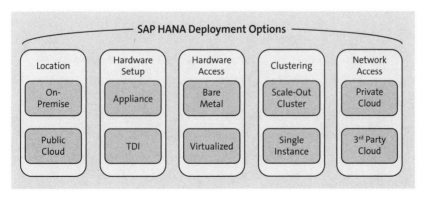

Figure 2.6 SAP HANA Deployment Options

The first decision that needs to be made when deploying on-premise is whether to purchase an SAP HANA appliance from a certified vendor or to use Tailored Datacenter

Integration (TDI). TDI provides more flexibility by allowing you to choose your preferred infrastructure components or leverage your existing hardware infrastructure for SAP HANA, which can reduce costs and increase flexibility. The second decision is whether to have SAP HANA on bare metal server(s) or to virtualize. Finally, you must decide to scale-out or scale-up.

Now that you understand the SAP HANA deployment options, let's move on to selecting hardware for your environment.

2.4.1   SAP HANA Hardware Options

SAP HANA is sold as an in-memory appliance, meaning that the software and hardware are included together from vendors. Because the hardware is unique in many ways and each vendor optimizes it to correctly support your chosen SAP solution, certified hardware vendors specialize in installing and supporting SAP HANA appliances; therefore, you shouldn't expect noncertified vendors to install or support SAP HANA. As of March 2017, you can purchase certified SAP HANA appliances from Bull SAS, Cisco Systems, Inc., Dell, Fujitsu Technology, Hewlett Packard Enterprise, Hitachi, Huawei Technologies Co., Inspur Electronic Information, Lenovo, NEC Corporation, Silicon Graphics International, Unisys Corporation, and VCE.

Before deciding what hardware to buy, you should understand that SAP HANA hardware can increase in size (scale-up approach), or multiple servers can be clustered together (scale-out approach). Choosing a scale-up or scale-out approach requires careful consideration by the SAP Basis team in your organization. Figure 2.7 illustrates scale-up versus scale-out options.

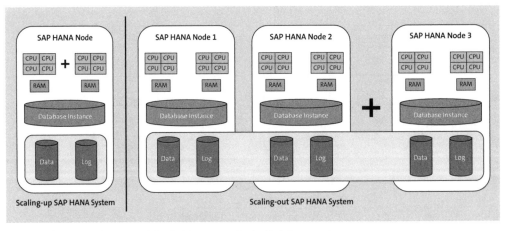

Figure 2.7 SAP HANA Scale-Up versus Scale-Out Approaches

Before we get into scale-up and scale-out in more detail, note that SAP HANA systems require specific CPU to RAM ratios for production systems. For analytic use cases, there must be 256 GB of RAM per socket; for SAP Business Suite, there must be 768 GB of RAM per socket.

In the next sections, we'll take a deeper look at the scale-up and scale-out scenarios.

2.4.2   Scaled-Up SAP HANA Systems

The scale-up method means you can use a more powerful server to process the work-load and, when needed, you can install more RAM and CPUs for processing. With a single system, you can enjoy the benefit of fewer servers to manage and purchase while still being able to scale-out in the future. As of the time of writing, SAP HANA appliances have the memory capacity of up to 20 TB for SAP Business Suite on SAP HANA and up to 4 TB for SAP BW powered by SAP HANA.

Scaling-up SAP HANA should always be the preferred approach. SAP HANA uses extremely efficient parallel query processing. When multiple users query the data-base at the same time, SAP HANA tries to use all available resources for maximum parallelization, creating a multiquery plan in which each query is then split into mul-tiple plan operators, like join and sort, which are executed in parallel over the CPU cores. Each time a multiquery plan is created, it's cached and reused for faster execu-tions later.

When the SAP HANA system's workload or RAM capacity is at its limit, adding more RAM and CPUs doesn't require changes to the database or to the application layer. This makes the process relatively easy and allows SAP HANA to be a self-contained unit.

Keep in mind the following points about scaling up:

- SAP HANA parallelism strongly supports the latest multi-CPU, multicore hardware architectures.
- SAP HANA scheduling and memory allocation is still under development and will continue to improve.
- Scaling up is the easiest way for SAP HANA to scale.
- This process requires no changes to the database or application layer.

Even with the current technology, there may be a point at which scaling up reaches the boundaries of a single server, which is one of the reasons that the scale-out method exists.

2.4.3   Scaled-Out SAP HANA Systems

The scale-out method combines multiple independent nodes into one system, called a *cluster*. It uses multiple processors as a single unit to allow businesses to reach beyond the capacity of a single server. It's important to look not only at current workloads but also at the characteristics of the amount of data that SAP HANA might need. As the workload increases, servers can be added incrementally to the cluster.

Scaling out requires a deep knowledge of SAP HANA applications, hardware, and the data that SAP HANA holds. For your SAP HANA system to function properly, internode communication must be minimized. *Server internode communication* is the communication between an index server on one host and an index server on another. If SAP HANA isn't set up properly, each node will saturate the network, resulting in meager performance. This is addressed by SAP HANA's *shared nothing architecture*, in which each node runs on its own data. The data in SAP HANA must be distributed to find the best balance between data models, usage, and workload to reduce internode communication.

In a scale-out solution, there are three types of nodes:

1. **Master node**
   The active master node coordinates global transactions and stores the metadata of the entire cluster. The master node role can only be assigned to one host at a time, but additional slave nodes will be assigned to take over if the master node fails.

2. **Slave node**
   The slave node buffers required metadata and preforms database operations assigned by the master node. One SAP HANA cluster can have multiple slave nodes.

3. **Standby node**
   The standby node is always running but doesn't take any orders from the master node. In the event of the failure of a slave node, the standby node automatically takes its place.

Now that we've discussed the basics of an SAP HANA scale-out system, let's take a deeper look at how it's deployed with SAP BW and SAP Business Suite.

SAP BW Powered by SAP HANA Scale-Out

SAP BW powered by SAP HANA workloads are generally OLAP rather than a static distribution environment. The master node handles OLTP loads and DDL statements for the ABAP system tables, metadata, operational tables, and all row tables. Although the slave nodes process OLAP loads exclusively, such as master data, cubes, DSOs, ADSOs, PSAs, and so on, they are distributed evenly across all the slave nodes. Figure 2.8 shows the basic layout of SAP BW powered by SAP HANA in an SAP HANA scale-out scenario.

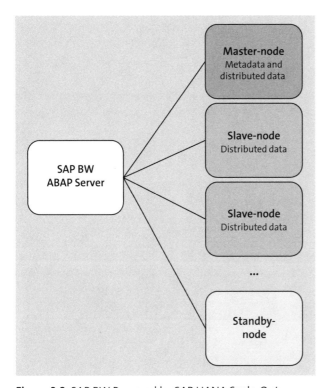

Figure 2.8 SAP BW Powered by SAP HANA Scale-Out

SAP Business Suite on SAP HANA Scale-Out

SAP Business Suite on SAP HANA has mixed OLTP and OLAP workloads that are spread across all nodes of the cluster. The table access patterns will differ from customer to customer, so the table distribution will be dynamic. Table groups aren't distributed across all nodes; instead, they're on the same node. Figure 2.9 shows the basic layout of SAP Business Suite on SAP HANA in a scale-out scenario. To combat inefficiency, SQL statements will be cached and prioritized in order to balance RAM and CPU usage across the nodes.

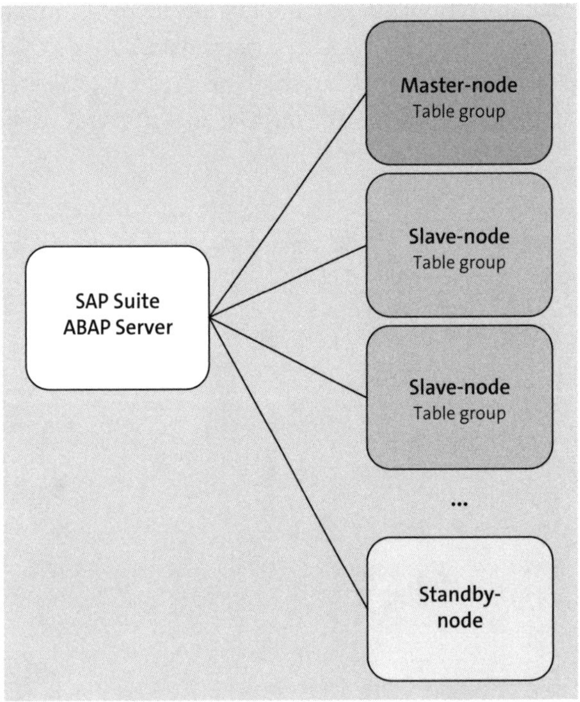

Figure 2.9 SAP Business Suite on SAP HANA Scale-Out

Keep in mind the following points about the scale-out solution:

- This option requires a deep understanding of SAP HANA and the data landscape.
- Scale-out works well in a static distribution environment.
- Scale-out with mixed OLAP and OLTP can be difficult to balance.
- Optimizing for performance can be a never-ending task.

Choosing an SAP HANA appliance and a scale-up or scale-out scenario can be very challenging. Qualified SAP HANA consultants can bring experience and knowledge to the table that will help to facilitate the decision. Overall, we recommend choosing the scale-up solution if, in the short term, you only need a 2 TB system. Later, when you need to, you can scale out. However, if your business needs exceed the availably of a single system, then the way forward is scaling out.

2.5 Virtualization

You've most likely heard about how virtualizing your IT environment can save money by cutting costs and increasing efficiency. In this section we'll discuss what virtualization is, how it applies to SAP HANA, and the different virtualization vendors currently certified by SAP.

2.5.1 What Is Virtualization?

You might be asking: What is virtualization? *Virtualization* is the process of creating a software-based representation of a computer rather than a physical one. Virtualization can apply to applications, servers, storage, and networks and is the most effective way to reduce IT expenses while boosting efficiency and agility for all business applications.

Is virtualization the same as cloud computing? In a word, no, although cloud computing uses virtualization technology. In cloud computing, hardware is owned by a company that sells virtual machines (VMs). A VM is an isolated software container with an operating system and application inside.

Organizations are faced with the limitations of today's servers, which are designed to run only one operating system and application at a time. This limitation causes organizations to deploy many servers that only operate at 5 to 10 percent capacity, which is extremely inefficient by any standard.

Virtualization allows for multiple operating systems to be installed on one server with the use of a hypervisor. The *hypervisor* is a thin layer of software installed directly on the server to simulate the existence of hardware. The server is now referred to as a *host*, and multiple VMs can then be installed on top of the hypervisor. Figure 2.10 illustrates how the hardware, hypervisor, and VMs work.

Each VM is completely independent from the host and other VMs. For example, six VMs could be on one host, with one running SUSE Linux, two running Red Hat Linux, two running Windows Server 2012 R2, and one running Windows 10. Each VM has its own IP address and can be moved to any other host running the same hypervisor.

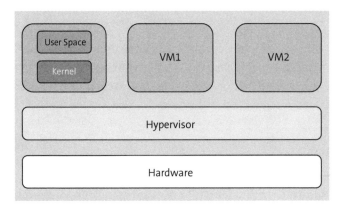

Figure 2.10 High-Level Virtualization View

Now that you have a better understanding of what virtualization is, let's look at the virtualization options for SAP HANA.

2.5.2   SAP HANA Virtualization

With the release of SAP HANA SPS 05, SAP announced support for VMware's hypervisor, the first technology supported to partition an SAP HANA server into smaller partitions or VMs. Since then, SAP has expanded its support for running SAP HANA in virtualized and multitenant environments by adding different scenarios and hypervisors.

Cost Control

Deploying SAP HANA in a virtualized environment allows you to control costs and run only the required memory for your system. As your data expands, you can expand within the infrastructure and not be bound to the physical limitations of an appliance. In addition, SAP HANA isn't tied to a specific server. The VM can be moved to another SAP-certified hardware appliance without losing the license.

High Availability

Many hypervisors, like VMware's, provide high availability, allowing for VMs to be migrated live to another host and to take snapshots for recovery and complete backup images of the machine. Combined with SAP HANA's high-availability technology, database snapshots and backups can make your environment virtually bulletproof.

SAP Note 17886655 is the master note for SAP HANA virtualization. This note will be regularly updated with the SAP HANA-supported hypervisors. Currently, VMware, Hitachi LPAR, Huawei, and IBM PowerVM are supported for production environments. KVM and XEN hypervisors may also be used for SAP HANA SPS 11 and later releases for nonproduction uses cases.

Following is a list of the currently-supported hypervisors for SAP HANA:

- **VMware**
  - VMware vSphere 5.1 with SAP HANA SPS 05 (or later releases) for nonproduction use cases
  - VMware vSphere 5.5 with SAP HANA SPS 07 (or later releases) for production and nonproduction use cases
  - VMware vSphere 6.0 with SAP HANA SPS 11/12 (or later releases) for single-VM and multi-VM use cases
  - VMware vSphere 6.5 with SAP HANA SPS 11/12 (or later releases) for single-VM and multi-VM use cases, up to 4 TB main memory
- **Hitachi LPAR**
  - Hitachi LPAR 2.0 with SAP HANA SPS 07 (or later releases) for production and nonproduction use cases
- **Huawei**
  - Huawei FusionSphere 3.1 with SAP HANA SPS 09 (or later releases) for production and nonproduction use cases for single-VM scenarios
  - Huawei FusionSphere 5.1 with SAP HANA SPS 10/11 (or later releases; details in SAP Note 2279020) for production use cases for single-VM, multi-VM, and scale-out scenarios
- **IBM PowerVM**
  - IBM PowerVM LPAR on IBM Power Systems for production use cases for single-VM and multi-VM scenarios, with up to eight LPARs on one server

> **Note**
>
> The SAP HANA system set up needs to be performed by an SAP HANA certified engineer on SAP HANA certified hardware and successfully verified with the SAP HANA hardware configuration check tool (SAP HANA TDI option) SAP Note 1943937. Alternatively, the system can be delivered preconfigured with a hypervisor and the SAP HANA software installed by an SAP HANA hardware partner (SAP HANA appliance option).

2.6 Summary

Hopefully, you now have a greater understanding of SAP HANA, how it's used as a database and an application platform, and the many deployment options that SAP offers. The most important takeaway from this chapter should be knowledge of each of the deployment options and how to find the best fit before making an investment into SAP HANA. We recommend that you don't make these decisions alone; consult experts to guide you through the process. The next chapter will cover the installation and configuration of SAP BW/4HANA.

Chapter 3
Installation and Setup

Installing any SAP application can be a daunting task. In this chapter, we'll try to take some the edge off of the process with a walkthrough of how SAP BW/4HANA is installed, configured, and made ready for general operation.

In this chapter, we'll walk through the installation and configuration of SAP BW/4HANA. We'll start by discussing the requirements of SAP BW/4HANA, the Product Availability Matrix (PAM), and the installation media collection and extraction. Then, we'll dive deeper into how to handle the installation process step by step and the postinstallation configuration activities.

This chapter will be focused on installing SAP BW/4HANA on SUSE Linux Enterprise Server 11. There are several other operating systems supported, which we'll go into detail about later on, but there are only minimal differences between the OSs for the installation process. For this installation, we'll be using the following applications: WinSCP, PuTTY, Xming, SAP GUI, and SAP HANA Studio.

3.1 Preparation

Before we begin, we must verify that all the requirements of the landscape have been met and that the installation media is up to date. Then, we'll walk through preparing the installation media.

3.1.1 Requirements

There are several combinations of operating systems and hardware in which SAP BW/4HANA can be implemented. Be sure to verify the current supported operating systems and databases on the PAM. The requirements for SAP BW/4HANA are as follows:

- SAP HANA 1.0 SPS 12 and SAP HANA 2.0
- 64-bit only

- 7.45_REL Kernel
- 7.49 Kernel, as DCK (see SAP Note 2195019)

There are several supported operating systems for SAP BW/4HANA (see Table 3.1).

	Windows (*2)	AIX	HP-UX	Solaris	Linux SLES 11, 12 RHEL 6, 7				IBM i	z/OS
	Server 2012 x64 (*3)	7.1 (*4) Power	11.31 IA64	10 (*5), 11 SPARC, x64	x86_64	Power BE (*6)	Power LE (*7)	System z	7.2, 7.3 Power	1.13, 2.1, 2.2 System z
SAP HANA DB 1.00	AS	AS	AS	AS	AS	&	&	AS	AS	HA (*8)
SAP HANA DB 2.0 (*1)	AS	AS	AS	AS	AS	&	AS	&	AS	HA (*8)

- *1: See SAP note 24020699
- *2: See SAP note 362379
- *3: Including Windows Server 2012 R2
- *4: Minimum AIX 7.1 TL 3
- *5: Min. Solaris 10 (U11)
- *6: Linux SLES 11 only
- *7: No SLES 11, RHEL 6, 7
- *8: See SAP Note 2177085
- AS: ABAP Application Server only
- HA: High Available Solution only
- &: Available for SAP HANA and AS

Table 3.1 OS Availability for SAP BW/4HANA

Installing SAP BW/4HANA works almost the same way on any supported operating system with the use of Software Provisioning Manager (SWPM), a tool for installation, system copy, duel stack split, and several other operations for SAP's core application servers. The differences between operating systems in the installation process lie in user permissions, file/directory permissions, and how to launch SWPM.

> **Note**
>
> Installing SAP BW/4HANA on the same system as SAP HANA isn't supported for production systems.

3.1.2   Installation Media

SAP provides installation media in three different ways:

1. Physical CDs containing the required media
2. Download via the maintenance planner
3. Download directly from SAP Software Download Center

We recommend that all installation media be downloaded from SAP whenever possible from either SAP Solution Manager's maintenance planner or the download center. This guarantees that the software is up to date and will save time down the road.

There are five required pieces in the installation package:

1. Software Provisioning Manager (SWPM)
2. SAP BW/4HANA Media (Export 1, Export 2, etc.)
3. Kernel
4. SAP HANA Database Client
5. SAPCAR, SAP's unzip utility (required for manual download)

If you're using SAP-provided CDs, please skip to Section 3.2.

Once you've downloaded the required files from SAP, you'll have to extract the files before they can be used. We've found that downloading, extracting, and then transferring the media from a Windows computer is the simplest way. Be sure to keep track of what you're downloading. The file names will be a series of numbers, so there's no easy way to identify which file contains what elements. Our recommendation is to create a directory named for what's being downloaded. Most of the files will be in SAR format and therefore will require SAPCAR for extraction. The process is as follows:

1. Move SAPCAR to the folder/directory where the SAR files are located.
2. Open a command prompt and change the directory to the location of the files.
3. In the command prompt, type "sapcar.exe -xffile.sar" (if you would like to see each file as it unpacks add "v" to visualized what the computer is doing, like "-xvf").
4. Run the unzip utility and extract the files.
5. Repeat the process until all the SAR files are extracted for SWPM, media, the kernel, and the database client.
6. Once all files have been extracted, move them to the server on which SAP BW/4HANA will be installed. Then, if required, change the file permissions recur-

sively for the installation package to read, write, and execute for the user installing SAP BW/4HANA (see Figure 3.1).

Figure 3.1 Installation Package Example

3.2   Installation

Now, we're ready to start the installation. This process will take approximately four to six hours to complete, depending on how much processing power is available. Before starting the installation, be sure to perform a database backup of SAP HANA. To begin, follow these steps:

1. Launch SWPM and change the directory to the SWPM directory.

2. Execute sapinst to launch the installation (see Figure 3.2).

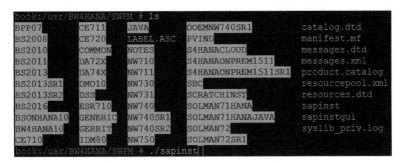

Figure 3.2 SWPM Launch

3. Once SWPM is open, navigate to **SAP BW/4HANA • SAP BW/4HANA Server • SAP HANA Database • Preparations** and double-click **Prerequisites Check** (see Figure 3.3).

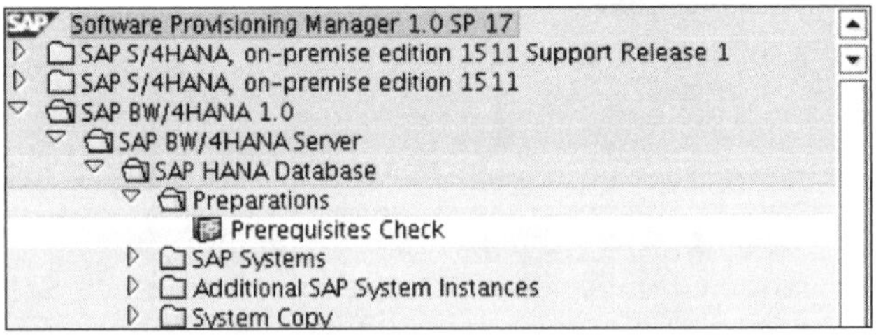

Figure 3.3 Prerequisites Check

4. Verify that the installation package includes all of the required media to complete the installation.

5. Once the check is completed successfully, close SWPM, then relaunch it. Follow the same path as before, select **SAP Systems • Application Server ABAP • Standard System**, and double-click **Standard System**.

6. On the next screen, select your **Parameter Mode**. There are two choices: **Typical** and **Custom**. Typical mode will only require responses to a limited number of prompts; all other options are set to their defaults. On the **Parameter Summary** screen, you can review and change any defaults that have been applied in the background. Custom mode will require input for all parameters, though they can also be changed again on the **Parameter Summary** screen. In order to fully explain each parameter, we'll use the custom mode for our example.

7. Enter your **SAP System ID (SAPSID)** and either accept the default **SAP Mount Directory** or define another location. Choose the SAPSID carefully; the renaming process is complicated and requires reinstallation of the system. When choosing an SAPSID, remember that no two systems can have the same SAPSID. We've found that the best practice for choosing an SAPSID is to make it reflect what the system is used for in a logical manner. For example, for your SAP BW systems, the first letter should be B; for production, quality assurance, and development, use BxP, BxQ, and BxD, respectively. This adds a layer of meaning to prevent users from mistakenly working in production when they should be in development.

   In the next box, accept the default location or change it to a location of your choosing. We recommended you keep the default location; it should only be changed if recommended by an SAP Note or by SAP directly (see Figure 3.4).

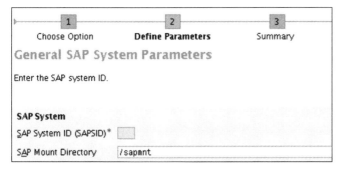

Figure 3.4 SAPSID Creation

8. Now that you've chosen an SAPSID, you need to set up your system domain name. SWPM will ask if you want to set a **Fully Qualified Domain Name (FQDN)**; check the box to do so, or leave it unchecked if you don't want to set an FQDN. If you decide to set an FQDN, you must enter your network's domain name. We recommend setting an FQDN; doing so will allow administrators to change internet protocol (IP) addresses. Also, if you want to use HTTP-based frameworks such as Web Dynpro applications, you'll need to set an FQDN.

9. Once you've set up your FQDN, you're asked to set a master password for your system. Doing so will set the password for all users that are created during the installation, such as <sid>adm and database users. If such a user already exists in the system, you'll be prompted to confirm the password for the user. You'll have the opportunity to set individual passwords on the **Parameter Summary** screen, but remember that if you decide to do so, the master password doesn't overwrite the individual settings.

10. The next screen gives the options for the SAP system administrator, <sid>adm. This screen doesn't appear in typical mode. Here, you have the option of entering a password other than the master password. By default, the master password is already entered. If the user already exists in the system, enter the existing password. You may also set the user ID, group ID, login shell, and the location of the home directory. If you don't want to change the password from the master password or change any of the other settings, you can leave them as is and accept the default settings (see Figure 3.5).

Figure 3.5 SAP System Administrator Setup

11. After verifying the SAP system administrator, you'll enter the information for the SAP HANA database. This will allow SWPM to create a schema for SAP BW/4HANA and to create the necessary users. Here, you must input the SAPSID of the database, the host, the instance number, and the password of the system administrator. If you want to install the system with a new database instance, you'll need to enter the database SID for the instance to be created. As before, be careful when choosing the new database SID; it can't be changed easily. If you're using a multitenant database container, you must use the database parameters and password for that tenant database and not for the system database.

12. On the next screen, you'll select either the media CD location, the directory downloaded from the maintenance planner, or the individual package locations within the manually downloaded kernel. For the CD, click **Add** and then browse to the location. Repeat for each CD. For the directory downloaded from maintenance planner, under **Download Basket** click the **Browse** button and navigate to the location of the directory. This will automatically populate the individual package locations. To choose the individual package locations from the kernel directory manually, select **SAPEXE.SAR**, **SAPHOSTAGENT.SAR**, **IGSEXE.SAR**, and **IGSHELPER.SAR** from the **DBINDEP** directory within the kernel, and select **SAPEXEDB.SAR** from the **HDB** directory within the kernel (see Figure 3.6).

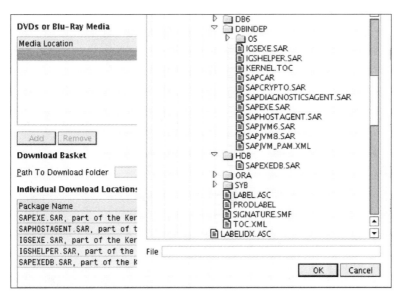

Figure 3.6 Media Selection

13. On the next screen, choose the client path strategy between the local client directory and central client directory. This will be based on your individual implementation; make the decision based upon the needs and availability of your infrastructure.

14. On the next screen, identify the location of the SAP HANA database client. Click **Browse** and select the client that matches the operating system and hardware you're installing on.

15. Now, you'll be prompted to review the DBACOCKPIT schema creation information. You can choose to keep the master password or set a unique one.

16. On the next screen, review the user for SAP BW/4HANA. Here, you can change the name of the schema. We recommend that you change it to a logical name; otherwise each ABAP system you install on the same database will be as follows: SAPA-BAP1, SAPABAP2, and so on. If you're reinstalling, you can choose to delete the existing schema and use the same name.

17. As shown in Figure 3.7, the next screen lets you select which import parameters should be kept after the import has finished. Select the **Keep after Import** checkbox for each parameter to be kept after the import has finished. You can change the parameters to optimize the import, but the exact parameters to set depend on your individual situation. Therefore, it's best to leave the default settings for most scenarios.

SAP HANA Import Parameters

Enter the import parameters.

SAP HANA Import

Import Parameters

Configuration File*	Section*	Parameter Name*	Parameter Value*	Keep after Import
indexserver.ini	distribution	client_distribution_mode	statement	☑
global.ini	table_placement	prefix	/	☑
global.ini	table_placement	method	2	☑
indexserver.ini	mergedog	critical_merge_decision_func	DMS>12000 and ...	☐
indexserver.ini	mergedog	num_merge_token	200	☐
indexserver.ini	mergedog	token_per_table	2	☐
indexserver.ini	mergedog	auto_merge_decision_func	DMS>5000 and ...	☐
indexserver.ini	optimize_compression	min_hours_since_last_merge_o...	0	☐
global.ini	persistence	savepoint_interval_s	300	☐

Figure 3.7 SAP HANA Import Parameters

18. On the next screen, choose to enable or disable decluster/depool ABAP tables. Make the decision that works best for your situation. See SAP Note 189235 for more information.

19. Next, indicate how many parallel jobs for exporting and importing data you'd like to run at the same time. SAP recommends using a maximum of two to three parallel jobs per CPU core. The higher the number you can use, the faster the installation process will be.

20. Now, enter the primary application server (PAS) instance number and host, as well as the ABAP central services (ASCS) instance and host. You can choose any two-digit number for either the PAS or ASCS. You mustn't use the same instance number more than once for any system on the installation host. If you're completing a high-availability system installation, use a virtual host name for the ASCS instance.

21. On the next screen, verify or change the ABAP message server ports. In most cases, you'll only verify the port; the default is 3600 plus the instance number. The only time this would change is if the port is already in use by another application.

22. After you've reviewed or changed the message server ports, the next screen will allow you to set a password for the internet communication manager (ICM) user management. The webadm user will be created to use the web administration interface for the ICM and web dispatcher. If you don't want to change the password from the master password, continue on to the next screen.

23. You're now prompted to either register the new system with the system landscape directory (SLD) or choose not to do so. We recommend registering the system; it will save time later on. Once completed, the data supplier is enabled to send OS information to the SLD.

24. Next, you can create a message server access control list (ACL), which defines the hosts that the message server will accept requests from. This should only be done if you won't be installing any additional instances on the host. When created, ACL will overwrite previous settings and inhibit any other instances to be created. This decision can be reversed later if there's a need for additional instances; simply delete the file manually and recreate it during the installation of the new instance.

25. Now, choose whether to encrypt confidential data by selecting an individual key or to use obfuscation by selecting a default key. The key is used to encrypt the secure storage in the database. SAP recommends that all production systems use encryption via an individual key. If you decide to use an individual key, when you click **Next**, a screen will open to show the key information (see Figure 3.8). As per the **Caution** note shown, imperative that a copy of this information be kept in a secure location in the event of a disaster. The information will be needed for recovery if such an event occurs.

Figure 3.8 Individual Key Information

26. The next selection screen allows you to accept the automatic unpacking of the system archives.

27. You've now completed the initial configuration of the installation. The next screen shows the **Parameter Summary**. It's very important that you go through each parameter to verify that it's correct. Once you start the installation process, the only way to change any of the parameters is to start all over again. As you can see in Figure 3.9, to make a revision, click the checkbox next to each parameter that you need to change, then click **Revise**. SWPM will then take you back to the selection screen for each parameter you want to change.

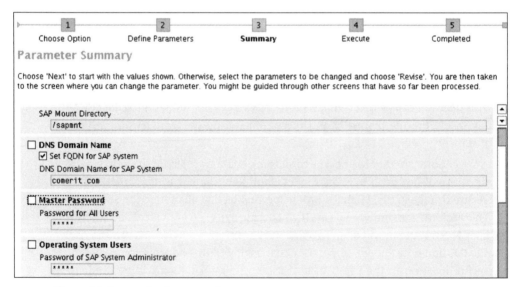

Figure 3.9 Parameter Summary Screen

28. Once you click **Next**, the installation will begin immediately. The slowest part of the installation will be the import ABAP phase, in which information is created and sent to the database. Figure 3.10 shows the complete list of all twenty-five phases of the installation.

If an error should arise, it's best to go to the location where the log file exists and read it directly, rather than use the SWPM log reader. Once you've corrected the error, click **Retry** and the process will pick up where it left off. If for any reason the host crashes or any other event happens, restart SWPM and follow the same steps as before. When it asks if you would like to continue with a new option or continue with the previous setup, select **New Option**. We've had mixed results when choosing **Continue**.

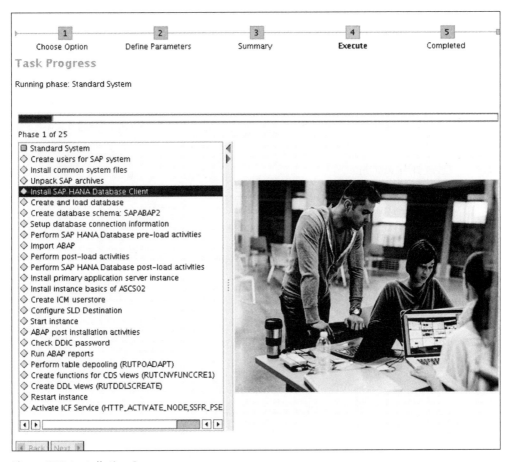

Figure 3.10 Installation Screen

Now that your installation is complete, SAP BW/4HANA will be started and ready for the postinstallation steps.

3.3   Postinstallation

In this section, we'll cover the postinstallation activities required before the system becomes operational. Before you begin, verify that your copy of SAP GUI is version 7.40 or higher.

After the installation is completed, refer to the central note for SAP BW/4HANA, SAP Note 234738. This note will be updated with relevant information for setup after an installation to include important notes that need to be implemented after installation or update and postinstallation activities.

Before starting the postinstallation activities, perform a database backup of SAP HANA.

3.3.1   SAP HANA Database Technical User Setup

As covered in SAP Note 2362807, first you need to verify the technical SAP BW/4HANA user (SAP<SID>) in the SAP HANA database to make sure it has the following permissions:

- Object permissions
  - SELECT for schema _SYS_BI
  - SELECT for schema _SYS_BIC
  - SELECT for the BW schema
  - EXECUTE for procedure REPOSITORY_REST (SYS)
- Analytic permissions
  - _SYS_BI_CP_ALL
- Package privileges
  - REPO.MAINTAIN_NATIVE_PACKAGES
  - REPO.READ
  - REPO.EDIT_NATIVE_OBJECTS
  - REPO.ACTIVATE_NATIVE_OBJECTS

You should also verify that the user _SYS_REPO_ has the following object permissions:

- SELECT on BW schema with GRANT option
- SELECT on tables mentioned in table RSOSTABLES

3.3.2   SAP BW/4HANA Setup

Now that the users in the database have been verified, a task list must run. This task list performs the basic system setup to create the background user, configuring the client and installing the necessary technical content, such as InfoObjects and variables.

To run the task list, follow these steps:

1. Login to the system using the user sap* and your master password.

2. Go to Transaction STC01.

3. Enter "SAP_BW4_SETUP_SIMPLE" into the text box.

4. Press ⌈F8⌋ or click **Generate Task List Run**. Your screen should look like Figure 3.11. You'll see each phase that will be run and a short description of what it does.

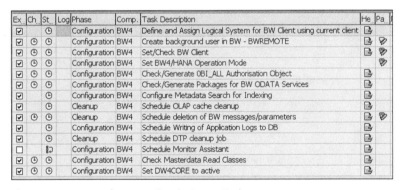

Ex	Ch	St	Log	Phase	Comp.	Task Description	He	Pa	
☑		⊕		Configuration	BW4	Define and Assign Logical System for BW Client using current client	📄		
☑	⊕	⊕		Configuration	BW4	Create background user in BW - BWREMOTE	📄	🐾	
☑	⊕	⊕		Configuration	BW4	Set/Check BW Client	📄	🐾	
☑		⊕		Configuration	BW4	Set BW4/HANA Operation Mode		🐾	
☑	⊕	⊕		Configuration	BW4	Check/Generate 0BI_ALL Authorisation Object	📄		
☑	⊕	⊕		Configuration	BW4	Check/Generate Packages for BW ODATA Services	📄		
☑		⊕		Configuration	BW4	Configure Metadata Search for Indexing	📄		
☑		⊕		Cleanup	BW4	Schedule OLAP cache cleanup	📄		
☑	⊕	⊕		Cleanup	BW4	Schedule deletion of BW messages/parameters	📄	🐾	
☑		⊕		Configuration	BW4	Schedule Writing of Application Logs to DB	📄		
☑		⊕		Cleanup	BW4	Schedule DTP cleanup job	📄		
☐		🔢		Configuration	BW4	Schedule Monitor Assistant	📄		
☑	⊕	⊕		Configuration	BW4	Check Masterdata Read Classes	📄		
☑	⊕	⊕		Configuration	BW4	Set DW4CORE to active	📄		

Figure 3.11 SAP BW/4HANA Simple Setup Tasks

5. Under the **Parameters** column, select **Fill** for **Create Background User in BW**.

6. Enter a password and click **Continue**.

7. Select display parameters for **Set/Check BW Client**.

8. Enter the client you want to use as the SAP BW client.

9. Select **Change Parameters** under the **Parameters** column for **Set BW/4HANA Operation Mode**. If you're using SAP BW/4HANA as a data warehouse, set the parameter to the maximum value, 16.

10. Select the **Fill Parameters** under the **Parameters** column.

11. Enter the number of days you want messages or parameters to be retained for.

12. Verify that all the information is correct.

13. Press [F8] or click **Start/Resume Task list** in **Dialog**.

3.3.3   RFC and Parameter Configuration

Once the task list has completed successfully, the next step is to configure a connection to an SAP router and add parameters to the default profile.

To configure a connection to an SAP router, follow these steps:

1. Login to SAP BW/4HANA from client 000 and go to Transaction OSS1.

2. Click **Parameter**, then click **Technical Settings**.

3. Click **Change** and add the information for your SAP router. Then, click the **Save** icon.

4. Go to Transaction SM59 and verify that ABAP connection SAPOSS has been created. Double-click **SAPOSS** and click **Connection Test** to verify that the connection to SAP router is complete.

To add parameters to the default profile, follow these steps:

1. Go Transaction RZ10, select the **DEFAULT** profile, click the **Extended Maintenance** radio button, and click **Change**.

2. Add the parameters from Table 3.2. (Replace $$ with the instance number of the system.)

3. Click **Exit**, click **Yes** to save the changes, save, accept the changes, click **Yes** to activate the profile, and accept the informational message by clicking **Yes**.

4. Restart SAP BW/4HANA to apply the parameter changes.

Parameter Name	Parameter Value
login/no_automatic_user_sapstar	0
icm/server_port_0	PROT=HTTP,PORT=80$$, PROCTIMEOUT=600, TIMEOUT=600
icm/server_port_1	PROT=SAPHTTP,PORT=80$$,PROCTIMEOUT=600, TIMEOUT=600

Table 3.2 Parameter Names and Values

Parameter Name	Parameter Value
icm/server_port_2	PROT=SMTP,PORT=25$$,PROCTIMEOUT=600, TIMEOUT=600
icm/server_port_3	PROT=HTTPS,PORT=52$$,PROCTIMEOUT=600, TIMEOUT=600

Table 3.2 Parameter Names and Values (Cont.)

3.3.4   Configuring SAP BW/4HANA Workspaces

Now that your system has restarted, you need to activate and configure the SAP BW/4HANA workspace. From client 000, go to Transaction SICF and activate the following services:

- RSL_UI_MY_WORKSPACE
- RSL_UI_CREATE_COPR
- RSL_UI_CREATE_PROVIDER
- RSL_UI_CHANGE_WORKSPACE
- RSL_UI_CHANGE_QUERIES
- RSL_UI_SUBMIT_DATA
- RSL_UI_CREATE_LCHA
- RSL_UI_CREATE_LCHY
- nwbc_launch

Now, you'll create the necessary roles and profiles required to meet your business needs. To give business users an environment to use SAP BW Workspace Designer, give them a link to SAP Business Client, or assign the SAP_BW_WORKSPACE_DESIGNER role or the com.sap.ip.i.bi_showcase portal role.

3.3.5   SAP BW/4HANA Table Placement

The next steps ensure that the tables of the system are partitioned correctly with SAP's recommendations. SAP Note 2334091 covers the table placement and landscape redistribution for SAP BW/4HANA. To complete these tasks, follow these steps:

1. Open a SQL console in SAP HANA Studio and run the following statement with user SAP<SID>: SELECT * FROM TABLE_PLACEMENT;.

2. If the result contains entries for the schema, verify the table placement settings meet current SAP recommendations. If they do, proceed to Step 6. If the result doesn't contain entries or isn't current, proceed to the next step.

3. Download *TABLE_PLACEMENT_BW4HANA.zip* from SAP Note 2334091, extract, select the correct database, select the correct landscape, and open the SQL file in Notepad.

> **Note**
>
> SAP Note 2334091 directs you to use *TABLE_PLACEMENT_BW4_FILL_PROC.txt*. The script will automatically detect your landscape and run the correct SQL statement. We've chosen to use the ZIP file to show what the script is doing.

4. In Notepad, in the menu, select **Edit • Replace**. Enter "<$$PLACEHOLDER>" in **Find What** and the SAP BW/4HANA schema name in **Replace With**, then click **Replace All**. Verify that your schema name has replaced all instances of <$$PLACEHOLDER>. Figure 3.12 shows what the SQL file looks like prior to inserting the schema name.

```
HdbTablePlacementParameters.SQL - Notepad
File  Edit  Format  View  Help
--[BEGIN HEADER]
-- VERSION 1
-- This is version 1 of the parameter file
--[END HEADER]

ALTER SYSTEM ALTER CONFIGURATION ('global.ini','SYSTEM') SET ('table_placement','max_rows_per_partition') = '1500000000

ALTER SYSTEM ALTER TABLE PLACEMENT
SET (LOCATION => 'master', MIN_ROWS_FOR_PARTITIONING => 0, INITIAL_PARTITIONS => 1, REPARTITIONING_THRESHOLD => 0);

ALTER SYSTEM ALTER TABLE PLACEMENT (SCHEMA_NAME => '$$PLACEHOLDER')
SET (LOCATION => 'master', MIN_ROWS_FOR_PARTITIONING => 0, INITIAL_PARTITIONS => 1, REPARTITIONING_THRESHOLD => 0);

ALTER SYSTEM ALTER TABLE PLACEMENT (SCHEMA_NAME => '$$PLACEHOLDER', GROUP_TYPE => 'sap.bw.dso')
SET (LOCATION => 'master', MIN_ROWS_FOR_PARTITIONING => 50000000, INITIAL_PARTITIONS => 1, REPARTITIONING_THRESHOLD =>

ALTER SYSTEM ALTER TABLE PLACEMENT (SCHEMA_NAME => '$$PLACEHOLDER', GROUP_TYPE => 'sap.bw.iobj')
SET (LOCATION => 'master', MIN_ROWS_FOR_PARTITIONING => 1500000000, INITIAL_PARTITIONS => 1, REPARTITIONING_THRESHOLD

ALTER SYSTEM ALTER TABLE PLACEMENT (SCHEMA_NAME => '$$PLACEHOLDER', GROUP_TYPE => 'sap.bw.psa')
SET (LOCATION => 'master', MIN_ROWS_FOR_PARTITIONING => 1500000000, INITIAL_PARTITIONS => 1, REPARTITIONING_THRESHOLD

ALTER SYSTEM ALTER TABLE PLACEMENT (SCHEMA_NAME => '$$PLACEHOLDER', GROUP_TYPE => 'sap.bw.dtp')
SET (LOCATION => 'master', MIN_ROWS_FOR_PARTITIONING => 1500000000, INITIAL_PARTITIONS => 1, REPARTITIONING_THRESHOLD

ALTER SYSTEM ALTER TABLE PLACEMENT (SCHEMA_NAME => '$$PLACEHOLDER', GROUP_TYPE => 'sap.bw.dsrc')
SET (LOCATION => 'master', MIN_ROWS_FOR_PARTITIONING => 200000000, INITIAL_PARTITIONS => 1, REPARTITIONING_THRESHOLD =

ALTER SYSTEM ALTER TABLE PLACEMENT (SCHEMA_NAME => '$$PLACEHOLDER', GROUP_TYPE => 'sap.bw.temp')
SET (LOCATION => 'master', MIN_ROWS_FOR_PARTITIONING => 0, INITIAL_PARTITIONS => 1, REPARTITIONING_THRESHOLD => 0);

ALTER SYSTEM ALTER TABLE PLACEMENT (SCHEMA_NAME => '$$PLACEHOLDER', GROUP_TYPE => 'sap.bw.openhub')
SET (LOCATION => 'master', MIN_ROWS_FOR_PARTITIONING => 0, INITIAL_PARTITIONS => 1, REPARTITIONING_THRESHOLD => 0);
```

Figure 3.12 SAP BW/4HANA Table Placement

5. Open a SQL console in SAP HANA Studio with user SAP<SID>, copy and paste the contents of the modified SQL file, and execute. Verify that the entries for the schema have been set by running `SELECT * FROM TABLE_PLACEMENT;`.

6. Verify that the parameters in the SAP HANA *database global.ini* file are set in accordance with your landscape from SAP Note 2334091 Step 2.

7. Download *REQUIRED_CORRECTION_NOTES_BW4HANA.xlsx* from SAP Note 2334091 and apply the notes listed in the spreadsheet.

8. To make sure that all SAP BW tables have been classified correctly, log in to SAP BW/4HANA from client 000 and run report RSDU_TABLE_CONSISTENCY from Transaction SE38. Execute the consistency check CL_SCEN_TAB_CLASSIFICATION and correct any errors.

9. Create a backup of the SAP HANA database.

10. Start the landscape redistribution.

3.3.6   Client Copy

Now that you've set the table placement for the system, the next step is to create a new client by performing a local client copy, as follows:

1. Login to client 000 and go to Transaction SCC4.

2. Click the **Change** button and accept the warning.

3. Enter a three-digit number for the client, the name of the client, the location, a logical system if applicable, the type of currency for the data used, and the type of client it will be.

4. Select the type of security measures for protecting changes and transports.

5. Click **Save**, then go back and verify that the new client was created.

6. Login to the new client with user <SAP*> and password <PASS>.

7. Go to Transaction SCCL. Select profile **SAP_ALL**, source client **000**, and source client user masters **000**.

8. Click **Schedule as a Background Job**. Client copy logs can be viewed from Transaction SCC3.

9. Once the client copy has completed, you can set the new client as the default client.

10. Go to Transaction RZ10 and select the **DEFAULT** profile.

11. Click the radio button for **Extended Maintenance** and click **Change**.

> **Note**
>
> During the client copy, all tables from SAP BW/4HANA will be brought into memory. For development and quality assurance systems, verify there is sufficient memory to complete the client copy.

12. Click **Create** and add the following parameter:
    - **Parameter Name**: login/system_client
    - **Parameter Value**: <Client number>
13. Click **Save**, go back, save, accept the message, and restart the system for the parameter to be active.

3.3.7   Service Pack Upgrade and SAP License Installation

Before your system is completely operational, you'll need to upgrade to the latest service pack. Each service pack contains new corrections and optimizations that should be applied prior to going live. Our recommendation is to connect the system to SAP Solution Manager. From there, you can upload the system information to SAP, use maintenance planner to download the service pack media, and use Software Update Manager (SUM) to complete the update. Alternatively, you can download the service packs directly from SAP and use Transaction SPAM to update.

The last remaining step before your system is operational is to install a permanent SAP license for your system; SAP installs a 90-day temporary license from the date of installation. From Transaction SLICENSE, you can view and install your license.

3.4   Summary

In this chapter, we walked through the installation and configuration of a standard SAP BW/4HANA system. There may be additional configurations required to meet an organization's specific needs. Therefore, the needs of the business should be understood and the installation should be planned in detail to prevent complications in the future. In the next chapter, we'll discuss the deployment of SAP BW/4HANA in the cloud.

Chapter 4

SAP BW/4HANA in the Cloud

With the rise of cloud deployments, it's important to consider whether to deploy SAP BW/4HANA on-premise or in the cloud. In this chapter, we'll discuss the latter option.

SAP designed SAP BW/4HANA for deployment in the cloud. As of April 2017, there aren't a lot of differences between SAP BW 7.5 powered by SAP HANA and SAP BW/4HANA, but some of the developments that SAP has promised around data integration will provide flexibility to help integrate SAP BW/4HANA in cloud systems. You can deploy SAP BW/4HANA on the following cloud offerings, among others:

- SAP HANA Enterprise Cloud
- Amazon Web Services (AWS)
- Microsoft Azure
- Virtustream by Dell EMC

Many of the providers offer infrastructure as a service (IaaS); hence, installing the SAP system still must be performed as described in Chapter 3.

In this chapter, we'll begin by discussing some of the criteria for choosing a cloud provider before looking at some specific providers. We'll end the chapter by briefly walking through the SAP BW/4HANA cloud deployment steps.

4.1   Choosing a Cloud Provider

Choosing a cloud provider is generally a separate process from SAP BW/4HANA system deployment. This section will cover some of the main selection criteria. However, before considering specific selection criteria, it's important for a company to define a cloud strategy.

Defining a company strategy for the cloud is recommended to avoid costly projects and later redeployments caused by changes in requirements and partners.

Several cloud providers offer cloud and datacenter strategy workshops that can provide initial strategy input and answer questions related to the specific provider.

The workshops normally include the following elements:

- An analysis of your business drivers, priorities, investment objectives, and technology enablers
- Enabling a high-level IT strategy that supports your specific business objectives, such as market differentiation, innovation, and cost-savings
- Determining the appropriate action plan for your organization to meet the outlined goals and priorities

The strategy should include a long-term vision of where the company wants to go with cloud deployments and a roadmap for how to get there.

We generally recommend starting small and growing the cloud footprint, and most deployments we've been involved in have been hybrid cloud deployments that make use of both on-premise and cloud.

With the cloud strategy in place, a more specific selection process to find a primary cloud provider follows. From what we've seen in the marketplace, most companies might have a primary and a secondary cloud provider, depending on the size of the company and the offerings provided. Now, in the following subsections, let's look at the primary cloud provider selection criteria:

- Performance
- Technology and certification
- Service level
- Ecosystem and community
- Security
- Cost
- Preferred providers

4.1.1 Performance

Performance is always a main concern when moving to a cloud provider. Performance is multifaceted: Both agility in deploying a new system and the technical performance of the hardware used plays a role in the overall performance rating. Performance issues include the geographical distance of the application and data to the end user, network performance within the cloud provider and to the end users, and disk I/O access speed between the compute and storage subsystems. Services and research reports such as CloudSleuth and CloudHarmony have attempted to measure the performance of cloud providers from various locations and for different application use cases.

4.1.2   Technology and Certification

Some cloud providers have focused their offerings on specific applications. Because we're looking at deploying SAP BW/4HANA, it's important to verify that the provider has experience with and is SAP-certified for SAP HANA deployments.

In addition to the certification, it's also important to look at the tools and APIs provided for managing the cloud platform.

4.1.3   Service-Level Agreements and Reliability

Cloud providers offer guarantees for levels of service; the guarantee is only an indication of the consequences when the service fails, however, and you should compare the consequences with the service-level agreement (SLA) before reading too much into the numbers provided. A high SLA does not mean much unless there's a significant penalty when the service is down unexpectedly. We recommend talking with existing customers and using comparison services such as CloudSleuth and CloudHarmony.

4.1.4   Ecosystem and Community

Cloud providers all offer tools and APIs to build and manage applications. If you've started building tools on one provider's APIs, it can be costly to rebuild on another provider's APIs.

Amazon, Virtustream, and Azure allow customers to implement in-house clouds using their tools and APIs. This allows for hybrid cloud deployments, with some systems in the cloud and others on-premise.

4.1.5   Security and Compliance

Two of the biggest barriers for companies considering cloud computing continue to be security and compliance. The real concern for enterprises is not truly security threats themselves, but rather the company's inability to achieve compliance with security-related standards. Many cloud providers have security and compliance standards that exceed what companies have been able to build internally, so this concern should be reviewed and an appropriate provider selected that meets or exceeds the standards you want.

4.1.6   Costs

Normally cloud providers are compared on costs, but this isn't always easy; costing models among cloud providers vary quite a bit. Some providers charge for the capacity you signed up for and other for the capacity you actually use. Providers offer VMs that vary widely in memory capacity, CPU clock speed, and other features. Also, the units provided to customers are often virtualized, creating further confusion as to what the customer is getting and how it might be impacted by shared infrastructure on the same cloud.

One way to measure the cost performance of different cloud providers is to conduct an experiment with the same application or prototype on multiple providers and compare the results. For SAP BW/4HANA, SAP has done this work and certified Azure and Amazon for certain SAP HANA sizes that you can expect to be very similar in performance.

4.1.7   Preferred Providers

Most companies have a list of preferred vendors that they work with, rather than send out requests to all possible vendors that could provide a service. Existing hardware and software providers like HP, IBM, Microsoft, and Dell EMC have cloud offerings that provide a similar setup as Amazon AWS. The most flexible one seems to be Azure, but also Dell EMC's Virtustream cloud has proven to be flexible specifically for SAP applications for which their tools exceed the capabilities of other providers.

It can sometimes be beneficial to work with providers that you have a long-term relationship with. However, it's important that a provider choice not made because of personal relationships or because it feels "safe" to choose one of the legacy companies.

Final Selection

When making a final selection, compare all the dimensions of the cloud offering. Once a cloud provider has been selected, it becomes easier to use that provider for subsequent systems because it's already set up and hence requires less effort to integrate into the network, security, and processes. Many large companies will have more than one provider to ensure that they can get the right costs and have flexibility to move workload between providers if needed.

4.2   Cloud Providers

In this section, we'll cover some of the cloud provider offerings for SAP BW/4HANA. Certified IaaS details can be found on the SAP HANA certification website at *http://global.sap.com/community/ebook/2014-09-02-hana-hardware/enEN/iaas.html*.

Some additional options are available from cloud providers that are certified as TDI solutions.

4.2.1   SAP HANA Enterprise Cloud

SAP HANA Enterprise Cloud offers a platform as a service (PaaS) option. SAP can provide services up to the SAP Basis layer, allowing companies to just make use of the application. More details on SAP HANA enterprise cloud can be found at *https://www.sap.com/product/technology-platform/hana-enterprise-cloud.html#*.

We recommend contacting your SAP account executive to discuss the details of SAP HANA Enterprise Cloud. The following are some aspects to keep in mind when considering SAP HANA Enterprise Cloud to serve as your cloud provider for SAP BW/4HANA:

- **Deployment**
  SAP provides systems through IaaS providers such as HP, IBM, and Virtustream. It can take a few days to get a system deployed, depending on the provider.

- **Licensing**
  SAP HANA Enterprise Cloud uses *bring your own license* (BYOL) for SAP ABAP-based systems.

- **Supported SAP HANA scenarios**
  SAP supports most SAP software, including SAP BW/4HANA, for deployment via SAP HANA Enterprise Cloud. For specific scenarios, discuss your options with SAP.

- **Pricing and sizing**
  SAP doesn't have a public price list for SAP HANA Enterprise Cloud.

- **Regions available**
  SAP HANA Enterprise clouds is available where SAPs providers operate; there is no official list of available areas.

4.2.2   Amazon Web Services

AWS provides a set of standard certified options for deploying SAP BW/4HANA on an IaaS platform. AWS worked closely with SAP to launch SAP BW/4HANA and had some of the first deployments running live when SAP BW/4HANA was announced in September 2016. Deploying SAP BW/4HANA on AWS generally takes less than a couple of hours to get a system provisioned, and then you can start development.

An overview of the SAP BW/4HANA options on AWS can be found at *https:// aws.amazon.com/sap/solutions/bw4hana/*. We will cover the main details in this section.

SAP HANA on AWS can be deployed on either the SUSE Linux Enterprise Server (SLES) or the Red Hat Enterprise Linux (RHEL) operating system. Certain SAP HANA scenarios are supported on a multinode cluster, providing up to 4 TB of total memory; see SAP Note 1964437 for additional details. The following are some aspects to keep in mind when considering AWS to serve as your cloud provider for SAP BW/4HANA:

- **Deployment**
  AWS Quick Start reference deployment for SAP HANA provides an automated process for deploying SAP HANA on AWS. This Quick Start option allows you to deploy single-node and multinode SAP HANA systems on AWS in less than one hour. The quick start reference can be found at *http://docs.aws.amazon.com/quickstart/ latest/sap-hana/welcome.html*.

- **Licensing**
  SAP BW/4HANA on AWS uses a BYOL model for the SAP HANA license and SAP BW/4HANA license.

  SLES and RHEL operating system licenses are provided by AWS, and their relevant license fees are combined with the base hourly fee of the corresponding Amazon Elastic Compute Cloud (EC2) instance type.

- **Supported SAP HANA scenarios**
  The SAP HANA scenarios listed in Table 4.1 are supported by SAP for production on AWS.

Supported Scenarios on AWS
SAP BW/4HANA
SAP Business Warehouse and SAP Business Planning and Consolidation (SAP BPC) on SAP HANA
Native SAP HANA applications

Table 4.1 Supported SAP HANA Scenarios on AWS

Supported Scenarios on AWS
Data marts and analytics
SAP S/4HANA
SAP Business Suite (SAP ERP, SAP CRM, etc.) powered by SAP HANA
SAP HANA Live/sidecar
SAP Business One, version for SAP HANA

Table 4.1 Supported SAP HANA Scenarios on AWS (Cont.)

For additional information about supported SAP HANA scenarios, including SAP BW/4HANA, see SAP Note 1964437.

- **Pricing and sizing**
  Scale-out/OLAP workloads like SAP BW/4HANA, data marts, analytics, SAP BW, and SAP Business Planning and Consolidation (SAP BPC) are supported on multinode/scale-out configurations providing up to 14 TB of memory when using the x1.32xlarge instance type. AWS provides two options for deploying SAP BW/4HANA: co-deployment of SAP HANA and the SAP BW/4HANA application, and a distributed deployment in which the SAP BW/4HANA application runs on separate VMs. The co-deployed option is the most efficient, because the network traffic is always internal to the VM between the application and the SAP HANA database.

  When the size of SAP HANA requires all the resources on the VM, we recommend distributing the SAP BW/4HANA application to a separate VM.

  Table 4.2 and Table 4.3 provide estimates of sample SAP BW/4HANA configurations on AWS. To estimate the pricing for a multinode/scale-out SAP BW/4HANA cluster, multiply the cost of a single SAP BW/4HANA node configuration by the number of nodes required. For additional information about estimating AWS infrastructure pricing for SAP solutions, see the SAP on AWS Pricing Guide at *https://d0.awsstatic.com/enterprise-marketing/SAP/sap-on-aws-pricing-guide.pdf*.

  Amazon EC2 offers both on-demand instances and reserved instances. We normally recommend using reserved instances unless for a temporary system, because the discounts are substantial.

- **Regions available**
  SAP HANA Infrastructure Services on AWS is currently available in all AWS regions except for Beijing.

EC2 Instance Type	vCPU	Memory (GB)	Supported for Production
r3.2xlarge	8	61	No
r3.4xlarge	16	122	No
r3.8xlarge	32	244	Yes
r4.16xlarge	64	488	Coming soon
x1.16xlarge	64	976	Yes
x1.32xlarge	128	1,952	Yes

Table 4.2 AWS Size Options for SAP BW/4HANA and SAP HANA Co-deployed

SAP HANA System				SAP NetWeaver AS System		
EC2 Instance Type	vCPU	Memory (GB)	Supported for production	EC2 Instance Type	vCPU	Memory (GB)
r3.4xlarge	16	122	No	r4.large	2	15.25
r3.8xlarge	32	244	Yes	r4.xlarge	4	30.50
r4.16xlarge	64	488	Coming soon	r4.2xlarge	8	61.00
r1.16xlarge	64	976	Yes	r4.2xlarge	8	61.00
x1.32xlarge	128	1952	Yes	r4.2xlarge	8	61.00

Table 4.3 1 Amazon EC2 Instance for the SAP HANA DB and 1 Amazon EC2 Instance for the SAP NetWeaver AS

4.2.3   Microsoft Azure

Microsoft Azure provides SAP HANA systems in different sizes, like AWS; Azure has a set of standard certified sizes and deployment options available, ranging from smaller systems to larger systems.

More details about the Microsoft Azure SAP HANA option and architecture is available on Microsoft's website at *https://docs.microsoft.com/en-us/azure/virtual-machines/workloads/sap/hana-overview-architecture.*

The following are some aspects to keep in mind when considering Microsoft Azure to serve as your cloud provider for SAP BW/4HANA:

- **Deployment**

  Microsoft Azure's deployment can be handled on standard provided VMs or in its large instance stamp infrastructure. SAP HANA on standard GS5 VMs is limited in size to 448 GB for production use; smaller sizes are available for nonproduction use. SAP Note 1928533 (SAP Applications on Azure: Supported Products and Azure VM Types) describes the details of SAP deployments on Azure, including SAP HANA VMs.

  The large instance option includes sizes up to 2 TB for SAP BW/4HANA and can be configured as scale-out. SAP Note 2316233 (SAP HANA on Microsoft Azure [Large Instances]) describes the large instances on Azure. Note that the large instances don't run on VMs but instead are installed on bare metal; hence, a failure or shutdown of the system won't automatically fail over to another server.

  The architecture of the large instances is depicted in Figure 4.1. The large instances run on certified hardware within Azure and on bare metal.

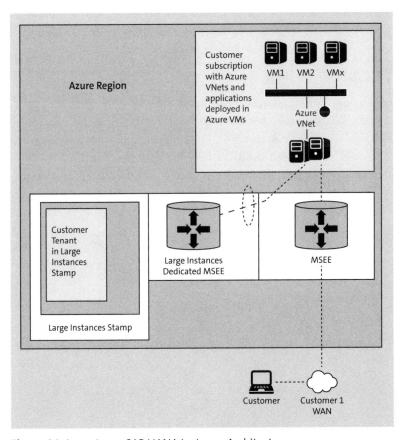

Figure 4.1 Azure Large SAP HANA Instance Architecture

Microsoft has a specific SLA for large instances, with 99.999 percent uptime. With 99.99 percent uptime, a 10 percent service credit is provided; with 99.9 percent uptime, a 25 percent credit is provided. The details are available on the Azure website at *https://azure.microsoft.com/support/legal/sla/sap-hana-large/v1_0/*.

- **Licensing**
  Azure provides IaaS; hence, it's required that licenses are purchased for the SAP HANA database and SAP BW/4HANA from SAP.

- **Supported SAP HANA scenarios**
  Azure supports most SAP software on their platforms, including SAP BW/4HANA, in both scale-up and scale-out approaches.

- **Pricing and sizing**
  Azure pricing is competitive with AWS, and pricing can be negotiated for large instances.

- **Regions available**
  SAP HANA is available in all Azure regions with large instance stamp infrastructure.

4.2.4   Other Providers

The list of other providers is long. Some of the big ones are IBM, Huawei, Virtustream, and HP, and as of April 2017 Google has been certified to run SAP HANA via Google Cloud. Most providers offer services, sizing, and pricing similar to those noted previously and provide certification via the SAP TDI certification. In addition, some providers have been certified for standard size deployments, which allows for easy sizing and deployment without additional TDI certification work. These providers can be found in the certified SAP HANA listing on SAP's website (see Table 4.4).

Vendor	Instance Type	RAM	Clustering	Scenarios/Limitations
Amazon Web Services	cr1.8xlarge	244 GB	No	OLAP/OLTP
Amazon Web Services	m4.10xlarge	160 GB	No	Sap Business One, SLES 11 SP 4
Amazon Web Services	m4.16xlarge	256 GB	No	SAP Business One, SLES 11 SP 4
Amazon Web Services	r3.8xlarge	244 GB	Yes	OLAP/OLTP

Table 4.4 Certified IaaS Platforms as of May 2017

Vendor	Instance Type	RAM	Clustering	Scenarios/Limitations
Amazon Web Services	r4.16xlarge	488 GB	No	OLAP/OLTP, SLES 12 SP 1
Amazon Web Services	x1.16xlarge	976 GB	Yes	OLAP/OLTP, RHEL 6.7, RHEL 7.2, SLES 12 SP 1
Amazon Web Services	x1.16xlarge	976 GB	No	SAP Business One, SLES 11 SP 4
Amazon Web Services	x1.32xlarge	1952 GB	Yes	OLAP/OLTP, RHEL 6.7, RHEL 7.2, SLES 12 SP 1
Google Cloud Platform	n1-highmem-32	208 GB	No	OLAP, SLES 12 SP 1
Huawei Technologies Co.	h2.2xlarge	512 GB	No	OLAP, SLES 11 SP 3
Huawei Technologies Co.	h3.xlarge	480 GB	Yes	OLAP, SLES 11 SP 3
IBM Bluemix	BI.S1.H1000	1 TB	No	OLAP/OLTP, RHEL 6.7
IBM Bluemix	BI.S1.H2000	2 TB	No	OLTP, RHEL 6.7
IBM Bluemix	BI.S1.H512	512 GB	No	OLAP/OLTP, RHEL 6.7
Microsoft Azure	GS5	448 GB	No	OLAP

Table 4.4 Certified IaaS Platforms as of May 2017 (Cont.)

The certification list changes frequently, so always check if your provider is certified and ask for details about the certification process (TDI or certified hardware).

4.3   SAP BW/4HANA Cloud Deployment Steps

SAP provides three options for free trials of SAP BW/4HANA:

- SAP BW/4HANA XL Edition
- SAP BW/4HANA 1.0 Developer Edition
- SAP BW/4HANA 1.0

In this section, we'll walk through deploying the SAP BW/4HANA 1.0 Developer Edition on AWS. The estimated cost for AWS for this instance is $1.40 per hour when active or $25.30 per month when suspended—the software cost is a free trial from SAP.

The deployments are available in the SAP Cloud Appliance Library, as shown in Figure 4.2. You can access SAP Cloud Appliance Library at *https://cal.sap.com/*.

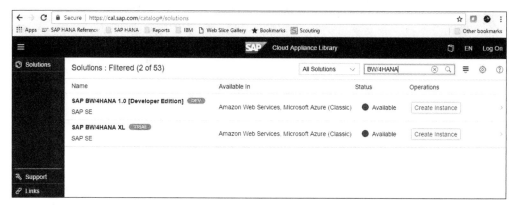

Figure 4.2 SAP Cloud Appliance Library SAP BW/4HANA Options

The deployment guides are updated frequently, so we recommend reviewing the latest documentation before deploying a system from the SAP Cloud Appliance Library.

4.3.1   Setting Up the Cloud Provider Account

The setup described in this section is specific to AWS, but similar steps are required for other providers. The first step is to set up an AWS account if you don't already have one. SAP recommends using a separate account to set up SAP Cloud Appliance Library instances and not use the root account used for other AWS instances. This example will go through the setup of a separate account.

To set up an account, go to *https://aws.amazon.com/* (see Figure 4.3).

The signup process includes quick steps such as adding contact information and billing information; it should only take a few minutes.

Once you've completed the signup process, you should be able to launch the management console (see Figure 4.4), from which you can manage your AWS instances and access the learning materials that AWS provides.

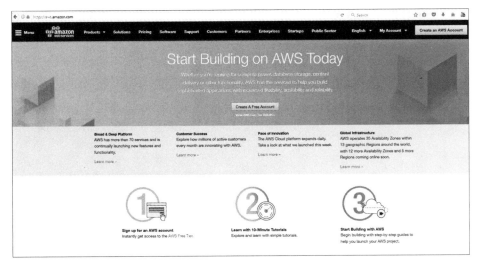

Figure 4.3 Creating New AWS Account

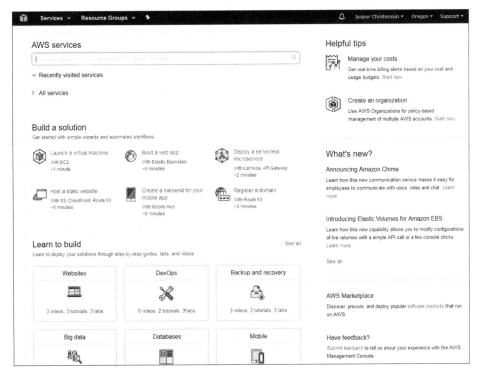

Figure 4.4 AWS Management Console

Click **Services** in the top-left corner (see Figure 4.4) and access the identity and access management (IAM) console, then create a user group so that you can grant only the required access for the SAP Cloud Appliance Library (see Figure 4.5).

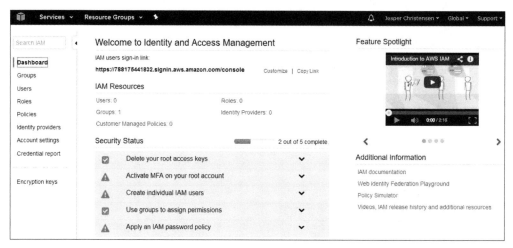

Figure 4.5 AWS IAM Console

Your IAM users for SAP Cloud Appliance Library require the following roles (see Figure 4.6):

- AmazonEC2FullAccess
- AmazonVPCFullAccess
- ReadOnlyAccess
- AWSAccountUsageReportAccess

Next, create a user that can be assigned to the user group. Make sure to select the **Programmatic Access** user option to generate an access and secret key pair (see Figure 4.7).

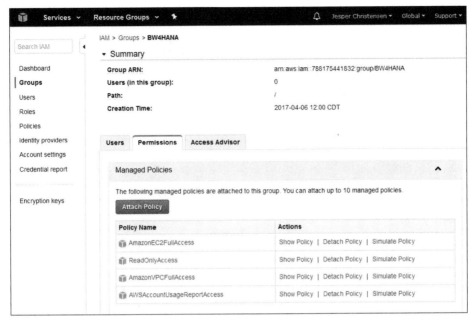

Figure 4.6 IAM User Group with Required Roles Assigned

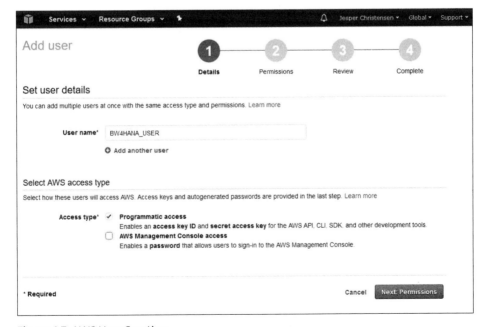

Figure 4.7 AWS User Creation

On the next screen, assign the user to the user group and click **Next** (see Figure 4.8).

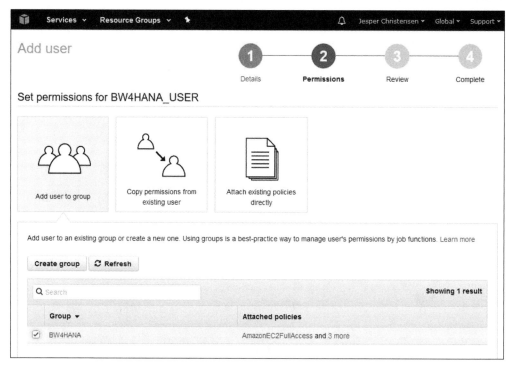

Figure 4.8 Assign User to User Group

A screen will show the user and the access key and secret key pair.

Now, you're ready to deploy an SAP BW/4HANA system from the SAP Cloud Appliance Library.

4.3.2   Selecting Your Deployment

Select the SAP BW/4HANA 1.0 Developer Edition in the SAP Cloud Appliance Library. Once selected, you should see the deployment options (see Figure 4.9).

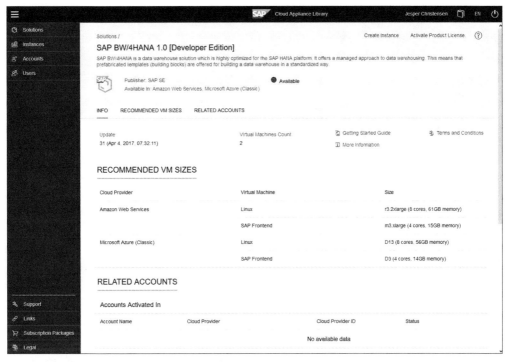

Figure 4.9 SAP BW/4HANA 1.0 Developer Edition Deployment Options

You'll see that the deployment uses two VMs on AWS (see Figure 4.9):

- One Linux r3.2xlarge (eight cores, 61 GB memory)
- One SAP frontend m3.xlarge (four cores, 15 GB memory); starting instance

We recommend reviewing the Getting Started guide before continuing, because some steps might change. The Getting Started guide can be found on the main page of the SAP Cloud Appliance Library.

Once you're ready, click the **Create Instance** button in the upper-right corner.

Enter the **Name** and **Description** and select a **Cloud Provider** (see Figure 4.10). Here, we've selected AWS, but you can also use Azure.

Figure 4.10 Naming Instance and Selecting Cloud Provider

Test the connection by clicking the **Test Connection** button (see Figure 4.10); you will be able to enter an instance **Name** and a master **Password**. Then, click **Create** in the bottom-right corner (see Figure 4.11).

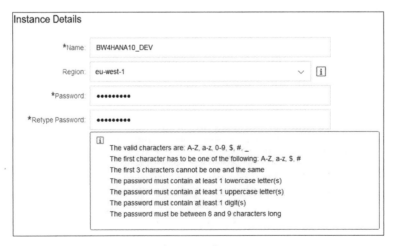

Figure 4.11 Name Instance and Password

A private key will be generated; download it for later use.

SAP will also display the restrictions that are enforced for the trial version and will note that the setup can take around one hour (see Figure 4.12). If you just created the AWS account, there might be a verification in progress for the account before the instance will be created.

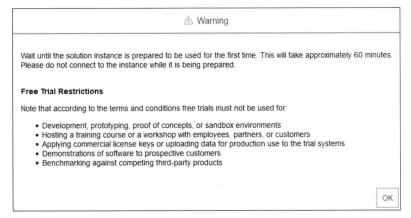

Figure 4.12 Instance Preparation on AWS

4.3.3   Logging On to the Instance

Once your instance has started, you can access it from SAP Cloud Appliance Library using your local SAP GUI, or via the remote desktop VM, which is part of the appliance deployment, using the **Connect** button at the top right (see Figure 4.13).

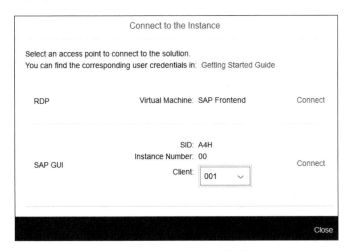

Figure 4.13 Connecting to Client 001 via SAP GUI

The user details are all included in the Getting Started guide, and the password is the master password created when setting up the instance.

The remote desktop protocol (RDP) provided with the SAP BW/4HANA 1.0 Developer Edition includes the components in Table 4.5.

Component	Version
SAP GUI for Windows 7.40	740.2.5.1110
SAP HANA Studio	2.3.8
SAP Development Tools for Eclipse: ABAP Development Tools	2.64.3
SAP Development Tools for Eclipse: BW Modeling Tools	1.15.1
SAP Development Tools for Eclipse: SAPUI5 Tools	1.38.7
SAP BusinessObjects Design Studio	1.6

Table 4.5 Components Installed on RDP VM

4.3.4   Managing Instances

The SAP Cloud Appliance Library interface shown in Figure 4.14 provides a few ways to manage your cloud appliance:

- **Connect**
  Provides easy access to RDP and SAP GUI
- **Start**
  Starts the instance
- **Suspend**
  Stops the instance
- **Reboot**
  Reboots the instance
- **Terminate**
  Stops the instance and discards it
- **Backup**
  Creates a backup of the instance
- **Create Solution**
  Creates a new instance based on the current instance

Figure 4.14 Options for Managing SAP Cloud Appliance Library Instance

It's also important to note that security is managed for the SAP Cloud Appliance Library instance from the **Security** section of the page. Only certain ports are open by default when the instance is created (see Figure 4.15). We recommend reviewing this information and closing ports that aren't used.

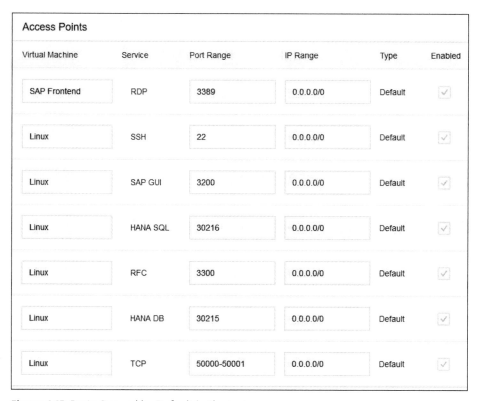

Figure 4.15 Ports Opened by Default in the Instance

In addition, you can set up schedules for when the instance will be running, and a default auto-stop feature will stop the instance from running after eight hours. These elements can all be managed from within the **Schedule** settings (see Figure 4.16).

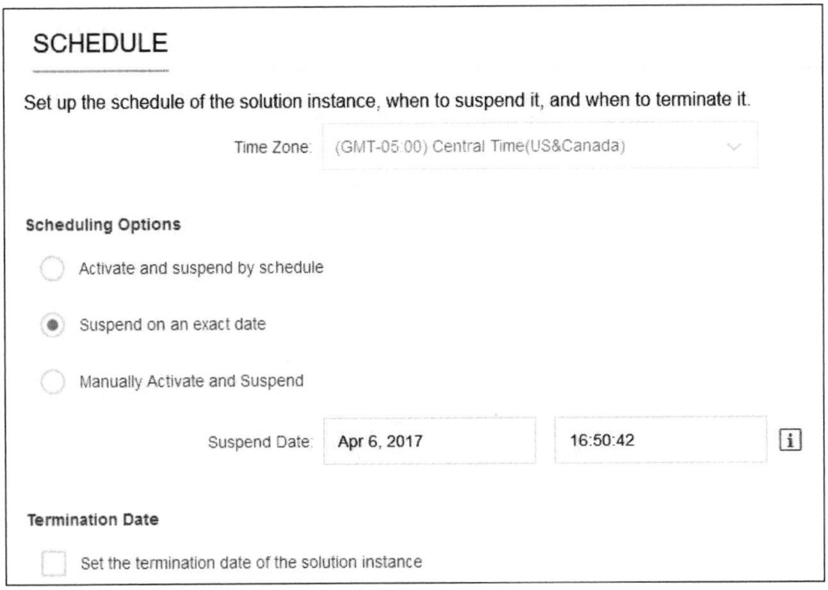

Figure 4.16 Schedule Options in the Instance

Most of these are basic management options; further options are available from within the AWS console.

4.3.5 Renewing Licenses

The licenses provided with the SAP BW/4HANA system are temporary, but it's possible to renew the licenses with a MiniSAP license key (see Figure 4.17). This option is described in detail at *https://wiki.scn.sap.com/wiki/pages/viewpage.action?pageId= 451058309.*

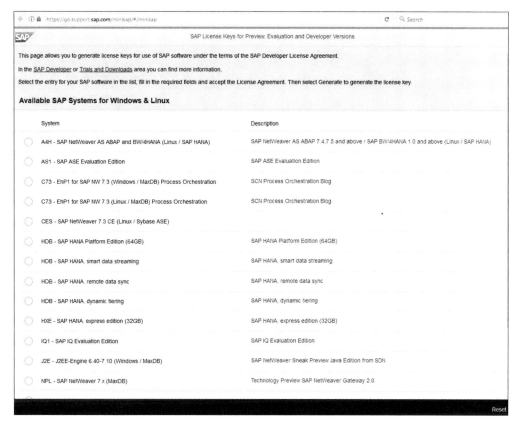

Figure 4.17 MiniSAP License Renewal

Renewing the license provides an additional 90 day extension beyond the expiration date.

4.4   Summary

It's clear that many companies look to the cloud for both cost savings and simplification of their IT organizations. SAP BW/4HANA is built for cloud, and many of the new features being included in SAP BW/4HANA in the future can be used with other cloud deployments for big data, data streaming, and analytics.

If you don't have a cloud strategy it may still make sense to consider deploying a sandbox system on one of the cloud providers to gain experience with cloud deployments. Later, you might decide to move your SAP BW/4HANA system fully to a cloud provider.

Chapter 5
Data Modeling

In this chapter, we discuss the modeling objects available in SAP BW/4HANA and how these elements can be configured to address typical data warehousing requirements, ranging from data virtualization to persistency, as well as agile reporting functionality.

To summarize data modeling with SAP BW/4HANA in three words: Less is more. *Less* because a reduced number of modeling objects is offered in SAP BW/4HANA compared to the SAP NetWeaver-based SAP BW application. *More* because these modeling objects, though reduced in number, are more versatile, pack together more features, and offer greater modeling flexibility than the several SAP BW applications combined.

In this chapter, we'll describe the SAP BW/4HANA modeling objects in detail, covering their features, their purposes, and how they can be configured using the BW modeling perspective of SAP HANA Studio. We'll discuss elements from the smallest SAP BW/4HANA modeling entities—known as InfoObjects and considered the information building blocks—to sophisticated information models represented by Advanced DSO and CompositeProviders—the former primarily acting as a persistent layer of SAP BW/4HANA and the latter having the role of a logical layer. The open integration nature of SAP BW/4HANA is reinforced by the availability of the Open ODS view modeling object, which corresponds to an agile data virtualization layer.

5.1 Modeling Perspectives

SAP BW modelers are very familiar with Transaction RSA1, which has been central to SAP BW since its inception. This transaction accesses the SAP BW Administrator Workbench, the main UI for performing tasks in data warehousing such as data modeling functions, as well as data loading control, monitoring, transport management, and maintenance processes.

Figure 5.1 shows the well-known Administrator Workbench, Transaction RSA1, in SAP BW. The left-side panel of the UI shows the many functionality groups available, with the **Modeling** functionality highlighted.

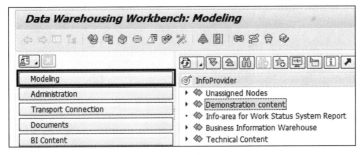

Figure 5.1 SAP BW Administrator Workbench

When accessing the same Administrator Workbench using Transaction RSA1 from SAP BW/4HANA, however, there's a striking difference. The modeling option of the left-side panel is absent, as shown in Figure 5.2.

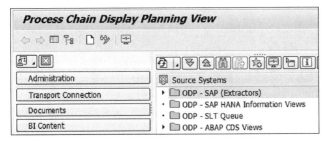

Figure 5.2 SAP BW/4HANA Administrator Workbench

The reason for this change is that modeling activities in SAP BW/4HANA are performed solely within Eclipse-based SAP HANA Studio. That doesn't mean that Transaction RSA1 has been made entirely obsolete; activities such as data load control, monitoring, authorization definition, and data source maintenance are still performed via the classic SAP BW Administrator Workbench.

Note

As SAP continues to migrate features from SAP NetWeaver to SAP HANA Studio, the SAP BW Administrator Workbench will eventually be made obsolete for SAP BW/4HANA.

The central SAP BW/4HANA modeling UI is the BW modeling perspective available in SAP HANA Studio. To access this perspective, choosing the **SAP HANA studio • Window • Perspective • Open Perspective • Other...** menu path and select **BW Modeling** from the list of available perspectives.

The first step for data modeling in SAP BW/4HANA is to set up a BW project if one isn't yet available. A BW project acts as a system connection to a corresponding application server. It's via a BW project that the metadata is exposed to SAP HANA Studio so that modeling activities can be performed.

Follow the menu path **File • New • BW Project** to create a new connection within the BW modeling perspective. The project type should be **Business Warehouse**, and the connection parameters should be entered as in the SAP Logon Pad; provide the SAP BW/4HANA system ID, client, user, and password.

Once you've defined a BW project, the next step is to connect to the SAP BW application layer by double-clicking the BW project itself. SAP HANA Studio will then connect to the corresponding application server and expose the repository of modeling objects, as seen in Figure 5.3, and organized under InfoAreas. InfoAreas are akin to folders into which modeling objects are organized.

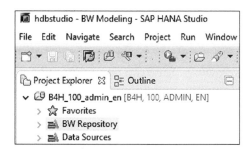

Figure 5.3 Modeling Perspective Exposing Metadata Repository

Right-click an InfoArea of the BW repository to open a context menu. Select **New...** from the context menu to create the following elements:

- **DataStore Objects (Advanced)**
- **InfoSource**
- **InfoObject**
- **Open ODS View**
- **InfoArea**

- Semantic Group
- CompositeProvider
- Open Hub Destination
- Data Flow

The elements of interest for data modeling in SAP BW/4HANA are InfoObjects, Open ODS views, Advanced DSOs, and CompositeProviders. The following sections dive into each of these objects in detail, describing their modeling purposes and configuration steps.

5.2   Modeling Objects

It helps to look at the past to better understand the present. Such is the case with modeling with SAP BW/4HANA. A quick comparison between the modeling objects available in the SAP BW application and those in SAP BW/4HANA may help illustrate the level of modeling simplification achieved with the latter.

For greenfield projects, this comparison may not be relevant, but for brownfield projects it can assist in determining objects to convert and those that need to be retired and replaced.

The main objects supporting data modeling in SAP BW/4HANA are InfoObjects, Open ODS views, Advanced DSOs, and CompositeProviders. The main purpose of each element is master data storage, virtualization, data persistency, and logical layer, respectively.

Table 5.1 lists each object and its main modeling purpose in SAP BW/4HANA.

SAP BW/4HANA Object	Main Modeling Purpose
InfoObjects	Master data
Open ODS Views	Data virtualization
Advanced DSOs	Data persistency
CompositeProviders	Logical layer

Table 5.1 SAP BW/4HANA Modeling Objects and Their Modeling Purposes

SAP BW applications have similar modeling requirements, achieved via classical objects such as InfoCubes, DSOs, InfoSets, MultiProviders, Virtual Cubes, Hybrid Providers, and Persistent Storage Areas (PSAs).

Table 5.2 lists the modeling objects available in SAP BW applications and their main modeling purposes.

SAP BW Object	Main Modeling Purpose
InfoObjects	Master data
DSOs	Data persistency
InfoCubes	Data persistency
Hybrid Providers	Data persistency with real-time option
PSAs	Inbound data persistency layer
InfoSets	Logical layer (join)
MultiProviders	Logical layer (union)
Virtual Cubes	Virtualization

Table 5.2 SAP BW Modeling Objects and Their Modeling Purposes

The larger number of modeling objects within SAP BW was a result of many years of development based on relational database technology concurrent with the evolution of the data warehouse concept itself.

SAP BW/4HANA, on the other hand, represents a fresh start. In terms of modeling, this translates into major simplification by means of a reduced number of objects required to cover key aspects of data warehousing: master data, data persistency, logical layer, and virtual integration.

A simple way of demonstrating the simplification represented by SAP BW/4HANA is to align the modeling objects from SAP BW with the SAP BW/4HANA objects based on their modeling purposes (see Table 5.3).

SAP BW Object	SAP BW/4HANA Object
InfoObjects	InfoObjects
DSOs	Advanced DSOs
InfoCubes	
Hybrid Providers	
PSAs	
InfoSets	CompositeProviders
MultiProviders	
Virtual Cubes	Open ODS Views

Table 5.3 Comparing SAP BW and SAP BW/4HANA Modeling Objects

SAP BW/4HANA modeling objects were designed to pack together features that belonged to different SAP BW objects. For example, Advanced DSOs can act as Info-Cubes or as DSOs, depending on the settings chosen during their definition.

This and other features of SAP BW/4HANA modeling objects are described in detail in the subsequent sections of this chapter. InfoObjects, as holders of master data and usually used as building blocks for defining other data providers, are the first objects discussed (see Section 5.3).

5.3   InfoObjects

Apart from a few new functionalities, SAP BW/4HANA InfoObjects are very similar in concept to the SAP BW versions. SAP professionals well-versed in this type of object from previous versions of SAP BW may find this section a breeze; it's intended to be an introduction for professionals new to SAP's BI world.

InfoObjects are considered the smallest modeling units in SAP BW. They act as building blocks for other modeling objects within the SAP BW data warehouse. A CompositeProvider or Advanced DSO can be defined by selecting a set of InfoObjects that represent the desired information.

There are four types of InfoObjects in SAP BW/4HANA: characteristic, key figure, unit, and XXL. To make an analogy to data warehousing fundamentals, *characteristic* types are contextual elements, whereas *key figures* represent the metrics of a data model.

Units are the standardized references required to establish the proper order of magnitude and comparison between the metrics of a data model. As for *XXL*, these are special InfoObjects that rely on deep ABAP types to allow for long content, up to 1,333 characters, to be stored as additional information for the model.

Example

Let's walk through an example. For this example, assume that sales information must be stored for reporting purposes. The first sales record indicates a total of $1,200,000. The second sales record shows a total of $200,000. Which one is more attractive for a business? That's a trick question: The contextual information hasn't yet been provided. The amounts of $1,200,000 and $200,000 are simple metrics until additional information can be used to contextualize them.

By assigning units to the metrics, some insights are possible. Let's say the first sales records is in US dollars (a total of $1,200,000). The second sales record is in Euros (€200,000). The first deduction here is that with orders of magnitude, the units, applied to the amounts, we can now say that based on market exchange rates the $1,200,000 amount is greater than the €200,000 amount.

However, this is maybe a limited view. To further contextualize the data, other elements can be added to the analysis. In this case, let's provide a time characteristic—for example, calendar month. It happens that the $1,200,000 amount was obtained during an entire year of sales at an average of $100,000 per month. The €200,000 amount was obtained in a single month.

As more characteristics are added to the model, more information and insights can be derived. Characteristics such as customer ID, product, region, and stores can assist in various analyses. Even some comments originating from customer feedback could be stored and assigned to related sales transactions. This intersection of data elements is modeled under datasets that in SAP BW/4HANA are commonly referred to as *InfoProviders*. InfoProviders thus are representations of a group of InfoObjects of different types as per analytical requirements.

5.3.1 Characteristics

Characteristic InfoObjects act as contextual elements for metrics in a data model. Characteristics in SAP BW/4HANA can be defined based on five ABAP dictionary data types:

1. Character string (CHAR)

2. Numerical text (NUMC)

3. Signed numerical characteristics (SNUMC)

4. Date in format YYYYMMDD (DATS)

5. Time in format HHMMSS (TIMS)

The data type is selected when defining a characteristic InfoObject (see Figure 5.4) and determines the format in which it should be displayed in the UI, including its maximum length and output template.

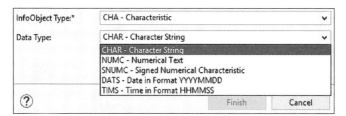

Figure 5.4 Data Types Selection during SAP BW/4HANA InfoObjects Definition

When an ABAP program consumes table data, the system converts the internal format of its contents per the ABAP data type for user visualization.

Table 5.4 describes the output template and length limitations of each of the five data types applicable to characteristics.

Data Type	Definition
Character string (CHAR)	Character field that can be filled with alphanumeric characters; limited to a maximum length of 1,333 characters in tables.
Numerical text (NUMC)	Character field in which only numbers can be entered; length of this field is limited to a maximum of 255 characters.
Signed numerical characteristic (SNUMC)	Character field in which signed numbers can be entered; similar to NUMC, but allows negative values.
Date in format YYYYMMDD (DATS)	Character field with a length set to eight characters; format is YYYYMMDD; output template can be set in user profile.

Table 5.4 Data Types for SAP BW/4HANA Characteristic InfoObjects

Data Type	Definition
Time in format HHMMSS (TIMS)	Character field with length set to six characters; the format is HHMMSS; template for input and output has the form '__.__.__'.

Table 5.4 Data Types for SAP BW/4HANA Characteristic InfoObjects (Cont.)

After specifying the data type applicable for the new InfoObject, the next step is to determine its general properties within the InfoObject definition UI, under the **General** tab, where the properties in Table 5.5 can be set.

Property	Definition
Usable as InfoProvider	This allows queries to be created on top of the InfoObject tables.
Authorization-relevant	Authorization objects for reporting that rely on this InfoObject can be created.
Attribute only	This InfoObject characteristic can only be modeled as a display attribute of another characteristic.
High-cardinality	No persistent SID table is created for this InfoObject.
Case-sensitive	Characteristic values aren't converted to uppercase by default.
Master data	Generates an attribute table.
Texts	Generates a text table.
Hierarchy	Generates a hierarchy table.

Table 5.5 General Properties of Characteristic InfoObjects

SAP BW/4HANA characteristic InfoObjects can be simple fields or sophisticated master data objects defined based on entity-relationship models. Examples of simple characteristics include postal codes, street names, and street numbers. These simple characteristics can be modeled as parts of a customer's addresses. The main characteristic customer would then be defined with these simple characteristics acting as its attributes.

Not only simple characteristics can be modeled as attributes. Characteristics with their own attributes can easily become attributes of other characteristics. For example, a characteristic such as city usually carries attributes such as state and country as part of its master data table. City is routinely mapped as an attribute of customer master data in entity-relationship models, as shown in Figure 5.5.

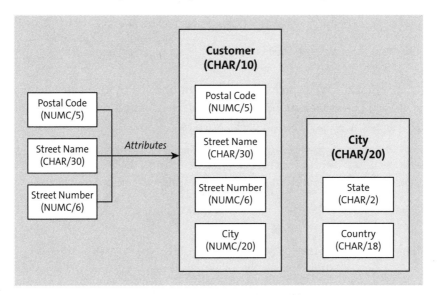

Figure 5.5 Entity-Relationship Model Applied to SAP BW/4HANA Characteristics

In addition to attributes, SAP BW/4HANA InfoObject characteristics can be configured with texts and/or hierarchy tables. *Texts* are the descriptions associated with the key values of a characteristic. *Hierarchies* are the tree structures against which the key values of a characteristic can be distributed, usually for rolling up and categorization purposes in reporting.

Attributes, texts, and hierarchies of a characteristic InfoObject are defined by flagging the **Master Data**, **Texts**, and **Hierarchies** properties (see Figure 5.6) during InfoObject definition. Tables are then generated in the SAP HANA database to store the related content.

The specifications of the master data tables storing attributes, texts, and hierarchies, including potential dependencies related to versioning or time validity, are determined by selecting the tabs made available during the InfoObject definition.

From the **Master Data/Texts** tab (see Figure 5.7), you can set the compounding parameters for the **Texts** table key, allowing multilanguage descriptions and time validity for such descriptions. To do so, set the **Language-Dependent** and **Time-Dependent** flags, respectively.

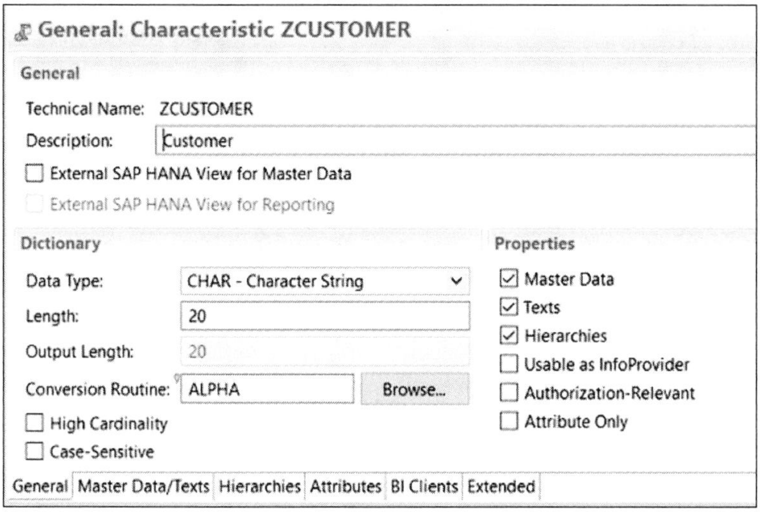

Figure 5.6 Configuring Characteristic InfoObject with Attributes, Texts, and Hierarchies

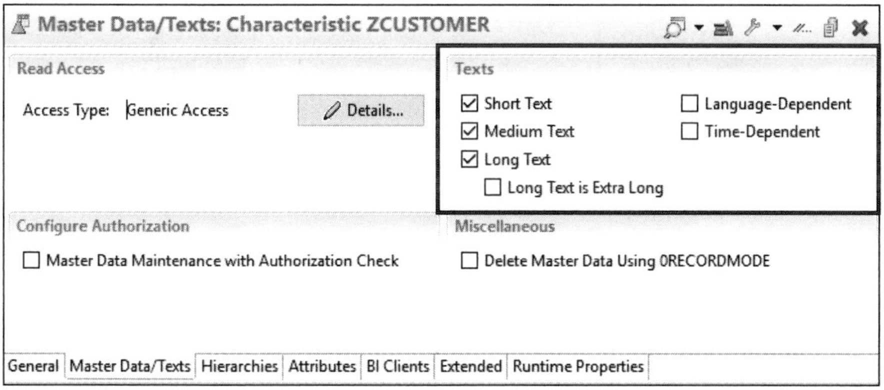

Figure 5.7 Defining Texts Table for Characteristic InfoObject

In the case of language dependency, the language is added as a compounding key to the characteristic's values, allowing multiple descriptions to be stored. For time dependency, setting the flag means compounding the characteristic's values with **Valid From** and **To** fields as keys for the text tables.

SAP BW/4HANA allows three lengths of text to be stored: short, medium, and long. Short texts have a maximum length of 20 characters, medium have a maximum length of 40, and long texts can vary from 60 up to a limit of 1,333 characters. This upper limit is enabled if the option **Long Text Is Extra Long** is chosen. In this case, the long text is associated with data type SSTRING.

For the hierarchy table of a characteristic InfoObject, the settings available under the **Hierarchies** tab (see Figure 5.8) allow time-dependency and versioning to be introduced to the hierarchy structure. Versioning (**Version-Dependent**), if set, is applied to entire structure. As for time-dependency (**Time-Dependent**), this can be set at the header level or structure level. At the header level, the entire hierarchy follows the validity set at the root level of the tree structure. If the time-dependency is set at the hierarchy structure level, then nodes within the tree structure can have their own dedicated validity periods.

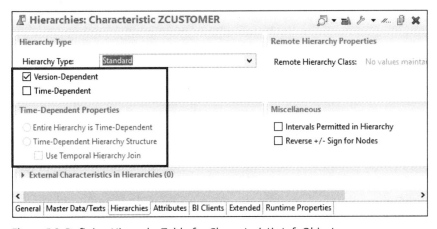

Figure 5.8 Defining Hierarchy Table for Characteristic InfoObject

Two other parameters are also available, under **Miscellaneous** in the **Hierarchy** tab. The first, **Intervals Permitted in the Hierarchy,** allows intervals to be set as nodes of the tree structure, minimizing maintenance effort when inputting the characteristic values to the tree structure. This is relevant when hierarchical values follow an interval pattern. The other parameter available, **Reverse +/- Sign for Nodes**, can be used to reverse the positive/negative sign for transaction data posted against the nodes of the hierarchy structure.

The **Attributes** tab (see Figure 5.9) is where attributes to be associated with the Info-Object can be entered. This is done by selecting other characteristics available within SAP BW/4HANA to act as attributes for the InfoObject being defined.

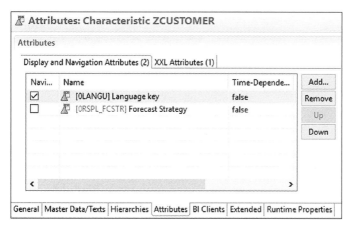

Figure 5.9 Adding Attributes to Characteristic InfoObject

Depending on the settings chosen, the attributes can be of a navigation or display nature. If an attribute is set as navigational, then it can be used for slicing and dicing at the query level. Display attributes won't have the same behavior and will only serve as an extension to the characteristic value on reports. They can be displayed side by side with the main characteristic. No slicing or filtering is possible with display attributes in queries.

It's also possible to logically assign XXL attributes to a characteristic. XXL attributes differ from regular attributes and can be further specified via MIME type. A *MIME type* is a standardized specification comprised of a two-part identifier that determines file format and content. Based on the MIME type selected, the system can interpret the XXL attribute as an audio file, a video file, text, or an image. XXL attributes first must be defined as an XXL InfoObject type before being available as XXL attributes for other characteristics.

5.3.2   XXL

XXL InfoObjects are available in SAP BW/4HANA to assist in storing large contents in different formats in the SAP HANA database. Subsequent modeling activities can then associate the contents stored as XXL InfoObjects with other characteristics.

There are two data types available when defining XXL InfoObjects, as noted in Table 5.6.

Data Type	Definition
Character string (CLOB)	*Character large object:* Used to store a large amount of character data, up to 1,333 characters.
Byte string (BLOB)	*Binary large object:* Used to store a large amount of binary data; further specification using MIME types is necessary to specify file format and content.

Table 5.6 Data Types for XXL InfoObjects

If an XXL InfoObject is created using the CLOB data type, then no further parameters are needed beyond the technical name and description of such an InfoObject. This is because the system recognizes CLOB as a text file by default.

If an XXL InfoObject type is created using the BLOB data type, then it's necessary to assign its MIME type. The MIME type specifies the file format and contents, assisting the system in determining how to store and interpret the file in question. MIME types available in SAP BW/4HANA include image types (PNG, IMG, BITF, PFX, etc.), video types (MPG, AVI, QT, VDO, etc.), Microsoft types (DOC, PPT, XLS, RTF, etc.), Adobe PDF, AutoCAD (DWG), and many others.

5.3.3 Key Figure

Key figure InfoObjects are the metrics used in data models. These metrics can represent amount, quantity, integer, number, date, or time. To accommodate these options, there are eight different data types applicable to key figures in SAP BW/4HANA. Table 5.7 describes the output template, length limitation, and properties of each of the eight data types applicable to key figures.

Data Type	Definition
Currency field (CURR)	Equivalent to an amount field DEC. A field of this type must refer to a field of type CUKY (reference field). The maximum length for this data type is 31 characters.
Floating point (FLTP)	The length (including decimal places) is set to 16 characters for this data type.

Table 5.7 Data Types for Key Figure InfoObjects

Data Type	Definition
Packed numbed (DEC)	Counter or amount field with decimal point, sign, and commas separating thousands. A DEC field has a maximum length of 31 characters.
Date in format YYYYMMDD (DATS)	Length set to eight characters. The format is YYYYMMDD. The output template can be set in the user profile.
Time in format HHMMSS (TIMS)	Length set to six characters. The format is HHMMSS. The template for input and output has the form '__.__.__'.
4-Byte integer (INT4)	The length for this data type is limited to 10 characters, with lower and upper limits set to -2,147,483,648 and +2,147,483,647, respectively.
8-Byte integer (INT8)	The length for this data type is limited to 20 characters, with lower and upper limits set to -9.2 × 1018 and +9.2 × 1018 respectively
Quantity field (QUAN)	Equivalent to an amount field DEC. A field of this type must always refer to a field type UNIT. The maximum length for this data type is 31 characters.

Table 5.7 Data Types for Key Figure InfoObjects (Cont.)

There's a relationship between the data type and the type of the key figure being defined. SAP BW/4HANA automatically restricts the data type options to the ones applicable to each key figure type. For example, if a key figure will represent an integer, then the data type options are restricted to INT4 and INT8 during the key figure definition. Table 5.8 presents the key figure types and related data types allowed.

Key Figure Type	Data Types Allowed
Amount	CURR, FLTP
Integer	INT4, INT8
Date	DATS, DEC
Number	FLTP, DEC
Quantity	QUAN, FLTP

Table 5.8 Key Figure Types and Related Data Types

Key Figure Type	Data Types Allowed
Time	TIMS, DEC

Table 5.8 Key Figure Types and Related Data Types (Cont.)

General key figure specifications are set during definition (see Figure 5.10). These range from aggregation procedures for reports (sum, minimum, maximum, no aggregation) to fixed or variable units to display behavior.

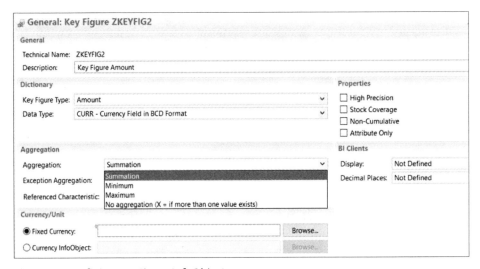

Figure 5.10 Defining Key Figure InfoObjects

In addition to the general key figure settings, SAP BW/4HANA also offers the opportunity to set four other special properties. These four special properties are **Non-Cumulative** and **Stock Coverage** (both commonly used for inventory management), **High Precision**, and **Attribute Only**.

The **Non-Cumulative** property enables snapshots of stock position by period. **Stock Coverage** determines the number of periods of supply against planned or expected demand.

High Precision is used to force the analytical engine to perform calculations using extra decimal places instead of rounding. The **Attribute Only** option can be set when a key figure is only to be used as an attribute of characteristics instead of for report calculation.

5.3.4   Unit

Unit InfoObjects are used in conjunction with key figures, setting the measuring standards between values and thus enabling proper comparisons and conversions. There are two data types available when defining unit InfoObjects, as noted in Table 5.9.

Data Type	Definition
Currency Key (CUKY)	Fields of this type are referenced by fields of type CURR. The length is set to five characters for this data type.
Unit Key (UNIT)	Fields of this type are referenced by fields of type QUAN. The length of this data type is set to two or three characters.

Table 5.9 Data Types for Unit InfoObjects

The steps for defining a unit InfoObject are restricted to selecting **Unit Type**, **Technical Name**, and **Description** (see Figure 5.11). The only further specification relates to the display behavior during reporting, which determines if the unit should be displayed as a key, text, or a combination of both.

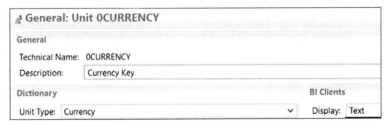

Figure 5.11 Defining Unit InfoObjects

5.4   SAP BW/4HANA InfoProviders

SAP BW/4HANA *InfoProviders* are modeling objects comprised of measures and contextual elements that represent a specific view of the data. Previous releases of SAP BW restricted the modeling of InfoProviders to be based solely on InfoObjects. Inbound data first was associated to InfoObjects during data provisioning before being made available in InfoProviders and queries. Data integration was a prerequisite for reporting functionality.

Any modeling activity started by making sure that all required InfoObjects, the smallest building blocks for an InfoProvider, were already available in SAP BW. If that wasn't the case, then the first step was to create the necessary InfoObjects. This could represent undesired overhead, especially for cases such as prototyping, one-time data loads, or ad hoc reporting requirements.

However, SAP BW/4HANA InfoProviders can be modeled based on InfoObjects or directly with fields that follow specifications from external sources. This new modeling option available for SAP BW/4HANA InfoProviders is known as *field-based modeling*; we'll discuss it next.

5.4.1 Field-Based Modeling

SAP BW/4HANA allows for field-based modeling in addition to InfoObject-based modeling when defining InfoProviders. With field-based modeling, InfoProviders can be defined with generic fields that follow the specifications of external data sources, such as for data type and length. Queries can be created on top of field-based InfoProviders the same way as with InfoObject-based ones. Reporting functionality in SAP BW/4HANA thus can be provided with or without associations with InfoObjects.

Choosing between field-based or InfoObject-based modeling depends on reporting requirements. If you want external content enhanced with attributes, hierarchies, and descriptions already stored in SAP BW/4HANA, then you should associate external fields with InfoObjects.

However, if your objective is more aligned with punctual analysis, prototyping, or even isolated data analysis, then the field-based approach could be effective. In this case, to allow queries on field-based InfoProviders the system will automatically convert the external fields into internal, temporary InfoObjects at the query level, with a naming convention following the pattern `2F<InfoProvider>-<field name>`.

Certain reporting restrictions are applicable to field-based InfoProviders, however (described in SAP Note 2185212, ADSO: Recommendations and restrictions regarding reporting). Only field names not longer than 20 characters are visible directly in reporting. Table 5.10 shows the required lengths for various fields for both characteristics and key figures.

Field	Length
Characteristics	
CHAR	1–250
NUMC	1–250
CUKY	5
UNIT	3
LANG	1
DATS	8
TIMS	6
Key Figures	
INT4	
FLOAT	
DEC	16–31; decimal places 0–14
CURR	Length 1–31; decimal places 1–14 (there must be an assignment to a CUKY characteristic, and the length must be greater than or equal to the number of decimal places)
QUAN	Length 1–31; decimal places 0 –14 (there must be an assignment to a UNIT characteristic, and the length must be greater than or equal to the number of decimal places)

Table 5.10 Required Field Lengths for Characteristics and Key Figures

5.4.2   Open ODS Views

Open ODS views are SAP BW/4HANA metadata objects that represent the structure of an external data source. Open ODS views, as the name suggests, are nonpersistent. They're mainly used for data virtualization and association of external data source fields with existing InfoObjects.

Data sources for an Open ODS view can vary, from SAP HANA tables to third-party tables located in external databases or data pools. Creating a new open ODS view follows similar steps as those for any other InfoProvider: Right-click an InfoArea and select the option to create a new Open ODS view. Basic parameters include technical ID and a meaningful description. Unique to Open ODS views, however, are the **Semantics** and **Source Type** parameters, as shown in Figure 5.12; these must be specified when defining such an InfoProvider.

Figure 5.12 Defining Open ODS View InfoProvider

These parameters can have the following effects:

- **Semantics**
  This parameter drives which structural elements are to be made available during the definition of the Open ODS view. An Open ODS view can have this parameter set to **Facts**, **Master Data**, or **Texts**:

  - **Facts** will allow for the definition of a structure containing a key field section for characteristics, acting as record keys, and a data field section, where other characteristics—in conjunction with key figures, currency, and units—can be added to the model.

- **Master data** will allow the definition of a structure comprised of elements typically associated with master data tables, including key, attributes, text, and validity fields for cases in which time-dependency is required.

- **Texts** will allow the definition of a structure comprised of elements typically associated with text tables, including language key, columns for short, medium, and long texts, and validity fields for cases in which time-dependency is required.

- **Source type**
  This refers to the API that specifies the data source type of an Open ODS view. It allows an Open ODS view to transparently connect to the data origin. This parameter for an Open ODS view can be set to **Database Table or View**, **DataSource (BW)**, **Transformation**, or **DataStore Objects (Advanced)**:

  - **Database Table or View** enables Open ODS views to connect to tables or views associated with any schema within an SAP HANA database. This source type also connects to virtual tables defined in the SAP HANA database via SAP HANA smart data access (SDA), thus enabling the consumption of remote, non-SAP data.

  - **DataSource (BW)** enables open ODS views to make use of existing SAP BW data sources. These data sources should support direct access and be associated with SAP source system types (i.e., SAP Business Suite, SAP BW) or DB Connect.

  - **Transformation** enables Open ODS views to connect to a transformation in SAP BW. This is useful when some level of data manipulation is desired between the source and the resulting data exposed through the Open ODS view.

  - **DataStore Object (Advanced)** enables Open ODS views to access data from SAP BW Advanced DSO InfoProviders. These InfoProviders are discussed in Section 5.4.3. For now, note that Advanced DSOs are modeling objects in SAP BW/4HANA used primarily as data-persistent repositories.

After providing the general specifications the next step for creating an Open ODS view is to complete the modeling of its structure. As an example, assume that table SALES_DATA was created directly in the SAP HANA database with sales data originating from a non-SAP system. The fields of such a table follow the naming conventions and definitions of the source system and differ from SAP terminology.

The goal here is to have this data reported alongside similar data coming from SAP sources. An Open ODS view can be created easily, allowing for the virtualization and consumption of this non-SAP sales data by the SAP BW/4HANA application.

To accomplish this, Open ODS view ZODSV1 is defined with **Semantics** set to **Facts** and **Source Type** set to **Database Table and View**. The system looks for the definition of the data source—in this case, the details of the table or view to supply data to the Open ODS view. It's necessary to indicate the SAP schema and table name for setting up the connection. Open ODS view ZODSV1 is then assigned to table SALES_DATA within the SAP HANA database.

To model the Open ODS view, we drag the fields of interest from table SALES_DATA, available under **Source Field**, and drop them into the corresponding folders of the Open ODS view, under **View Field**, as shown in Figure 5.13.

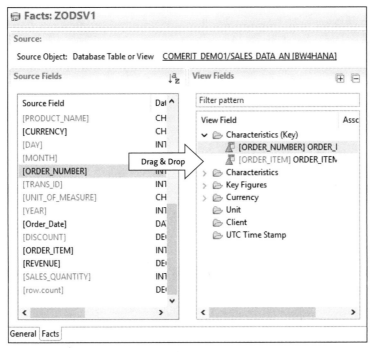

Figure 5.13 Modeling Open ODS View Structure

After completing the modeling, the Open ODS view can be activated and queries can be built directly on top of it. In such a scenario, SAP BW/4HANA queries would rely on field modeling, because associations with InfoObjects have been made during the Open ODS view definition.

Right-clicking the Open ODS view opens a context menu containing the option to create a new SAP BW/4HANA query (see Figure 5.14).

Figure 5.14 Creating SAP BW/4HANA Query on Field-Based Open ODS View

Because the Open ODS view ZODSV1 is based on field modeling, any query created on top of it will contain elements with the naming convention 2FZODSV1-<field name> (for example, 2FZODSV1-ORDER_DATE; see Figure 5.15).

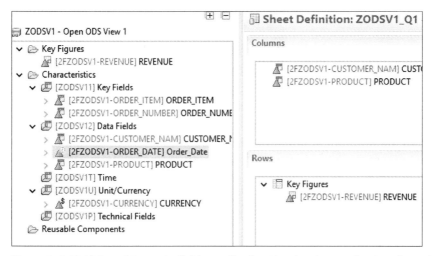

Figure 5.15 Field-Based Query Definition Following Naming Convention 2<InfoProvider>-<field name>

It's also possible to enrich the external content view via an association feature available in the Open ODS view definition screen. *Association* refers to assigning the fields of an Open ODS view to existing SAP BW/4HANA elements such as an InfoObject, thus inheriting the InfoObject's master data content, including attributes, text, and hierarchies.

To demonstrate the association feature, the definition of Open ODS view ZODSV1 can be modified. The CUSTOMER_NAM field can be associated with InfoObject ZCUSTOMER, as shown in Figure 5.16. This InfoObject is of type characteristic and contains *language and forecast strategy* attributes.

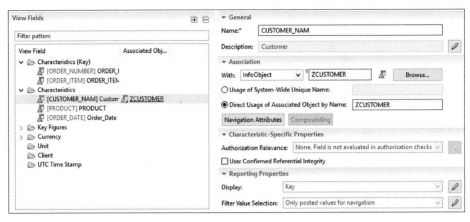

Figure 5.16 Modified Open ODS View Definition

The **Direct Usage of Associated Object by Name** property can also be set to ZCUSTOMER. By doing so, the CUSTOMER_NAM field will be presented as InfoObject ZCUSTOMER to subsequent SAP BW procedures and queries.

After this, the CUSTOMER_NAM field will act and feel like InfoObject ZCUSTOMER. The attributes of ZCUSTOMER will be made available during query definition, and any display property will, by default, follow the InfoObject definition. The field-based modeling is thus superseded by the associated SAP BW data model. Figure 5.17 shows the Open ODS view ZODSV1 fields during query creation after association has been set. As shown, ZCUSTOMER and its related attributes are now available for selection instead of the CUSTOMER_NAM field.

Figure 5.17 ZCUSTOMER InfoObject and Related Attributes Made Available for Query Definition after Association at Open ODS View Level

5.4.3   Advanced DataStore Objects

Advanced DSOs are the central objects for data persistency in SAP BW/4HANA. These are very flexible modeling objects that can be configured to address different data retention scenarios, including data overwriting, additive behavior, and change log-based delta processes.

Advanced DSOs are comprised of three tables: the inbound table, active table, and change log. The modeling properties of an Advanced DSO are set according to data-retention requirements and determine which of these three tables are to be generated.

The options available for modeling Advanced DSOs are centered on data-writing procedures and how existing data content is to be updated against potential changes triggered by inbound data.

Inbound data is commonly written to the inbound table of an Advanced DSO. From there, it can be transferred to the active table following a process known as activation/compression. The activation can generate change logs that may then be stored in the change log table.

As shown in Figure 5.18, the general definition screen of an Advanced DSO contains the modeling options available in the left panel and predefined model templates on the right panel. Model templates cover the most typical data architectural requirements. After selecting a model template, the corresponding modeling properties are set automatically.

The modeling properties can also be set manually by flagging the options related to activation needs and special types of data input. The system validates the options as they're selected by inactivating certain property combinations. The modeling properties available to be set manually are as follows:

- **Activate Data**
  - **Write Change Log**
  - **Keep Inbound Data, Extract from Inbound Table**
  - **Unique Data Records**
  - **Snapshot Support**
- **Special Types**
  - **Direct Update**
  - **All Characteristics Are Key, Reporting on Union of Inbound and Active Table**
  - **Planning Mode**
  - **Inventory**

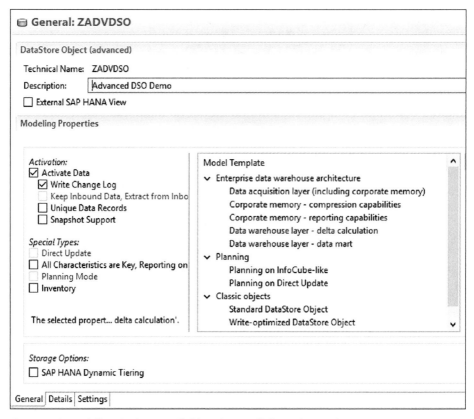

Figure 5.18 Modeling Options Available When Defining Advanced DSOs

Let's dive into each of these modeling options with the assistance of diagrams depicting the three Advanced DSO tables:

- **Activate Data**

    Selecting this property for an Advanced DSO tells the system that data should be moved from the inbound table to the active table following a process known as activation/compression. This scenario is depicted in Figure 5.19, in which the inbound and active tables are generated, as well as process logic to move the data between these two tables. No change log table is generated with this property setting alone.

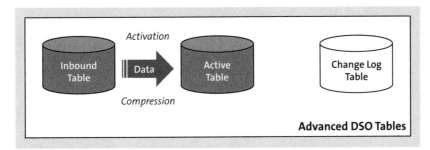

Figure 5.19 Advanced DSO Scenario for Activate Data

- **Activate/Write Change Log**

  This modeling property is only enabled if the **Activate Data** property is set first. It determines that a change log table should be generated to capture new or changed records. By capturing the change history as records are written to the active table from the inbound table, the change log table acts as a delta mechanism for subsequent data movements. The Advanced DSO can thus act as a delta-enabled source for other providers. Figure 5.20 depicts the modeling scenario of data activation with change log writing enabled, resulting in all three Advanced DSO tables being generated.

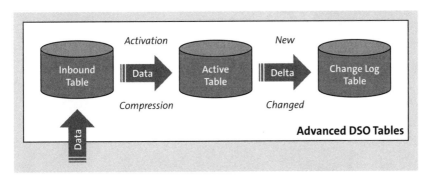

Figure 5.20 Advanced DSO Scenario for Activating Data and Writing to Change Log

- **Activate/Keep Inbound Data, Extract from Inbound Table**

  This modeling property is only enabled if the **Activate Data** property is set first. It determines that no change log will be captured, regardless of changes to the original data set. Without delta pointers, only the afterimage of the full data set is kept in the Advanced DSO for subsequent loads or analysis. Figure 5.21 depicts this modeling scenario.

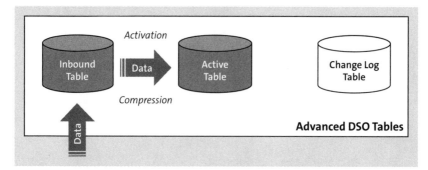

Figure 5.21 Advanced DSO Scenario for Activating Data and Keeping Inbound Data

- **Activate/Unique Data Records**
  This modeling property is only enabled if the **Activate Data** property is set first. If this property is enabled, the system won't check if the inbound record already exists in the active table. No aggregation is thus possible, and the inbound data set shouldn't contain duplicates. Figure 5.22 depicts this modeling scenario.

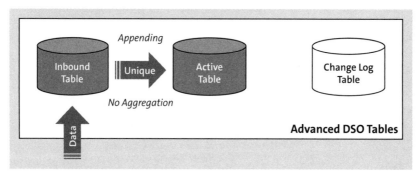

Figure 5.22 Advanced DSO Scenario for Unique Data Records

- **Activate/Snapshot Support**
  This modeling property is only enabled if the **Activate Data** property in conjunction with **Write Change Log** is set first. As the property name suggests, any new data load will be considered a new dataset snapshot. No aggregation against previous snapshots already stored in the active table will occur. In this case, it's important to have the entire data set during any load to the Advanced DSO. Figure 5.23 depicts this modeling scenario.

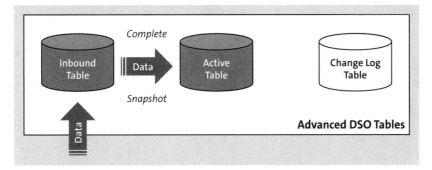

Figure 5.23 Advanced DSO Scenario for Snapshot Support

- **Special Type/Direct Update**
  This is considered a modeling configuration for special scenarios in which the data is to be written via an API directly to the active table. If set, the system will generate an Advanced DSO that omits the inbound table and change log table. Figure 5.24 depicts this modeling scenario.

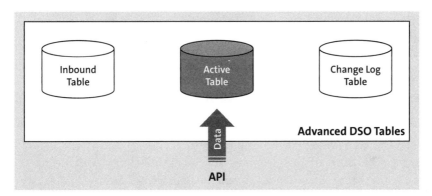

Figure 5.24 Advanced DSO Scenario for Direct Update

- **Special Type/All Characteristics are Key, Reporting on Union of Inbound and Active Table**
  In this modeling scenario, the Advanced DSO will make all characteristics part of the key section, thus not allowing overwriting of existing records. In this case, any delta load is considered additive in nature. SAP describes this setting as making an Advanced DSO play the role of an InfoCube, a classic SAP BW modeling object. Figure 5.25 depicts this modeling scenario.

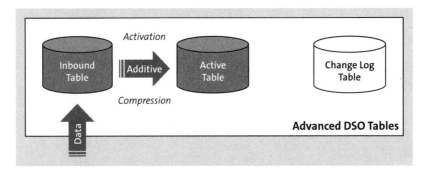

Figure 5.25 Advanced DSO Scenario for All Characteristics Are Key

- **Special Type/Planning Mode**
  This modeling scenario is only possible in conjunction with special type proper-ties **Direct Update** or **All Characteristics Are Key, Reporting on Union of Inbound and Active Table**. With this setting, the Advanced DSO makes use of the SAP HANA Planning Application Kit (PAK) with optimized writing procedures. A few con-straints exist, as described in SAP Note 2189829, Details and Conditions for Plan-ning on Advanced DataStore Object. If the **Planning Mode** property is set in conjunction with **All Characteristics are Key, Reporting on Union of Inbound and Active Table**, then the modeling constraints are as follows:

  - All characteristics must be mapped to SAP BW/4HANA InfoObjects.
  - InfoObjects with high cardinality aren't allowed.
  - InfoObjects with stock cover inventory properties aren't supported.
  - InfoObjects with constant values aren't allowed.

  Figure 5.26 depicts the planning modeling scenario in conjunction with **All Charac-teristics are Key, Reporting on Union of Inbound and Active Table**.

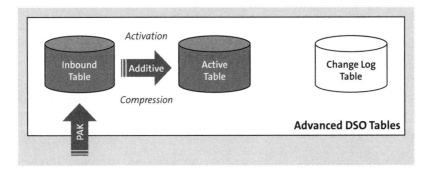

Figure 5.26 Advanced DSO Scenario for Planning with All Characteristics Are Key

If the **Planning Mode** property is set in conjunction with **Direct Update**, then modeling is limited in such way that InfoObjects with constant values aren't allowed to be part of the model. However, high cardinality and field modeling are allowed. Figure 5.27 depicts the planning modeling scenario in conjunction with **Direct Update**.

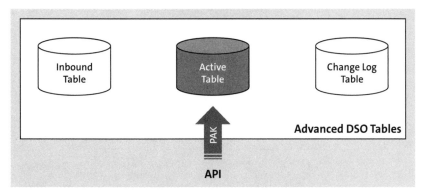

Figure 5.27 Advanced DSO Scenario for Planning with Direct Update

- **Special Type/Inventory**
  This modeling property is only enabled if the **All Characteristics are Key, Reporting on Union of Inbound and Active Table** property is set first. It adds a tab to the Advanced DSO definition screen named **Inventory**, in which inventory-related parameters can be specified. This includes reference time characteristics for the noncumulative nature of inventory key figures and a related list of validity characteristics, as shown in Figure 5.28. Validity characteristics are the characteristics for which noncumulative, inventory-related key figures are applicable.

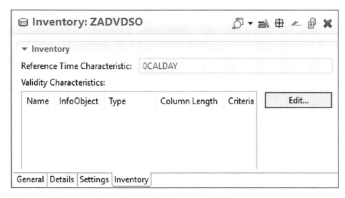

Figure 5.28 Inventory Tab of Advanced DSO

131

Figure 5.29 depicts the modeling scenario with the **Inventory** property. As expected, an Advanced DSO under this setting will act like an Advanced DSO set as **All Characteristics are Key, Reporting on Union of Inbound and Active Table** but also enhanced with pointers for point-in-time, noncumulative snapshots of inventory positions.

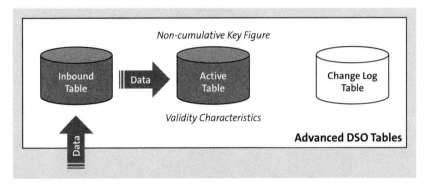

Figure 5.29 Advanced DSO Supporting Noncumulative Snapshots of Inventory Positions

- **No Setting of Modeling Properties**
  This final modeling scenario is one in which none of the modeling properties are set. In this case, an Advanced DSO is generated with the inbound table only. This table could be comprised of fields or InfoObjects. If field modeling is used, then the Advanced DSO will play a role more like that of a data-acquisition layer, acting as a landing pad for inbound external data without any association with existing Info-Objects.

  If, on the other hand, the Advanced DSO is modeled using InfoObjects, then it will be similar in nature to a corporate memory layer enhanced with associated master data tables. Figure 5.30 depicts this modeling scenario.

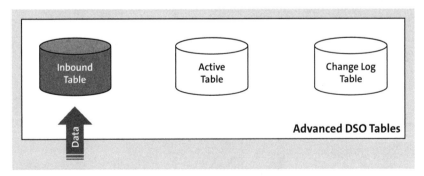

Figure 5.30 Advanced DSO with No Modeling Property Set

As noted earlier, SAP offers model templates that consist of predefined Advanced DSO property settings. These settings create Advanced DSOs to address the most common data warehousing modeling scenarios.

Some of these model templates use a naming convention that refers explicitly to classic SAP BW metadata modeling objects, such as InfoCubes or standard DSOs. Table 5.11 lists each model template and its corresponding modeling properties set in the Advanced DSO configuration.

Model Template Group	Model Template Name	Advanced DSO Modeling Properties
Enterprise data warehouse architecture	Data-acquisition layer (including corporate memory)	▪ None
Enterprise data warehouse architecture	Corporate memory—compression capabilities	▪ Activate Data
Enterprise data warehouse architecture	Corporate memory—reporting capabilities	▪ Activate Data ▪ Keep Inbound Data, Extract from Inbound Table
Enterprise data warehouse architecture	Data warehouse layer—delta calculation	▪ Activate Data ▪ Write Change Log
Enterprise data warehouse architecture	Data warehouse layer—data mart	▪ Activate Data ▪ All Characteristics are Key, Reporting on Union of Inbound and Active Table
Planning	Planning in InfoCube-like manner	▪ All Characteristics are Key, Reporting on Union of Inbound and Active Table ▪ Planning Mode
Planning	Planning on direct update	▪ Direct Update ▪ Planning Mode
Classic objects	Standard DSO	▪ Activate Data ▪ Write Change Log
Classic objects	Write-optimized DSO	▪ None

Table 5.11 Model Templates and Related Advanced DSO Properties

Model Template Group	Model Template Name	Advanced DSO Modeling Properties
Classic objects	InfoCube	■ **Activate Data** ■ **All Characteristics are Key, Reporting on Union of Inbound and Active Table**

Table 5.11 Model Templates and Related Advanced DSO Properties (Cont.)

5.4.4   CompositeProvider

CompositeProviders are metadata objects of a nonpersistent nature. Their primary purpose is to act as a logical layer that combines the content of different datasets for reporting and analysis. CompositeProviders make use of union and join SQL operations to harmonize data from SAP BW/4HANA InfoProviders and SAP HANA views, forming an output structure for query consumption. The modeling complexity is thus transparent for the report user.

A CompositeProvider is created like any other SAP BW/4HANA InfoProvider: Select an InfoArea within the SAP BW/4HANA application, right-click, and choose **New • CompositeProvider**. After providing a technical name and a description, the next step is to select the datasets (i.e., InfoProviders) and SQL operation types (union or join) required for the desired modeling output.

For example, let's imagine a modeling scenario in which three objects must be combined in a report. The first is InfoObject type characteristic ZCUSTOMER and stores the customer master data, which includes, in addition to customer IDs, the language and forecast strategy attributes.

The other two objects are transactional repositories containing sales transaction data. One is an Advanced DSO, ZADVDSO, storing sales data originating from SAP sources and persisted in the SAP HANA database. The other is Open ODS view ZODSV1, which allows for visualization of sales data from external sources. The reporting requirement is to have the sales revenue combined and summarized by customer in one dataset enriched with attributes for reporting purposes. A possible solution could be to create a union combining the two sets of sales transactions first, followed by a join of the resulting data set with the master data attributes.

For this, a CompositeProvider using a SQL union operation can be created to combine the contents of Advanced DSO ZADVDSO and Open ODS view ZODSV1. This CompositeProvider will then be joined subsequently to master data ZCUSTOMER. The first step is to provide a technical name (ZCP_U1) and a description (**Composite Provider Union 1**) for our union-based CompositeProvider, as shown in Figure 5.31.

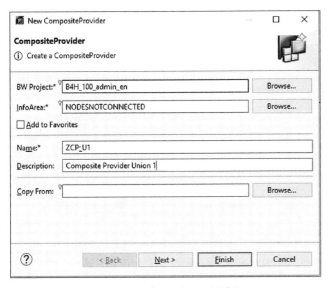

Figure 5.31 CompositeProvider Union Initial Screen

Click **Next** at the bottom of the composite initial screen. On the next screen, select the SQL operation and InfoProviders that should be part of the model. For this example, these parameters define a union between Advanced DSO ZADVDSO and Open ODS view ZODSV1. This is done by adding these two InfoProviders under **Union Providers** (see Figure 5.32). Click **Finish** to proceed to the CompositeProvider definition screen.

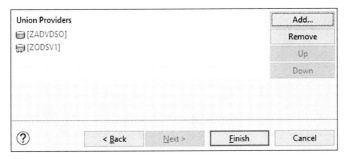

Figure 5.32 Selecting Union of InfoProviders for CompositeProvider ZCP_U1

The CompositeProvider definition screen contains three tabs: **General**, **Scenario**, and **Output**. On the **General** tab, runtime properties can be set that cover many aspects, such as parallel processing, access to near-line storage data, data integrity checks, and caching, among others.

In our example the CompositeProvider union ZCP_U1 will be used in a subsequent join with customer master data, so the property **This CompositeProvider Can Be Added to Another CompositeProvider** is selected in the **General** tab (see Figure 5.33).

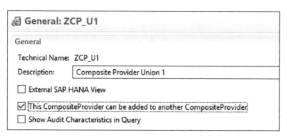

Figure 5.33 Allowing CompositeProvider Union to be Used by Other CompositeProviders

The modeling of the output structure is defined in the **Scenario** tab by dragging and dropping the fields from each InfoProvider within the **Source** section into the output structure within the **Target** section of the CompositeProvider. The union procedure is established automatically if the same InfoObjects are dragged from different Info-Providers, as shown in Figure 5.34.

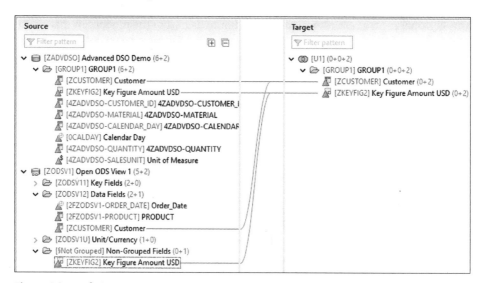

Figure 5.34 Defining Output Structure and Union Operation of CompositeProvider via Scenario Tab

The semantics of a CompositeProvider output structure can be further enhanced in the **Output** tab. This could include updates to the descriptions of the structural elements and association with InfoObjects, pertinent when field-based modeling objects are being combined under a CompositeProvider but should be reported based on InfoObjects at the query level.

When modeling is complete, the ZCP_U1 CompositeProvider union can be activated. The next step is to create a second CompositeProvider to perform the join operation between ZCP_U1 and InfoObject ZCUSTOMER. This is done by defining a new CompositeProvider, ZCP_J1 (CompositeProvider join 1), combining both InfoProviders using a SQL union operation. The steps are very much like those we used to create the first CompositeProvider, ZCP_U1.

After providing a technical ID (ZCP_J1) and description (**CompositeProvider Join 1**) for the new CompositeProvider, click **Next** to add ZCP_U1 and ZCUSTOMER to the **Join Providers** section (see Figure 5.35).

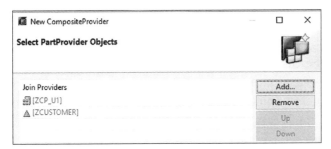

Figure 5.35 Selecting Join Operation PartProviders for CompositeProvider ZCP_J1

The join type can be inner or left outer. For CompositeProviders with left-outer joins, the sequence in which the InfoProviders are added to the **Join Providers** section is important. If a left outer join is chosen, then the first InfoProvider added to this section will drive the join.

The sequence of providers and the join type can be changed in the CompositeProvider screen during modeling, however, under the **Scenario** tab. To do so, right-click on top of the join element and select an option from the context menu (see Figure 5.36):

- **Switch Inputs**
  Change the sequence of InfoProviders within the join operation

- **Join Type**
  Change the join type from **Inner** to **Left Outer** or vice versa

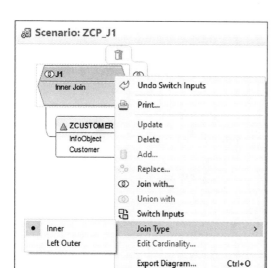

Figure 5.36 Switching Join Type and InfoProvider Sequence during Modeling of CompositeProvider ZCP_J1

In our example, CompositeProvider ZCP_J1 will use an inner join type. The next step is to drag and drop the elements from the source section to the target section, thus defining the output structure of **CompositeProvider Join 1**. Because this is a join instead of a union, the customer ID available in both InfoProviders only needs to be dragged over once to be available in the output structure.

The **Customer ID** and related **Language** and **Forecast Strategy** attributes are dragged from the source area represented by ZCUSTOMER InfoObject into the target structure. The key figure **Amount USD** is dragged from the CompositeProvider ZCP_U1 which reflects the union of sales transactions from SAP sources (Advanced DSO ZADVDSO) and external sources (Open ODS view ZODSV1).

Now, it's time to define the join condition. Right-click **ZCUSTOMER** under **Source** and choose **Create Join Condition Field** from the context menu. Now, you can define the join between the two InfoProviders. The join in this case will be based on InfoObject ZCUSTOMER, available in both InfoProviders (see Figure 5.37).

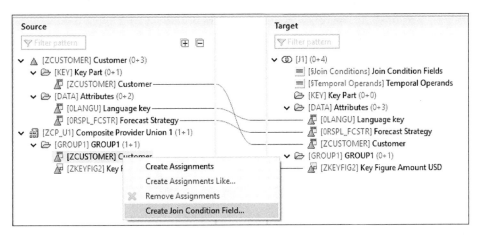

Figure 5.37 Defining Join Condition Field between InfoProviders

Now, the join condition is integrated into the output structure, as shown in Figure 5.38. CompositeProvider ZCP_J1 can now be activated and made available for reporting and analysis.

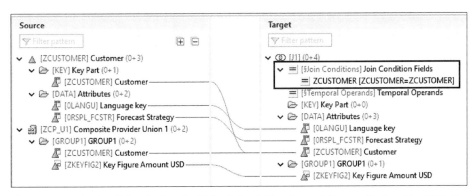

Figure 5.38 Join Condition Defined within Output Structure of CompositeProvider ZCP_J1

5.5 Summary

Modeling in SAP BW/4HANA is based on the Eclipse-based UI via the BW modeling perspective of SAP HANA Studio. In this chapter, we described the modeling objects available in SAP BW/4HANA in detail, from the smallest units of modeling in SAP

BW/4HANA (InfoObjects) to InfoProviders, including Open ODS views (mainly used for data virtualization of external sources), Advanced DSOs for data persistency, and CompositeProviders acting as the logical layer. We also discussed the concept of field-based modeling, which enables SAP BW/4HANA to consume external data as-is, in a flexible, agile fashion without the need of data staging or integration.

Chapter 6
Data Acquisition

One of the biggest challenges when implementing a business ware-house system is integrating it with other source systems. In this chapter, we'll discuss important tools and mechanisms available in SAP BW/4HANA to simplify this integration among different types of source systems, including big data in Hadoop.

One of the important processes in *business intelligence (BI)* is the ability to access, collect, persist, and harmonize data that came from different source systems or was manually entered. This process of extracting data from different source systems, harmonizing it, and consolidating it into a generic format in a business warehouse system is called *extraction, transformation, and loading (ETL)*.

The technical innovations and frameworks available in SAP BW/4HANA allow you to enter data manually, use ETL processes to transfer and persist data in SAP BW/4HANA, or directly access data from source systems virtually.

The following types of source systems are available for integration:

- SAP applications: Data from SAP source systems is accessed using the Operational Data Provisioning (ODP) framework. This framework allows you to transfer data from various SAP repositories either using the Service Application Programming Interface (S-API), which is the common method of communication used in several versions of SAP BW systems or via Operational Delta Queues (ODQ), which is the new method of communication to SAP applications including SAP Data Services.

- Database source systems: Data from different non-SAP HANA database systems can be accessed through ODBC connectors. SAP HANA systems are accessed via the HODBC (SAP HANA ODBC) connector provided by SAP. You can also use SAP HANA smart data integration (SDI) and SAP HANA smart data access (SDA) frameworks for this integration.

- Local or tenant database: Data from a local database or from multitenant databases linked to SAP BW/4HANA is accessed directly.

- Big data source systems: Data from big data systems such as Hadoop can be accessed using the SAP HANA Spark Controller adapter from the SAP HANA smart data access framework.

- Files: Data can be transferred from flat files with specific delimiters or fixed-length structures and from Microsoft Excel workbooks.

This chapter describes end-to-end data flow creation to support the integration of SAP BW/4HANA with different source systems. We will discuss connecting it with source systems, creating DataSources, and the transformations necessary to transfer and persist data from the source systems into InfoProviders in SAP BW/4HANA. This chapter also covers creation and monitoring of data load processes using data transfer processes (DTPs) and process chains.

Eclipse SAP HANA Tools

The functions described in this chapter require the installation of the following add-ons in SAP HANA Studio or Eclipse:

- ABAP Development Tool (ADT)
- Modeling Tools for SAP BW powered by SAP HANA
- SAP HANA Tools

For installation links to use in the Eclipse installation path, visit *https://tools.hana.ondemand.com*.

6.1   SAP BW/4HANA Source Systems

Source systems are objects in SAP BW/4HANA used for connecting different sources of data and defining which protocols will be used for these connections. These source system objects are grouped by communication protocols under the **Data Sources** tree, as shown in Figure 6.1.

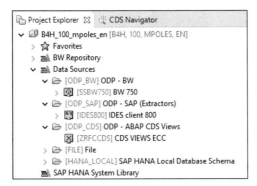

Figure 6.1 Source System Types in SAP BW/4HANA with Three Source Systems Created

You can find the source systems via the following path in Eclipse or SAP HANA Studio: **BW Modeling tools perspective • Project Explorer panel • Data Sources tree**.

The following subsections describe in detail the creation of source system objects in SAP BW/4HANA, using the following connection types: local and tenant database schema (Section 6.1.2), SAP HANA smart data access and big data (Section 6.1.3), file-based (Section 6.1.4), and Operational Data Provisioning (Section 6.1.5).

6.1.1   Creating a Source System

SAP BW/4HANA contains an Eclipse-based wizard to facilitate the creation of source systems. There are different ways to start the source system creation wizard:

- Right-click the source system type and choose **Source System**.
- Right-click the **Data Sources** node and choose **Source System**.
- Right-click the **BW project** node and choose **New… • Source System**.
- From the main menu, choose **File • New • Other… • Business Warehouse • Source System**.

When you open the source system creation wizard, the initial screen will show the main source system identification parameters (see Figure 6.2).

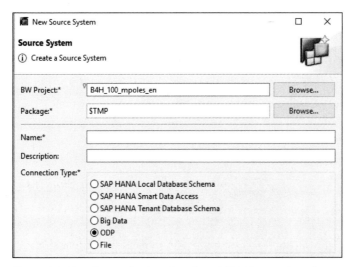

Figure 6.2 New Source System Creation: Initial Parameters Screen

The main source system properties are as follows:

- **BW Project**
  Project name that identifies the SAP BW/4HANA system, client, username, and language to store the source system being created.

- **Package**
  Defines the transport strategy for the source system being created. You can create the source system as a local development by assigning it to the package $TMP or you can assign a package that has a transport path in case you need to move the source system to other systems, such as quality assurance or production.

- **Name**
  This is the technical name of the source system in SAP BW/4HANA that identifies the source of data. For SAP source applications, this source system technical name also becomes the name of the Remote Function Call (RFC) connection created and associated with this source system.

- **Description**
  Optional description for the source system.

- **Connection Type**
  Defines the source system connection framework to be used for connecting to the source.

For each connection type, the wizard has a distinct set of connection-specific parameters to be entered, as described in the following subsections.

6.1.2   Connection Type: SAP HANA Local and Tenant Database Schema

SAP HANA local and tenant databases can be accessed directly when they're connected to SAP BW/4HANA. Each source system object created in SAP BW/4HANA for this connection type specifies one schema on the source database to be used as a data provider.

> **Prerequisites**
>
> The connection to the local or tenant database schema uses the *SAP<SID>* user. This user needs to have SELECT object privileges for the schema that will be used as a source of the data.

After starting the wizard for creating source systems, as described in Section 6.1.1, and choosing either the **SAP HANA Local Database Schema** or **SAP HANA Tenant Database Schema** connection type, click **Next** to specify further properties for these connection types, starting with the schema selection (see Figure 6.3).

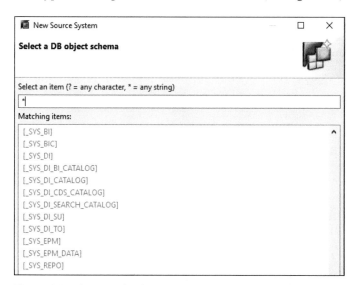

Figure 6.3 Schema Selection Screen in SAP HANA Database Source System

> **Note**
>
> SAP BW/4HANA InfoProviders and SAP HANA views are available under the _SYS_BIC schema.

Once the schema used as a source is selected, click the **Finish** button to move to the summary screen and activate it by clicking the **Activate** button (✏). This makes this source system available for use; you can find it in the **Project Explorer** panel, as shown in Figure 6.4.

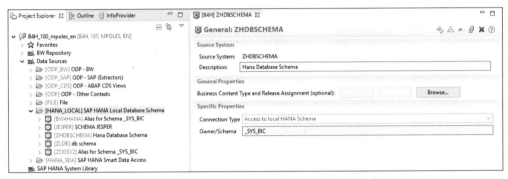

Figure 6.4 SAP Local Database Schema Created and Active in Project Explorer

6.1.3   Connection Type: SAP HANA Smart Data Access and Big Data

SDA is a framework that enables you to connect different source systems, including big data source systems such as Hadoop, and create a combined *enterprise data warehouse (EDW)* landscape, allowing you to access data directly from these source systems and make it available in SAP BW/4HANA system virtually. It also provides the option to stream data from the connected source systems in near real time.

> **Tip**
>
> Depending on the volume of data being merged in an SAP HANA view with multiple source systems, the performance of the select operation may be affected by the non-SAP HANA source systems and network capacity. Consider, in these cases, replicating the data from these non-SAP HANA systems into SAP BW/4HANA to optimize the performance of your views and queries.

> **Prerequisites**
>
> Create the remote connection as discussed in Chapter 8, Section 8.1.

Once the remote connections are created in SAP HANA, you can start the wizard for creating source systems as described in Section 6.1.1 and select the **SAP HANA Smart Data Access** or **Big Data** connection types.

For each source system object created in SAP BW/4HANA for these connection types, specify one schema on the source database to be used as a data provider.

Click **Next** to specify further properties for these connection types, starting with the remote connection selection. You can use the wildcard character (*) to display all possible and active remote connections available, as shown in Figure 6.5.

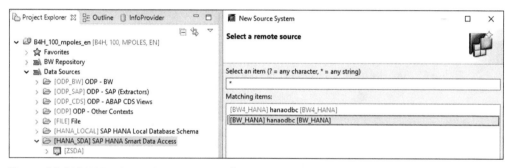

Figure 6.5 SAP HANA Smart Data Access and Big Data Remote Source Selection

Next, choose the remote connection to use for this source system, then proceed to the next part of the source system creation—that is, select the database to use for the connection. Choose **[<NULL>]** or the desired database (if available) and proceed as shown in Figure 6.6.

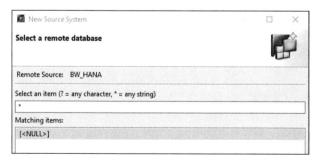

Figure 6.6 SAP HANA Smart Data Access and Big Data Remote Database Selection

The database source system connected may have different schemas for the tables or views to be used as sources for this source system. Select the schema to be used in this connection, as shown in Figure 6.7.

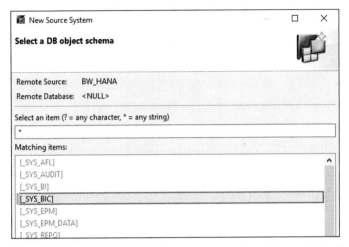

Figure 6.7 SAP HANA Smart Data Access Database Schema Selection

After proceeding to the confirmation page, click **Finish** to exit the wizard. The source system screen will appears with its properties and the system will be available for use after you click **Activate** ✎ , as shown in Figure 6.8.

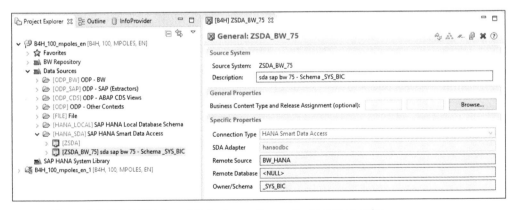

Figure 6.8 SAP HANA Smart Data Access Source System Properties

6.1.4 Connection Type: File

This source system connection type is used when you want to transfer data from flat files in different formats or from Microsoft Excel spreadsheets into SAP BW/4HANA.

After starting the wizard for creating source systems as described in Section 6.1.1 and choosing the connection type **File**, click **Next** to specify further properties for this connection type (see Figure 6.9).

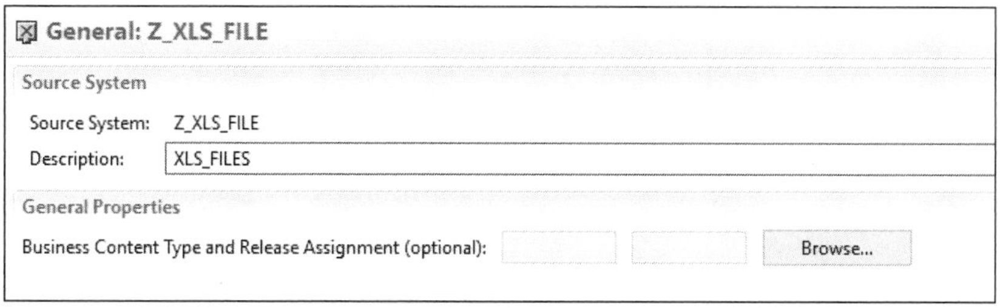

Figure 6.9 Additional Properties for File Type Source System Connection

Optionally, you can specify a version and release number for the source system if it's available in your installation. After completing these additional parameters, the system will be available for use after you click **Activate** 🖉.

6.1.5 Connection Type: Operational Data Provisioning

ODP is the framework used in SAP BW/4HANA for data extraction and replication from SAP source systems via *RFCs* or via *Simple Object Access Protocol (SOAP)* web services. ODP also allows you to transfer data in real time via the SAP *Landscape Transformation* replication server. This ODP framework creates data transfer queues in the source system for tables accessed by the SAP Landscape Transformation server or DataSources accessed directly from SAP BW/4HANA.

Therefore, the ODP framework works as a central component for managing these data transfer queues. Systems and objects connected to the ODP framework have two main roles: *providers* and *consumers*. Providers are systems or data objects responsible for sending data to the ODP framework; consumers are systems or objects that receive data from the ODP framework, as shown in Figure 6.10.

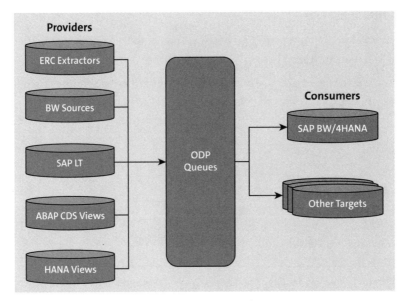

Figure 6.10 ODP High-Level Communication Schema

The ODP framework can of receive and provide data to multiple targets due to the new concept of connection used in this framework called *subscriptions*. These subscriptions contain the provider and consumer objects paired and identified on each of the data transfer queues available in ODP queue management.

The ODP Queue Monitor is accessed via Transaction ODQMON for following up the delta queue processing status and performance administrative activities, such as clean up queues.

Prerequisites

The following SAP Notes contain the support packages and prerequisites for ODP provider implementation in SAP source systems:

- SAP BASIS < 730: SAP Note 1521883 (ODP Replication API 1.0)
- SAP BASIS ≥ 730: SAP Note 1931427 (ODP Replication API 2.0)
- Release SAP Source Systems Extractors for ODP Usage: SAP Note 2232584

The following subsections describe the procedure to enable ODP extractors in an SAP source system and the creation of an ODP source system object in SAP BW/4HANA linked to this SAP source system.

Source Application Extractors for ODP

Most of the SAP extractors are already released for ODP replication according to SAP Note 2232584 (Release of SAP Extractors for Operational Data Provisioning [ODP]). This note contains an up-to-date list of SAP extractors that are already released to be used in this method.

However, there might be occasions that you may need to create a custom extractor to transfer data to SAP BW/4HANA or other target systems and you want to use that extractor in the ODP framework.

In SAP source systems, you can create a custom or generic extractor in Transaction RSO2. Figure 6.11, for example, shows a generic/custom extractor created to transfer exchange rates from table TCURR with delta enabled and controlled by the **Exchange Rate Date** field. This way, the delta loads only transfer new exchange rates with dates greater than those of the last delta execution.

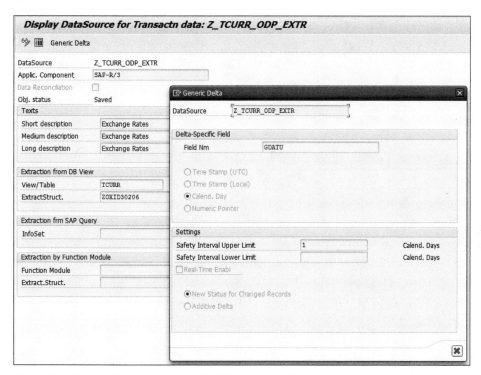

Figure 6.11 Generic Extractor Created in SAP Source System

Generic/customer DataSources aren't released to be used in ODP automatically (see SAP Note 2350464, Creation of Generic DataSource in RSo2, Automatic Release for

ODP). You need to use program RODPS_OS_EXPOSE via Transaction SA38 to release the DataSource for ODP usage.

After running the program, enter the DataSource name or pattern to retrieve a list of DataSources available to be released for ODP, then click the **Release DataSource(s)** button. The list of available DataSources to be released is displayed in Figure 6.12.

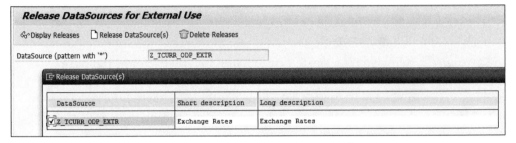

Figure 6.12 Releasing Generic DataSources for ODP Use

Once the release is complete, you can see the releases created by clicking **Display Releases**. Alternatively, you can check the **EXPOSE_EXTERNAL** activation flag in table ROOSATTR for the available DataSources released for ODP (see Figure 6.13).

Figure 6.13 ODP Released DataSources List from Table ROOSATTR

Creating an ODP Source System

After starting the wizard for creating source systems as described in Section 6.1.1 and selecting the **ODP** connection type, click **Next** to specify further properties for this connection type, starting with the **ODP Page Selection**, as shown in Figure 6.14. The ODP page specifies the type of connection to the source system.

There are three main options for ODP pages:

- **RFC with Remote System**
  Used to connect SAP systems to SAP BW/4HANA

- **RFC in the Same BW System**
  Used for self-connection of the SAP BW/4HANA system

- **HTTP**

  Used for SAP systems that don't support RFC connections, such as SAP Business ByDesign

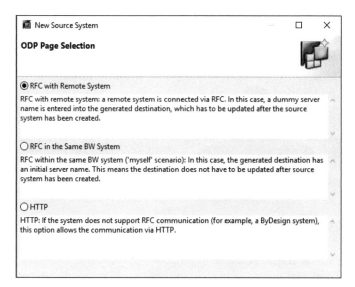

Figure 6.14 ODP Page Selection

After confirming the selection, the system displays the specific parameters for the ODP page selected. Figure 6.15 shows an example of the specific properties of the ODP page option **RFC with Remote System**.

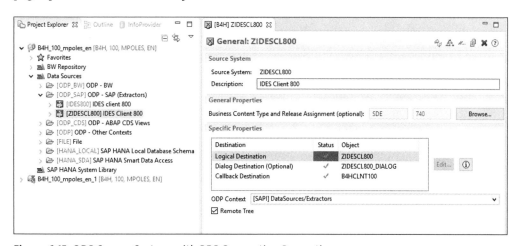

Figure 6.15 ODP Source System with RFC Connection Properties

The specific parameter details for the three options are as follows:

- **RFC with Remote System**
  - The first time the source system is created, SAP BW/4HANA automatically creates an RFC destination with the same name as the DataSource and uses a dummy value on the target host field. Maintain this RFC connection with the correct target host details and login information by selecting the **Logical Destination** line and clicking **Edit....** The system will call Transaction SM59 to open the RFC connection editor in an Eclipse tab.
  - For **ODP Context**, select **[SAPI] DataSources/Extractors**.
- **RFC in the Same BW System**
  - The logical destination already exists and should display without any errors.
  - For **ODP Context**, select **[BW] BW/4HANA**.
- **HTTP**
  - Click the **SOA Manager** hyperlink to navigate to **Web Service Configuration** in the SOA Manager. There, create a logical port *using the same name as your source system name* inside the default consumer proxy **CO_RSDSPX_ODP_IN**.
  - Select an ODP context applicable to your source system.

The **Remote Tree** parameter allows for the replication of the application component hierarchy from the source system to SAP BW/4HANA. If this option isn't selected or the source system can't replicate the application component hierarchy, then the application component hierarchy defined locally in SAP BW/4HANA is used as the **Data Sources** tree.

If the **Remote Tree** parameter is selected, you can update changes to the application components tree in the source system by clicking the **Upload Tree** button ⬚ in the **Editor** toolbar.

Once the specific parameters of the ODP page are set and validated, you can use the source system after clicking **Activate** ✎. This makes this source system available for use, and you can find it in under the **Project Explorer** panel.

6.2   SAP BW/4HANA DataSources

DataSources are SAP BW/4HANA objects that contain a collection of rules, parameters, and fields that allow you to access or extract data from source systems and make them available in SAP BW/4HANA. This set of fields can be organized either in a flat structure or in multiple flat structures, for example, the extraction of hierarchies.

DataSources are defined according the type of data they process. These DataSources types are as follows:

- Transaction data
- Master data (attributes, texts, hierarchies)
- Segmented data

These DataSources are grouped in application component hierarchies under each source system the DataSource is linked to. New application component nodes can be created locally in SAP BW/4HANA via the source system's context menu or via any application component context menu by selecting **New... • Application Component**.

> **Note**
>
> File-type DataSources still use the SAP GUI DataSource editor embedded in an Eclipse session. Other source system connection types, such as ODP, big data, and SAP HANA, use the native Eclipse wizard for creating DataSources.

The following subsections describe the creation of DataSources using the Eclipse-based native wizard and discuss the special case of file-based DataSources, which use Transaction RSDS.

6.2.1   Creating a DataSource with the Native Eclipse-Based Wizard

You can create a DataSource in different ways:

- Right-click the BW project and select **New... • DataSource...**.
- From the main menu, select **File • New... • DataSource...**.
- Right-click the source system and select **New... • DataSource...**.

After accessing the DataSource creation menu option, the **New DataSource** screen is displayed where you can enter the main properties for the DataSource.

The first part of the main properties, as shown in Figure 6.16, includes the following items:

- **BW Project**
  Project name that identifies the SAP BW/4HANA system, client, username, and language for the DataSource.

- **Package**
  Defines the transport strategy for the DataSource. Local developments use the package $TMP.

- **Source System**
  The technical name of the source system to be used as a source of data for this DataSource.

- **Source System Type**
  A display-only property showing the selected source system type.

- **Application Component**
  The hierarchical group node to assign the DataSource being created. This helps group DataSources that share the same functional areas.

- **Add to Favorites**
  A flag to add the DataSource shortcut to your favorites.

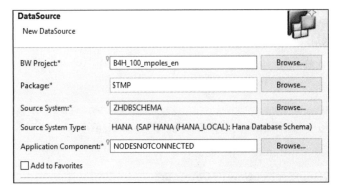

Figure 6.16 SAP HANA Database DataSource: General Parameters 1

The second part of the main properties, as shown in Figure 6.17, includes the following items:

- **Name**
  The technical name of the DataSource.

- **Description**
  Optional meaningful description of the DataSource.

- **DataSource Type**
  The DataSource type according to the data being sourced. It may be master data, hierarchies, or transactional data.

- **Copy From**
  Indicates the reference DataSource that will be used as a template for the one being created.

6

Name:*	Z_SALES_BY_COUNTRY
Description:	
DataSource Type:*	Transactional Data ⌄
Copy From:	⁹ Browse...

Figure 6.17 SAP HANA Database DataSource: General Parameters 2

The last part of the DataSource main parameters, as shown in Figure 6.18, creates the association of the DataSource with the source system object used as the data provider. The available options depend on the selected source system type.

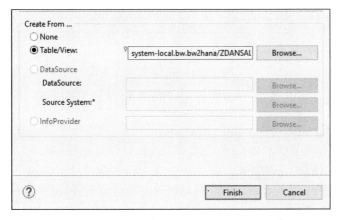

Figure 6.18 SAP HANA Database DataSource: General Parameters 3

After completing the first part of the wizard, the DataSource configuration is shown as in Figure 6.19. It has three main sections, each with its own tab: **Overview**, **Extraction**, and **Fields**.

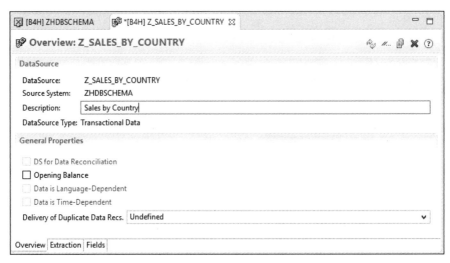

Figure 6.19 SAP HANA Database DataSource Overview Tab

The **Overview** tab includes the following main properties:

- **Description**
  Optional meaningful description of the DataSource.

- **DS for Data Reconciliation**
  Allows you to have a DataSource with direct access to the data provider in the source system and make the data available in SAP BW/4HANA via a Virtual Provider. This enables you to easily perform a consistency check on the data that was transferred by the official DataSource.

- **Opening Balance**
  This option is used to perform an initial load into noncumulative key figures in the InfoProviders.

- **Data Is Language-Dependent**
  This option is set to avoid data duplication or data loss when the data being transferred to SAP BW/4HANA has a language dependency. DataSources in this case must have a field to identify the language of the record. In SAP systems, standard fields for language are LANGU and SPRAS.

- **Data Is Time-Dependent**
  This option is set to avoid data duplication or data loss when data being transferred to SAP BW/4HANA has a time dependency, such as validity periods. DataSources in this case must have at least one field to define either the lower limit or

the upper limit of the validity period of the record. In SAP systems, standard SAP fields for validity period limits are DATEFROM and DATETO.

- **Delivery of Duplicate Data Recs**
  This indicator sets the behavior of the DataSource when processing duplicate records during the data load. The options to here are **Undefined**, **None**, and **Allowed**. Except for the **Undefined** option, you must set the fields in the DataSource that will be used as the primary key for the validation of duplicate records.

The **Extraction** tab, shown in Figure 6.20, provides a set of properties to define how data will be extracted or accessed from the source system:

- **Extraction Properties (general DataSource properties):**
  - **Delta Process**
    Defines the processing mode according to the data being loaded. For this DataSource type, we have the following options:
    - **No Delta, Only Full**
      Records are transferred as-is to the targets and you are also allowed to add filters to the data being extracted.
    - **Overwrite Delta without Deletions**
      Records are transferred with new values/status for all key figures and characteristics. The data selection is based on the delta pointers and conditions set in this DataSource and are replicated to the source system.
    - **Pure Additive Deltas**
      Records are transferred with only the modification to the key figure values and not their final value. The final value may be calculated by aggregation on the target object during the load or during reporting.
  - **Direct Access**
    Defines if the DataSource can establish direct access to the source provider and additional operations that can be performed on the data during the extraction.
  - **Streaming**
    Defines if the DataSource can stream data in real time.
  - **Adapter**
    Method used to access and load data from the source system to the SAP BW/4HANA.
- **Extractor-Specific Properties**
  This group contains information about the source system and the object that sources the data to the DataSource. You can modify the source object if necessary.

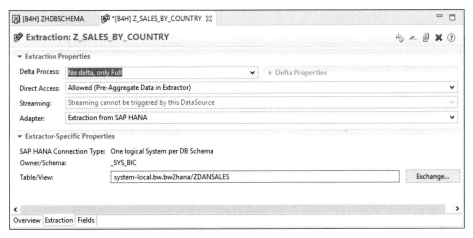

Figure 6.20 SAP HANA Database DataSource Extraction Tab

The **Fields** tab, shown in Figure 6.21, provides the available fields for the source in the left panel; and you can set the group of fields to be used to transfer data from the source to SAP BW/4HANA by selecting the **Transfer** checkbox for each field you want to use.

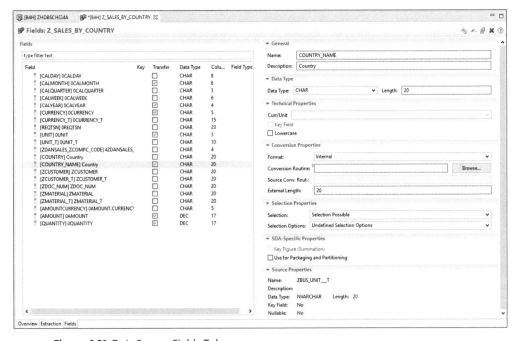

Figure 6.21 DataSource Fields Tab

Each field has a set of properties displayed in the right panel. You can further customize the properties of each field as follows:

- **Field Name**
  Technical name of the field in the DataSource structure. It can be different from the field name in the source table/view/object. You can see the field name in the source linked to the field in the DataSource in the **Source Properties** panel, as shown at the bottom right of Figure 6.21.

- **Field Description**
  A meaningful description for the field.

- **Data Type**
  Defines the technical information for the field, type of data, and length. For numeric values, you can also define the number of decimal places.

- **Technical Properties**
  Associate a field for unit of measure or currency for amount or quantity fields. For alphanumeric fields, you can define if lowercase characters are acceptable. Also, when you use duplicate records verification in the DataSource, you can set the **Key Field** flag to consider the field as part of the primary key for this validation.

- **Conversion Properties**
  Defines a conversion routine to be used in the transformation of the field and indicates if the values at the source are using the external format or the internal format of the conversion routine—for example, adding leading zeros for customer numbers.

- **Selection Properties**
  Defines if the field can be restricted during the data load with filters and indicates which filter operators can be used in this field.

- **SDA-Specific Properties**
  Used to specify which fields are used for creating packages or partitions of data during the data transfer and which key figures can be summarized during real-time replication when all delta records (including new records, changes or deletions) are processed internally using INSERT command.

You can use the DataSource in the system after clicking **Activate** (🖉). As shown in Figure 6.22, this makes this DataSource available for use, and you can find it in under the **Project Explorer** panel.

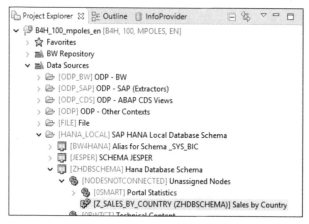

Figure 6.22 DataSources in Project Explorer Panel

6.2.2   Creating a DataSource for File-Type Source Systems

File-type DataSources have been widely used in SAP BW since the very first version of the product; they're also available in SAP BW/4HANA.

You can create a file-type DataSource via the same menu paths as described in Section 6.2.1, which are:

- Right-click the BW project and select **New... • DataSource...**.
- From the main menu, select **File • New... • DataSource...**.
- Right-click the source system and select **New... • DataSource...**.

The first two options will open the Eclipse wizard, because the source system type isn't yet selected. Once a file-type source system is selected and you proceed, the Eclipse wizard will open Transaction RSDS to complete the creation of the file type DataSource in an embedded session in Eclipse. The last option opens Transaction RSDS directly, because the source system is already preselected.

Figure 6.23 shows the first screen of a file-type DataSource creation. Here, you specify which source system will be used to establish a connection to your file system, the name of the DataSource, and the type of data being transferred. You can also create the DataSource using another object as a template. For example, we can use a target Advanced DSO as the basis for the field structure of this DataSource.

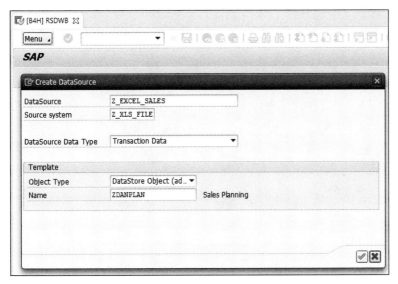

Figure 6.23 File-Type DataSource Creation: Initial Screen

The **General Info** tab shown in Figure 6.24 allows you to enter a **Description** to identify the DataSource, enter the **Application Component**, identify if the DataSource has unique records or if duplicates are allowed, and set if it's an **Opening Balance** Data-Source.

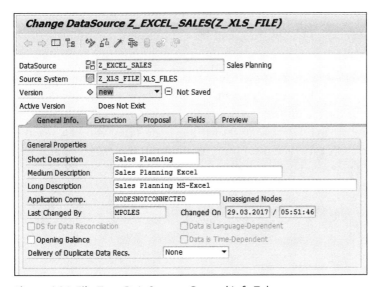

Figure 6.24 File-Type DataSource: General Info Tab

The **Extraction** tab shown in Figure 6.25 allows you to define the source of the data being transferred to SAP BW/4HANA and the extraction method.

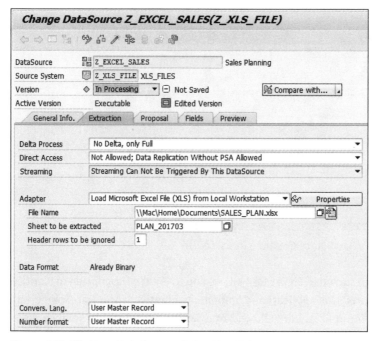

Figure 6.25 File-Type DataSource: Extraction Tab

The source of the data is identified by the **Adapter** and **Data Format** as follows:

- **File Adapter**

   The type of file and location to be used to load the data. In flat files, you can write an ABAP routine to make the file names dynamic and determined during the load process, then access the file in the local machine from the application server file system. For Microsoft Excel types (as shown in Figure 6.25), you can see the **Adapter Load Microsoft Excel File (XLS) from Local Workstation** selected and you can specify the file name and the tab of the workbook to be used.

- **Data Format**

   Applicable to flat file types. You can define the structure of the file, such as the columns separator, text delimiter, or fixed length.

> **Note**
>
> Local machine adapters and MS Excel can't have data processed in the background, including load via process chains. For background data loads, use the flat file adapter type with files stored on a file-system directory accessible by SAP BW/4HANA and the files visible in Transaction AL11.

The **Proposal** tab shown in Figure 6.26 allows you to automatically receive a proposal for the DataSource field names, data types, and field lengths based on a sample of the existing records in the source file. The number of records to be used for this sampling process is defined in the **No. of Data Records** field.

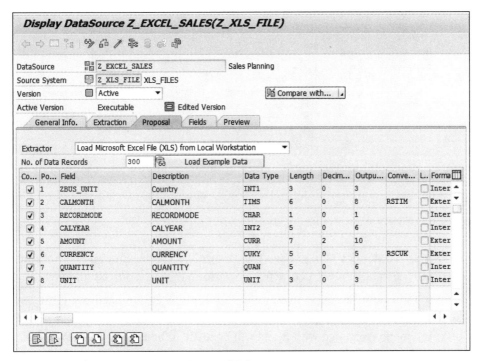

Figure 6.26 File-Type DataSource: Proposal Tab

The **Fields** tab shown in Figure 6.27 allows you to define the field structure of the DataSource. You can manually define the data types, length, case-sensitivity, primary key, conversion routines and the data format present in the source in case of using the conversion routines, which data selection operators are allowed, and time or language links for each field present in the DataSource structure.

You can also associate an InfoObject to the DataSource field as a template to retrieve the definitions of the InfoObject to the DataSource field. You can adjust those definitions according to the source of the data you're loading into SAP BW/4HANA.

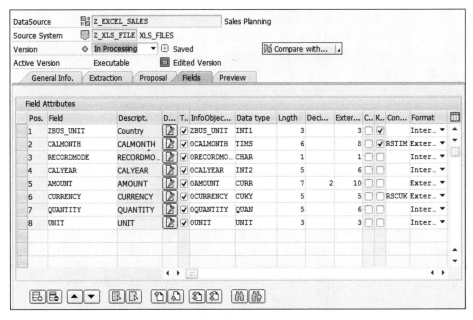

Figure 6.27 File-Type DataSource: Fields Tab

The **Preview** tab allows you to preview the data with all conversions and field characteristics in the DataSource structure to help perform the DataSource's unit test.

Once the DataSource is created, you must activate it by clicking **Activate** (✎). The DataSource will be in the **Project Explorer** panel under the source system and application component associated with it and will be ready to be used in SAP BW/4HANA data flows.

6.2.3   ODP DataSources

ODP DataSources are usually created in SAP source systems and their metadata replicated to SAP BW/4HANA. Besides metadata replication, you can create manually

ODP DataSources in SAP BW/4HANA and during their creation establish the link between the available ODP provider in the SAP source system.

For DataSources replication, navigate to the desired source system node in the **Data Sources** tree of the **Project Explorer** panel; for faster selection of available Data-Sources, you can navigate to the **Application Component** node to which the desired DataSources are linked.

Once you select the node for which you want DataSources to be replicated, right-click it and choose **Replicate**; a list of available DataSources for replication will appear, as shown in Figure 6.28.

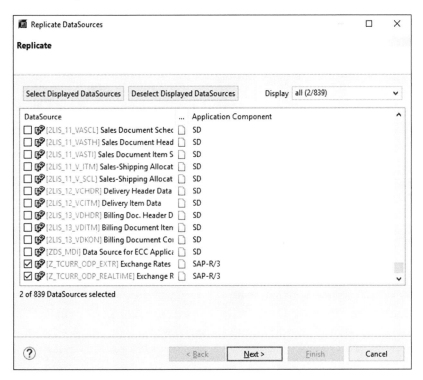

Figure 6.28 List of Available ODP DataSources to Replicate

From the list of available DataSources for replication under the selected application component, you can select either all DataSources or just specific ones to replicate the metadata from the source system to SAP BW/4HANA. This way, you can avoid repli-cating unchanged DataSources currently in use, which may also be time consuming.

Proceeding to the next step, as shown in Figure 6.29, you can confirm the number of DataSources being replicated and can activate them after the replication by setting the **Activate New DataSources** flag.

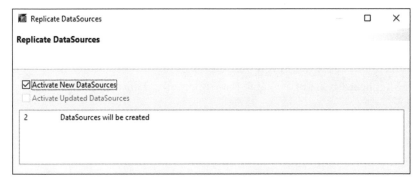

Figure 6.29 Confirmation of ODP DataSources Replication

The replication of the DataSources will start in the background, and SAP BW/4HANA will open Transaction SM37 (Job Monitor) to help you monitor the progress of the replication. Once the job is finished, the selected DataSources are replicated and activated if the corresponding option was selected.

Once you refresh the respective **Data Sources** tree, you can see the DataSources active and ready for use in SAP HANA flows.

6.3   SAP BW/4HANA Data Flows

Data flows are visual modeling elements to help you connect several InfoProviders and create transformations of data among them. Figure 6.30 shows an example of an SAP BW/4HANA data flow using an SAP ERP DataSource and linked to an Advanced DSO as a target.

You can save the data flows you create, and several flows can be defined that share the same DataSources and InfoProviders. You can check which objects in SAP BW/4HANA use another by right-clicking the object you want to check and selecting **Where-Used....**

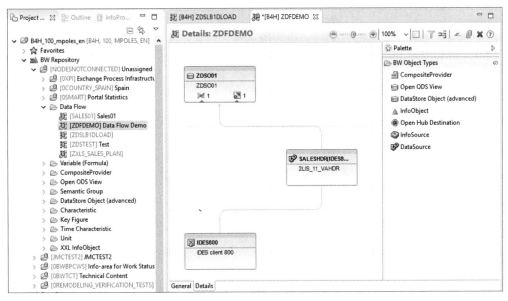

Figure 6.30 Example SAP HANA Data Flow

An example of the where-used list for the DataSource SALESHDR is shown in Figure 6.31. You can see that this DataSource is used in two data flows, one transformation, and one data transfer process.

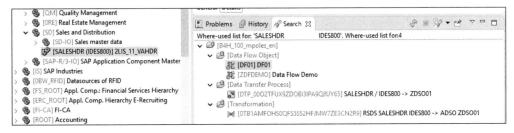

Figure 6.31 Where-Used List for DataSource

The following subsections describe the creation of an SAP BW/4HANA dataflow, how to connect objects in the data flow, and creation of transformations between a source and target objects.

6.3.1   Creating a Data Flow

You can create a data flow via the **File • New • Data Flow...** menu or via the context menu of an InfoArea node, project node, or data flow node under an InfoArea. On the parameters screen (see Figure 6.32), define the technical name of the data flow and its description. Also, you can associate it with an InfoArea and a package for transporting it to other environments. Then, click the **Finish** button.

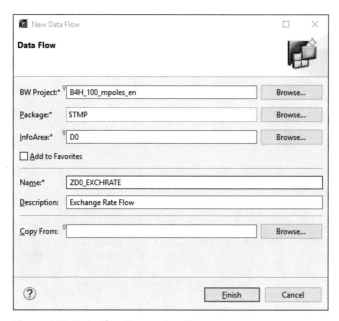

Figure 6.32 Data Flow Parameters Screen

The data flow designer screen will appear, ready to create the data flow. You can add SAP BW/4HANA objects into the data flow by dragging and dropping them from the **Project Explorer** panel or from the **Palette** panel on the right side of the screen (shown in Figure 6.30).

Once you added the necessary InfoProviders in the data flow, you can connect them via connections. To create a connection, hover your mouse pointer over the object you want to be the source of the connection; action buttons will appear, as shown in Figure 6.33.

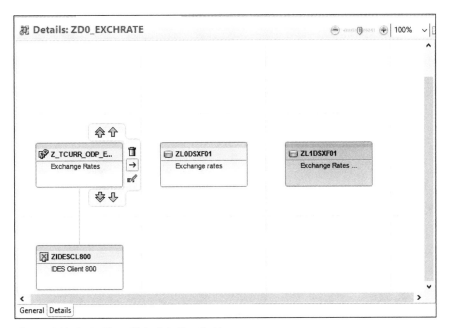

Figure 6.33 Data Flow Object Action Buttons

Click and hold the right-pointing arrow button from the source object and drop it into the target. Once the connections are created (see Figure 6.34), options to create transformations and data transfer processes are available.

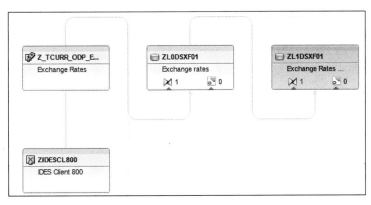

Figure 6.34 Data Flow with Connections

6.3.2   Creating Transformations

Transformations are sets of rules and programming logic to consolidate, cleanse, and apply business rules to the data being transferred from a source provider to a target provider in SAP BW/4HANA.

You can create transformations in the following ways:

- Via the data flow by right-clicking the target object and choosing **Transformations**, as shown in Figure 6.35.

- Via right-clicking the target object in **Project Explorer** and selecting **New • Transformation**. For this option, you need to enter the **Source** object.

- Via the main menu path **File • New • Other • Business Warehouse • Transformation**. For this option, you need to enter the **Source** and **Target** objects to be used.

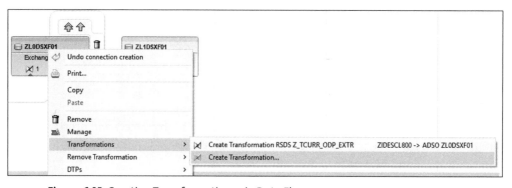

Figure 6.35 Creating Transformations via Data Flows

The other options in the **Transformations** submenu are the existing transformations already created for the object, a proposed transformation according to the connection created, and the **Create Transformation...** option, which allows you to create a different transformation from another source.

Once you select the option to create a new transformation, a pop-up screen will display to confirm the source and target for your transformation. Once you proceed, the transformation designer screen will appear, and the system may propose mappings for the source and target fields. You can change the proposed options and create new rules.

On the left side of the screen, as shown in Figure 6.36, you'll see the source object and its fields. On the right side of the screen, you see the rule group. To show the target as well, click the **Switch Detail View On/Off** button 🗔 .

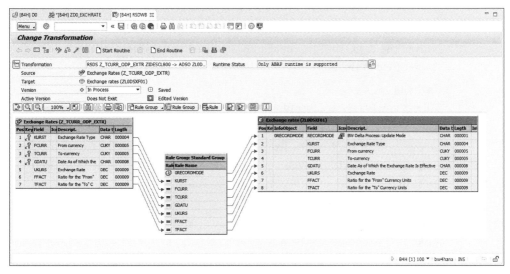

Figure 6.36 Transformation Designer Screen

The transformation designer allows you to apply different sets of transformations and rules to fields and to the overall transformation itself.

During the transformation process, you have four main stages in which you can apply rules:

1. **Before record transformation**

   You can create a set of rules to be applied to the data available in the source structure before it's passed to the transformation of records step that will create the data in the target structure. This set of rules is a programming routine created via the **Start Routine** application button.

2. **During record transformation**

   You can create a set of rules to be applied to each field of the data during the transformation of each record when creating the data in the target structure. This set of rules is run inside of each field mapping and has the following options, as shown in Figure 6.37:

- **No Transformation**
  Keeps the target field set to null or unassigned value.

- **Constant**
  Allows you to apply a constant to the target field.

- **Direct Assignment**
  Moves the data from the field indicated as a **Source Field of the Rule** to the **Target field of the Rule**.

- **Formula**
  Allows you to create a formula using a wizard.

- **Read Master Data**
  Allows you to read values from an InfoObject provider—for example, if the source field is **Customer Number** and you want to retrieve the **Account Group** to be stored in the target InfoProvider of this rule.

- **Read from Data Store (Advanced)**
  Allows you to perform a lookup on an Advanced DSO to retrieve an information according to the key of the Advanced DSO. For example, from the **Sales Order** number as a source field of the rule, you can read the **Sales Order Header** DSO details and have the **Sales Order** type stored in the target InfoProvider for this rule.

- **Routine**
  When more complicated logic is necessary to map the data from a list of source fields for this rule to a target field, you can create programming routines.

3. **After the record transformation**
   You can create a set of rules to be applied to the data available in the target structure after the data in the target structure is created and before the aggregation operations. This set of rules is a programming routine created via the **End Routine** application button.

4. **Aggregation operations**
   You can define aggregation operations for each numeric field in the transformation. These operations are either **Overwrite** or **Summation**. **Overwrite** replaces the key figures for the records with the same key on the Advanced DSO while **Summation** performs an addition operation on these key figures. They're performed after the completion of the data in the target structure creation, meaning after the **End Routine** process in the transformation (if it exists).

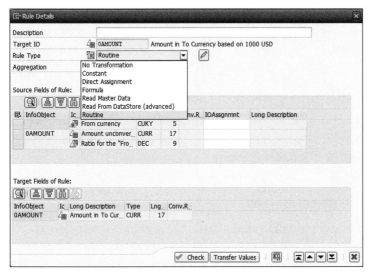

Figure 6.37 Field Routine Options

Rules for each field as shown in Figure 6.36 are created by dragging the source field and dropping it on the target field. This creates a direct mapping from the source field to the target. Alternatively, you can double-click the target field to access the **Rule Details** screen, as shown in Figure 6.37, from which you can select the **Rule Type** and add the **Source Fields** manually.

The following subsections describe additional properties and functions of the transformation and the process to enable the transformation to be fully processed by the SAP HANA database in the SAP BW/4HANA system.

6.3.3   Currency Conversions and Unit of Measures Validation

You can perform automatic currency or unit of measure translation during the transformation in the settings for currencies and units, accessed via the menu path **Menu • Edit • Settings: Currencies and Units**.

> **Prerequisites**
> - All currencies and units of measure must be contained in the key of the target InfoProvider.
> - When using Advanced DSOs, translation/conversion of currencies and units is only supported with InfoObjects.

You can also activate the consistency check for units of measure in the settings for currencies and units. This prevent records with initial values in units of measure fields from being updated in the target.

6.3.4   Transformation Version Management

You can track the changes for the transformation of a given period, fall back to a previous version, compare versions, or create a new version via the Version Management tool: **Menu • Goto • Version Management**.

6.3.5   Transformation Metadata View

Via **Menu • Extras**, you can view the ABAP-generated program, view the generated SAP HANA transformation, or view the transformation metadata in a tabular form (the **Tabular Overview** option), as shown in Figure 6.38.

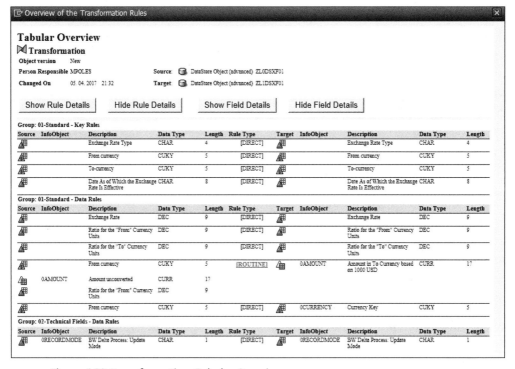

Figure 6.38 Transformation: Tabular Overview

6.3.6   Transformation Runtime Status

Depending on the method of programming you selected for the transformation, if you use ABAP-Managed Database Procedures (AMDPs) for all routines, the transformation may be executed in the SAP HANA database. To check if SAP HANA execution is possible, click the **Check** button to the right of the **Runtime Status** field. The check function simulates the creation of the transformation in the SAP HANA database. If it is successful, then the transformation is marked as possible to be executed in SAP HANA. Additionally, during the activation of the transformation, the system performs the same checks and if it is successful then the SAP HANA transformation is generated.

The generated SAP HANA transformation details can be found via **Menu • Extras • Display Generated HANA Transformation**.

When you've completed all the rules and there are no inconsistencies in the transformation, you can activate the transformation and return to the SAP HANA data flow. The transformation icon will be green, indicating the transformation is active.

6.3.7   ABAP Managed Database Procedures

Routines can be programmed in the ABAP language as in previous versions of SAP BW for any database or as AMDPs for SAP HANA execution. When using an AMDP, the system creates an ABAP class associated with the transformation routine. This class has the following sections:

- **Class Definition**
  Contains the variable declarations to be used by the mapping routine, where you can add your code and the definition of the PROCEDURE method. This method receives source values from the transformation via the inTab parameter, returns the calculated values back to the transformation via the outTab parameter, and returns all error messages that needs to be sent to the error handler via the errorTab parameter.

- **Class Implementation**
  Contains the PROCEDURE method, in which you can add your logic.

Figure 6.39 shows an example of an exchange rate conversion of an amount. The fields **Amount** (AMOUNT) and **Exchange Rate** (FFACT) are mapped from the source structure to the AMOUNT field as the target. This routine is applied in this transformation. This transformation doesn't return any errors to the handler.

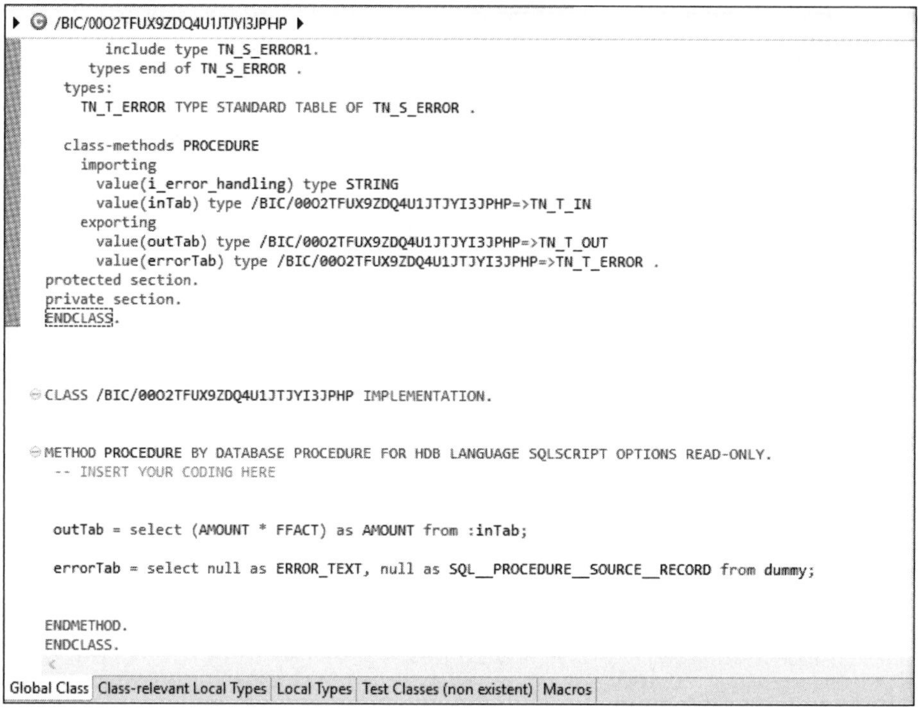

```
▶ ⊙ /BIC/00O2TFUX9ZDQ4U1JTJYI3JPHP ▶

        include type TN_S_ERROR1.
      types end of TN_S_ERROR .
    types:
      TN_T_ERROR TYPE STANDARD TABLE OF TN_S_ERROR .

    class-methods PROCEDURE
      importing
        value(i_error_handling) type STRING
        value(inTab) type /BIC/00O2TFUX9ZDQ4U1JTJYI3JPHP=>TN_T_IN
      exporting
        value(outTab) type /BIC/00O2TFUX9ZDQ4U1JTJYI3JPHP=>TN_T_OUT
        value(errorTab) type /BIC/00O2TFUX9ZDQ4U1JTJYI3JPHP=>TN_T_ERROR .
  protected section.
  private section.
  ENDCLASS.


⊖ CLASS /BIC/00O2TFUX9ZDQ4U1JTJYI3JPHP IMPLEMENTATION.


⊖ METHOD PROCEDURE BY DATABASE PROCEDURE FOR HDB LANGUAGE SQLSCRIPT OPTIONS READ-ONLY.
    -- INSERT YOUR CODING HERE


  outTab = select (AMOUNT * FFACT) as AMOUNT from :inTab;

  errorTab = select null as ERROR_TEXT, null as SQL__PROCEDURE__SOURCE__RECORD from dummy;


  ENDMETHOD.
  ENDCLASS.
  <

Global Class │ Class-relevant Local Types │ Local Types │ Test Classes (non existent) │ Macros
```

Figure 6.39 AMDP Routine to Perform Exchange Rate Conversion

6.4   SAP BW/4HANA Data Loading

SAP BW/4HANA data loading is performed via DTPs, generated programs with several settings to extract, gather, and process data from source systems and post the data directly to target InfoProviders according to transformations defined between the source and target InfoProviders.

DTPs have optimized parallel processing, which improves the performance of the data load. You can also have multiple DTPs created for the same transformation to separate delta processes from full load processes and apply different filters to be used.

In full load mode, the entire dataset of the source is transferred to the target; in delta mode, only the data that was posted to the source since the last data transfer is transferred. Multiple targets can be fed by different delta processes from one source because DTPs have delta management mechanisms to control these delta loads.

> **Note**
>
> In previous SAP BW systems, you used InfoPackages to read data from the source system and stored the data read in a PSA before transferring the data to the target Info-Providers. SAP BW/4HANA reads the data from the source system to the target InfoProviders via DTPs directly without using the PSA explicitly. DTPs also allow you to perform delta initialization without data transfer.

When a data load is triggered, a request number is generated to identify the load. The data is extracted and organized into packages with a limited number of records inside the request. In the request, SAP BW/4HANA logs and stores all the steps performed by the DTP and their properties such as extraction method, filters used, messages, and execution statuses.

You can access the status of the request via the DTP monitor or by right-clicking the target object in the SAP HANA data flow and selecting **Manage**. The following subsections describe the creation of the DTPs and process chains used to schedule and perform data loads in SAP BW/4HANA system.

6.4.1   Creating DTPs

DTPs are created in different ways:

- Via the data flow by right-clicking the target object and choosing **DTPs • Create DTP...**.
- Via right-clicking the target object in **Project Explorer** and selecting **New • Data Transfer Process...**. For this option, you need to enter the **Source** object.
- Via the main menu path **File • New • Other • Business Warehouse • Data Transfer Process**. For this option, you need to enter the **Source** and **Target** objects to be used.
- Via the process chain in Transaction RSPC.

After confirming the source and target providers, the DTP maintenance screen appears with the **Extraction** tab selected, as shown in Figure 6.40.

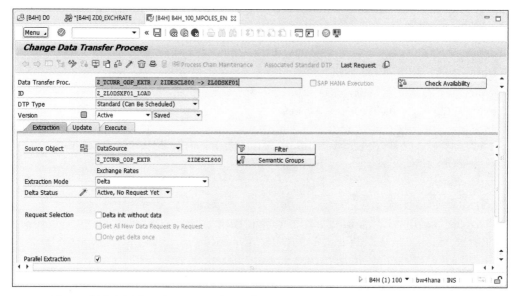

Figure 6.40 DTP Creation: Extraction Tab

The header data for the data transfer process shows the description, ID, type, version, and status of the DTP. You can also see whether the DTP can be executed in SAP HANA execution process mode by clicking the **Check Availability** button. If the DTP can be executed into the SAP HANA database, you can set the property **SAP HANA Execution** to enable the DTP execution in the SAP HANA database. **SAP HANA Execution** improves the performance of the data load since the routines and transformations are pushed down to the SAP HANA database level.

The following parameters can be defined in the **Extraction** tab:

- **Filter**
  Allows you to restrict the data selected from the source to be transferred to SAP BW/4HANA.

- **Semantic Groups**
  Used to group data that shares the same key in the packages of data transferred from the source provider. This means that the number of records in the packages will be close to the limit established in the DTP. For example, sales document line items are kept together during the splitting of the packages or parallel processing.

- **Extraction Mode**
  Defines if the data will be extracted in delta mode or full load mode.

> **Note**
>
> In full mode, the DTP supports CompositeProviders as sources. In delta mode, the DTP supports CompositeProviders as sources if they're composed only of Advanced DSOs.

- **Request Selection**
  You can specify that you want to initialize the delta without data transfer. This is useful when you have a large amount of historical data that can't be gathered together in a single request. Once the delta pointer is set on the source system, you can perform partial full loads to transfer the historical data if necessary by creating another DTP for these ad hoc full loads.

- **Parallel Extraction**
  Set the data extraction from the data provider to be processed in parallel or sequentially.

- **Package Size**
  Define how many records will be placed in each data package.

- **Parameters of the Data Source block**
  Shows the definition of the DataSource for DTPs created with a source provider as a DataSource.

The **Update** tab contains more parameters relevant to the type of target provider used in the DTP. For example, for Advanced DSOs, you can set the following:

- **Trigger Database Merge**
  Performs the data merge operation on the database for the Advanced DSO.

- **Error handling options**
  Determines whether to cancel a request after a failure and provides an option to track errors.

- **Master Data validation**
  Determines whether to continue processing the data transfer for items without master data.

The **Execute** tab contains parameters for the execution of the DTP, such as the following:

- **Technical Request Status**
  This parameter sets the status to green or red in case of warnings in the log.

- **Overall Status of Request**
  Allows you to manually or automatically set the overall status of the request. If the overall status is set manually, this status initially remains unchanged, even if the DTP execution was complete successfully or with errors. Therefore, data contained in a successful request isn't released for reporting or further processing until the overall status is manually set as successful either by the user or by the process chain step: **Quality Status/Set Data Release**.

- **Automatically Repeat Red Requests in Process Chains**
  Specifies whether requests in error should be automatically repeated when the DTP is executed in process chains. Therefore, if this property is set, the previous request containing errors is automatically deleted and a new one is started, processing both the new data and the data that was previously in error. Otherwise, the DTP ends in an error since a new load to the target is only possible if the previous request is free from errors. In this case, you may need to resolve the error on the previous request prior to repeating the DTP.

- **Processing Mode**
  Allows you to define additional options for the DTP execution besides the background process that is automatically determined by the system. You can choose from the following modes:

  - **No Data Transfer; Delta Status in Source: Retrieved** is used to set existing data in the InfoProvider source as already processed in this transfer.

  - **Serially in the Dialog Process (for Debugging)** is used when you want to perform a simulation of the DTP for debugging the code and stop at defined breakpoints in the program.

Once the parameters of the DTP are set, you can save and activate it by clicking **Activate** ✏.

6.4.2   Creating Process Chains

Process chains are collections of load steps and target actions grouped together and logically sequenced that can be triggered by an event or scheduled to run in the background.

You can create a process chain via Transaction RSPC. To open the SAP GUI screen embedded in Eclipse, select **Navigate • Open SAP GUI** from the main menu.

Transaction RSPC opens the **Planning View** of process chains, as shown in Figure 6.41, and lists all available process chains grouped by **Display Components**.

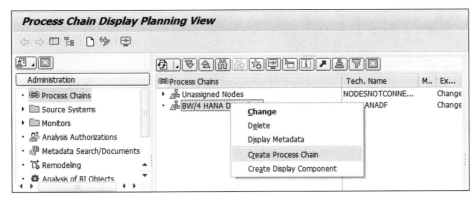

Figure 6.41 Process Chain Planning View

To create a new process chain, right-click the display component that you'll associate the new process chain with and select **Create Process Chain**.

The first step when creating a new process chain is to define the **Start Process**, which contains the definition of the process chain trigger. There are two options:

- **Scheduled**
  This option allows you to schedule the process chain execution or trigger the process chain manually or from an external scheduling tool.

- **External start only** (via API or metachain)
  This option permits the process chain execution only when called via an API or when it's inside another process chain as a subchain.

Once the start process is created, you can add steps of the process chain in the logical sequence.

To add a DTP in the process chain, open the **Load Process and Postprocessing** node and double-click the **Data Transfer Process** node.

In the pop-up, enter the ID of an existing DTP or choose to create a new DTP. If you create a new DTP, the dialog box for creating a new DTP appears as shown in Figure 6.42, and you can select the **Source** and **Target** providers for this process and continue. Otherwise, the DTP is added into the process chain.

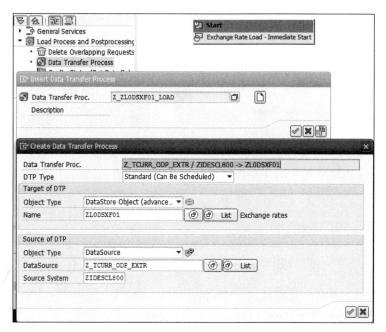

Figure 6.42 DTP Creation via Process Chain

Once the start process, DTPs, and other processes are added in the process chain, you can connect these processes by dragging and dropping the selected source process to the target process. When dragging and dropping, the mouse cursor becomes a pencil. The system may ask if the process chain should continue to the next process only if the current process is **Successful**, when it has **Errors**, or **Always**, as shown in Figure 6.43.

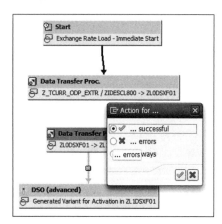

Figure 6.43 Process Chain Planning View: Linking Processes

Once the process chain is created, click **Activate** (✐) to be able to execute or schedule it.

The process chain log (see Figure 6.44) can be accessed via the menu path **Menu • Goto • Log View**.

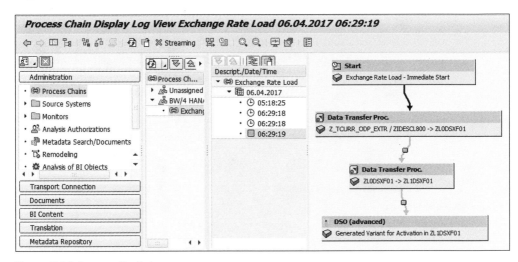

Figure 6.44 Process Chain Log

6.5   Manual Data Acquisition

In addition to loading data into SAP BW/4HANA, you can also enter data manually for master data attributes, texts, and hierarchies. This master data maintenance is performed using the Web Dynpro ABAP interface.

Prerequisites

This option has the following prerequisites:

- Activate the following Internet Communication Framework (ICF) services:
  - /default_host/sap/bc/webdynpro
  - /default_host/sap/public/bc
  - /default_host/sap/public/bc/ur
  - /default_host/sap/public/bc/icons
  - /default_host/sap/public/bc/icons_rtl
  - /default_host/sap/public/bc/webicons

- /default_host/sap/public/bc/pictograms
- /default_host/sap/public/bc/webdynpro/*
- /default_host/sap/bc/webdynpro/sap/RSDMDM_MD_MAINTENANCE_APP
- /default_host/sap/bc/webdynpro/sap/RSDMDM_MD_NEW_APP
- /default_host/sap/public/myssocntl

- Characteristic InfoObjects must have at least one of the following master data properties enabled to store master data: master data, texts, and/or hierarchies, as discussed in Chapter 5, Section 5.3.1.

The master data maintenance, as in the example shown in Figure 6.45, is accessed when you display a characteristic and click the **Miscellaneous** 🔧 button.

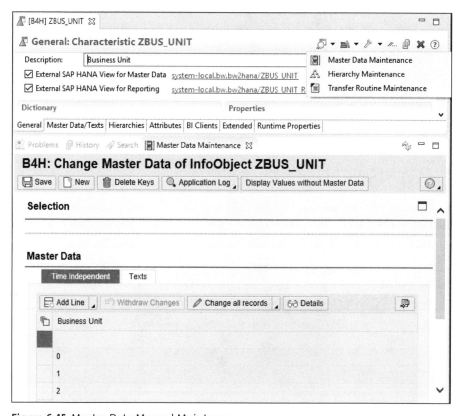

Figure 6.45 Master Data Manual Maintenance

The following options may be available:

- **Master Data Maintenance**
  For maintaining master data attributes and texts.
- **Hierarchy Maintenance**
  For maintaining hierarchies for the characteristic.
- **Transfer Routine Maintenance**
  To allow you to create a conversion routine for the characteristic to be used globally during transformations. You can define different conversion routines in this option depending on the source system.

Once the master data is maintained, click **Save and Activate** to make the master data changes effective and available for reporting.

6.6   Summary

SAP BW/4HANA has become a central enterprise data warehouse system for data integration, harmonization, and persistency due to its ability to integrate with different types of source systems, to federate data objects, or to manually receive data changes.

This chapter discussed the details of setting up source systems, DataSources, data flows, and data load processes for all available types of source systems.

The consolidated view of SAP BW/4HANA's data acquisition capabilities and its integration methods with different source systems described in this chapter enables you to identify, model, and implement different integration solutions applicable to your platform and business requirements in order to create a powerful EDW landscape.

The next chapter covers the capabilities and improvements in SAP BW/4HANA for reporting and analytics that we can leverage to read and further transform the data present in the modelled EDW landscape to provide business tailored solutions for data visualization and analytical reporting.

Chapter 7
Reporting and Analytics

Reporting and analytics are key processes in business intelligence, and several SAP and third-party tools are available to support different analysis needs. In this chapter, we'll discuss SAP BW/4HANA's high-performance tools and connectors that enable reporting and analytics in different visualization systems.

Reporting and analytics are crucial functions in business intelligence that collect and organize data available in your EDW landscape into different data visualizations. These visualizations can be used to understand certain *key performance indicators (KPIs)* and establish actions to improve them.

SAP BW/4HANA provides significant performance improvements by pushing *OLAP* operations and complex reporting calculations down to the database. In previous SAP BW systems, these reporting calculations and OLAP operations were processed in the application server layer by the OLAP engine.

This ability to process data in the database layer is one of the key factors that contributes to the efficiency in using advanced analytics methods, such as complex statistics functions, scenarios simulation, and predictive analysis.

There are several tools within SAP HANA that can be used together for complex analytic reporting, including SAP HANA analysis process, Application Function Library, Predictive Analysis Library, R scripts for statistical computing and data mining, and text analysis.

In this chapter, we'll examine important available resources for reporting in SAP BW/4HANA, including its core component, the SAP BW/4HANA query, its integration with SAP BusinessObjects and third-party business intelligence tools, and its ability to make queries available as SAP HANA calculation views to be used as data sources in SAP HANA native developments.

Simple query examples will be used throughout the chapter to illustrate some of the capabilities from each tool presented.

7.1   SAP BW/4HANA Queries

SAP BW/4HANA queries are objects that contain several functions and properties to help you to perform multidimensional analyses on multi-scale datasets and to address different business requirements.

In SAP BW/4HANA, the component responsible for retrieving, processing, and formatting data requested by a query from its InfoProvider is called *analytic manager*. This is the main interface between you and the database and it makes multidimensional data available to different frontend tools via special integration protocols and components tailored for each of them.

Queries are defined and linked to a specific InfoProvider that contains the data you want to report on. The performance of the query execution is directly related to the precision of the query definition and the query size. A query with several calculation levels, few filters, or with a large number of fields may have longer runtime during its first execution and navigation.

Queries in SAP BW/4HANA have the following main parts:

- **Query properties**
  A combination of settings to define the query execution procedures and visibility to third-party tools. These query properties are subdivided into general properties and runtime properties.

- **Sheet definition**
  A combination of query elements to form a worksheet that provides a mechanism to organize data according to your reporting needs.

- **Query elements**
  These are characteristic InfoObjects; basic, restricted, and calculated key figures; structures; formulas; and selections.

- **Filters**
  A combination of restrictions that affects the data reported, allowing you to restrict the data volume retrieved from the InfoProvider and used in the report.

- **Variables**
  Objects that can be defined and associated with InfoObjects to help make filters and selections flexible and incorporate complex rules.

- **Conditions**
  A combination of rules to further restrict the information displayed, such as top N records according to a specific key-figure.

- **Exceptions**

    A combination of rules and alerts to highlight certain figures on the report.

Before we examine these elements in more detail, it's important to highlight the process of creating new queries in SAP BW/4HANA and how it differs from previous SAP BW systems.

7.1.1   Creating a Query with Eclipse-Based Query Designer

SAP BW reporting users will be familiar with the SAP Business Explorer (SAP BEx) query designer tool. SAP BEx queries have been the main reporting feature for all previous versions of SAP BW. In SAP BW/4HANA, this feature was migrated from the SAP BEx toolset to the Eclipse platform.

Figure 7.1 shows the well-known SAP BEx query designer. The **InfoProvider** panel is where all available InfoObjects for reporting from the InfoProvider linked to the query are listed and ready for drag and drop to the desired section of the report. The central section, called **Rows/Columns**, is reserved to build the query sheet definition, the **Properties** panel shows all properties related to a certain query element, and the **Messages** panel shows all messages related to the query being designed.

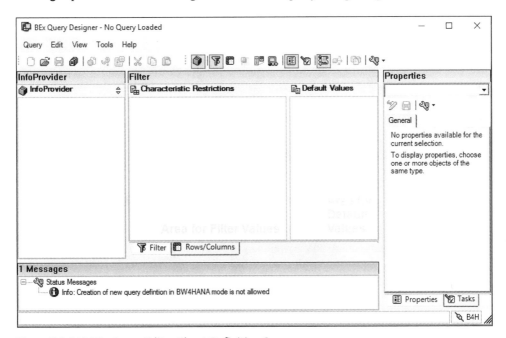

Figure 7.1 SAP BEx Query Editor Sheet Definition Screen

> **Note**
>
> During SAP BW migration, existing SAP BEx queries are migrated via the SAP BW/4HANA Starter Add-On for SAP BW 7.5 powered by SAP HANA. After the migration, you need to **Open** each query using the Eclipse-based query designer, fix any inconsistencies, and **Save** it.

Figure 7.2 shows the new SAP BW/4HANA query editor based in Eclipse. The elements of the query in this editor are divided into tabs; each tab contains the different query design elements.

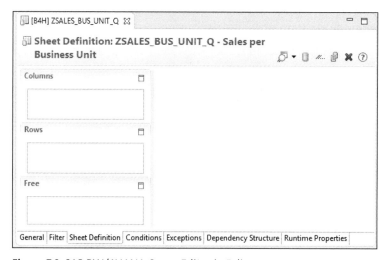

Figure 7.2 SAP BW/4HANA Query Editor in Eclipse

> **Note**
>
> Functions described in this chapter require the installation of the following add-ons in SAP HANA Studio or Eclipse:
>
> - ABAP Development Tool (ADT)
> - Modeling Tools for SAP BW Powered by SAP HANA
> - SAP HANA Tools
>
> For installation links to use in the Eclipse installation path, visit *https://tools.hana.ondemand.com*.

You can create a query in SAP HANA Studio in the BW modeling perspective in the **Project Explorer** panel in two ways:

1. Select the node that has the BW project name or an InfoProvider and select the menu path **File • New • Query...**, as shown in Figure 7.3.
2. Right-click the selected node and select **New • Query...**.

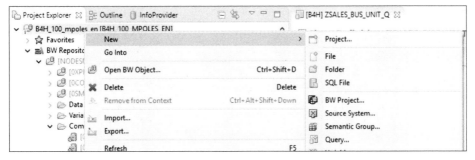

Figure 7.3 Creating Query via Context Menu from SAP BW Project Node

Also, you can create a new query as a copy of an existing one by right-clicking an existing query and selecting **Copy...** from the context menu, as shown in Figure 7.4.

Figure 7.4 Creating Query via Context Menu from Existing Query as Copy

The first pop-up screen in the query creation, shown on Figure 7.5, asks for the main general properties of the query.

These main general properties are as follows:

- **BW Project**
  Shows the name of the SAP BW/4HANA project that identifies the SAP BW/4HANA system ID, client, username, and language to in which you're creating the query.

- **Package**
  Allows you to select which development package this query belongs to. The **$TMP** package is used for local developments. Transporting queries is discussed in Section 7.1.9.

Figure 7.5 Create New Query Initial Screen

- **InfoProvider**
  Shows the technical name of the InfoProvider that will be used as the basis of the query.

- **Name**
  Stores the technical name of the query.

- **Description**
  Stores a meaningful description of the query.

- **Copy From**
  References the technical name of a query that will be used as a template for this new one.

> **Note**
>
> The query used as a copy from when creating a new query must be from the same InfoProvider.

7.1.2 Query Properties

Query properties are organized into two groups: general properties and runtime properties. We'll discuss each group in turn.

General Properties

The **General** tab shown in Figure 7.6 is the first tab viewed when creating a new query. It contains the general settings and properties of the query.

Figure 7.6 New SAP BW/4HANA Query: General Tab

This screen is divided into the following sections:

- **Output Settings**
  Select options to modify the default format of the report when the query result is shown.

195

- **Result Location**
Select the default location of the total and subtotal columns and rows.

- **Zero Suppression**
Hide rows or columns either when their result values are equal to zero or when all individual values for that row or column are zero.

- **Remote Access**
Use the following options in this section if you want to run your query using a different frontend:

  - **By OLE DB for OLAP**
  Enable the query to be accessed by MDX-enabled frontends, such as SAP BusinessObjects tools.

  - **External SAP HANA View**
  Enable the query to be accessed by SQL-based ODBC third-party tools, such as Tableau. SAP BW/4HANA queries automatically generate SAP HANA calculation views when this property is selected. The generated **SAP HANA View** hyperlink will sit beside this property. You can get the location of the SAP HANA view by hovering your cursor over the link or open it by clicking the hyperlink. The SAP HANA view is displayed in the SAP HANA Studio modeling perspective.

  - **OData**
  Enable the query to be accessed by applications based on Representational State Transfer (REST), such as Qlik.

- **Universal Display Hierarchy**
Limits the hierarchy levels that are read from the database when you design your query to have characteristics displayed in a hierarchical mode. For example, if you have a report with country, state and city arranged hierarchically and you set this property to **Up to level 2**, then the query only retrieves data up to the state level.

- **Variables Order**
View and configure the screen order of the variables used in the query. When the query is executed, the system generates a variable input window, which displays the variables in the order specified in this section.

- **Extended**
Manage data selection parameters for backend processing, particularly when you use near-line storage for cold data storage and you want to incorporate archived data with current data in your query. Also allows you to enable links to documentation created for values in master data, InfoProvider and to the query metadata. Near-line storage solutions are discussed in Chapter 9.

- **Planning**
  This section lets you change planning mode options for queries.

> **Note**
>
> The **External SAP HANA View** option is only enabled for the query if the InfoProvider has also the **External SAP HANA View** option enabled.

You can save the query by following the menu path **File • Save**.

Runtime Properties

In the **Runtime Properties** tab (see Figure 7.7), you can override settings from the Info-Provider to provide specific values needed for the query. This tab is divided into two sections:

1. **Common Runtime Properties**

   - **Process Key Figure with High Precision**
     This property is used to set the precision level for the calculations in the query. Two levels are possible: 16 places (short decimal floating) and 34 places (long decimal floating). Short decimal floating is used by default in SAP BW/4HANA to minimize main memory usage when data is stored in the OLAP cache.

   - **No Parallel Processing**
     When the query is executed, it can be split into several subqueries internally. This happens according to the complexity of the objects and formulas, especially when the query contains calculated or restricted key figures and hierarchy conditions. With this property, you can set the processing of these subqueries to be either sequentially or in parallel. For parallel processing, if you have an InfoProvider with non-cumulative key figures, the query processing happens in two stages: subqueries that are not related to the non-cumulative key figures are processed in parallel first and then the remaining ones which are related to non-cumulative key figures are processed sequentially to avoid extensive memory consumption.

   - **Calculating Commutative Formulas After Aggregation**
     Commutative formulas, such as addition and subtraction, can be calculated before or after aggregation, returning the same result. The before aggregation option ensures that the formula calculation is executed for every record in the dataset transferred from the InfoProvider to the OLAP engine. If the formula is calculated after aggregation, the number of calculations depends on the granularity level of the formula in your query.

- **Query Is used as InfoProvider**
  This setting allows the query to be used as an InfoProvider in data flows.

- **Generation Log**
  This property is set to store the log created during query generation.

- **OLAP Effort**
  This property is used for setting the OLAP effort expectations and limits for queries that have InfoProviders with a high volume of data. It is also used when the query structure is extensive or has complex calculations that result in a large result set to be processed by the OLAP engine.

Figure 7.7 Query Runtime Properties in Query Editor

2. **Runtime Profile Properties**

   − **Data Integrity Profile**
     Allows you to specify the method of retrieving data from the InfoProvider either via predefined available profiles or via expert mode for custom settings.

   − **Query Read Mode**
     Defines how the OLAP processor acquires data from the InfoProvider during the initial query execution and navigation of the query results.

   − **Query Cache Mode**
     Defines different options and algorithms for using the SAP BW/4HANA cache to optimize the query runtime by saving OLAP calculation results in the cache highly-compressed by default in SAP BW/4HANA. You can maintain cache compression parameters for the query via Transaction RSRCACHE. It is recommended the query cache compression size to be close to 2GB and with compression threshold greater than 5000 rows in the cache.

   − **Cache Usage Mode**
     Defines whether the cache entries are used to display the query results.

   − **Update Cache Objects in Delta Process**
     Specifies that new data retrieved in a query is added to the cache; also called *delta caching*.

   − **Type of SP Grouping for Delta Caching**
     Helps optimize the behavior of the delta cache. For example, if a query is based on a CompositeProvider with several InfoProviders, you can set it so that data from each InfoProvider is stored separately in the cache. The advantage of this option is that when you execute the query, only InfoProviders with changed data are read again. On the other hand, it consumes more memory to store these individual datasets.

   − **Operations in SAP HANA/BWA**
     This is the setting that allows you to push complex calculations normally performed in the OLAP engine down to SAP HANA database. SAP Note 2063449:

Push down of BW OLAP functionalities to SAP HANA contains the available functions that will be executed in SAP HANA database.

- **Materialize Intermediate Query Result**
  SAP BW/4 HANA offers an option to materialize intermediate query results and it is used in conjunction to the property **Operations in SAP HANA/BWA**; when **Operations** in SAP HANA is set to **Exception Aggregation** or **Formulas Calculated in SAP HANA**, a large part of query processing takes place in the SAP HANA database. This way, intermediate results of queries are calculated and materialized to be reused during drill-down operations and providing a better performance for queries with large datasets. Although, for cases of smaller datasets or depending on the level of performance optimizations used when creating the query, it might be quicker to keep recalculation of intermediate results each time the query is executed.

- **Use Selection of Structure Elements**
  This property ensures that only elements present in the structure and their selections are passed to the database for retrieving the query dataset. For example, if you have records with amounts in January and February, and you display only January column in your query structure. This property ensures that only records with values in January are processed. This way, you might have improvement in performance if you have many selections or restricted key figures that either are not displayed initially during the initial query execution or used in several operations, such as **Filter and Drill Down by**.

- **Also Read Child Members**
  This setting complements the property **Use Selection of Structure Elements** when it is active. It automatically incorporates all hierarchical successors in a filter of a hierarchy-type structure element for the data retrieval.

- **Optimization Mode**
  Defines the frequency with which the OLAP processor memory is optimized for existing queries. By default, this optimization happens on the first execution of the query and subsequently 31 days after the last optimization. It can also happen according to the Optimization Periods property definition.

- **Optimization Periods**
  Defines the period to be used in the optimization of the OLAP processor if you've set the **Optimization Mode** to **Query Optimization with Individual Period in Days**. This setting can be used if the InfoProvider is consistently fully dropped and reloaded.

– **Stat. Detail Level**

displays the detail level for statistic details of the query runtime, as defined in Transaction RSDDSTAT (Maintenance of Statistic Properties) for the query object type (see Figure 7.8).

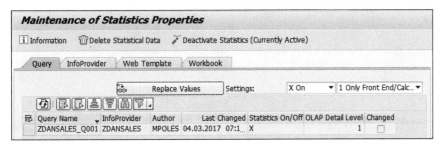

Figure 7.8 Maintenance of Statistics Properties

7.1.3   Filters

Query filters are mechanisms to restrict the data selection for the query. They can be defined locally in the query or globally in the InfoProvider to be used in multiple queries. The following subsections describe the properties and use of filters and creation of global filters.

Query Filters

Filters are restrictions on the data selection for the entire query. These filters are sent to the database to reduce the volume of data retrieved and sent to the OLAP processor during the query execution.

The **Filter** tab (see Figure 7.9) allows you to create fixed-value filters and default-value filters for the characteristics available for the InfoProvider selected for the report. Fixed-value and default-value filters differ as follows:

- **Filters with fixed values**

  The characteristic values used as the filter selection can't be changed after the query result is displayed.

- **Filters with default values**

  The characteristic values are used as the filter selection in the background; they aren't displayed on the selection screen, but you can change or remove these values after the query result is displayed.

Figure 7.9 SAP BW/4HANA: Filter Tab

In both sections, you can associate variables with query filters, allowing them to receive flexible values during query execution (see Section 7.1.4).

Special Feature: Query Definition without Key Figures

Say that you want to define a query that only contains characteristics in the query structure (rows/columns), but every query must contain at least one key figure. In this case, you can add a key figure to the **Filter: Fixed Values** panel and, if required, add filters to it. For example, you can create a list of customer details with individual sales order amounts greater than $10,000.

Global Filters

Global filters are reusable elements created to be present in different queries sharing the same InfoProvider. This allows you to have a group of queries with the same filter logic. When a change in logic is needed, you won't need to change each query individually; instead, you only need to change the logic in the global filter and regression test the queries involved.

If you have a filter collection in your report and you want to make it a global filter to be reusable for different queries sharing the same InfoProvider, right-click any filter element in the filter area and choose **Save as Global Filter…**, as shown in Figure 7.10.

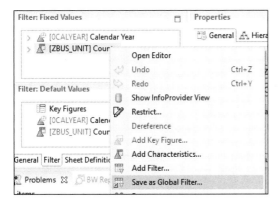

Figure 7.10 Context Menu of Filter with Save as Global Filter Highlighted

A create **Filter** screen will appear, in which you can enter the technical name and the description of the filter.

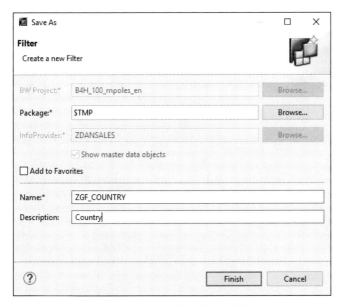

Figure 7.11 Input Screen for Creating Global Filter

After clicking **Finish**, you'll see the new global filter created in your query, with all fil-ter elements associated with your query.

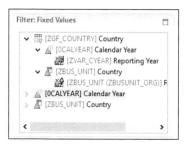

Figure 7.12 Global Filter and Its Definition Created from Existing Query Filters

You can clean up the filter area by removing the local filters made into global filters. You also may want to change the global filter definition, which you can find under the InfoProvider associated with it, as shown in Figure 7.13.

Figure 7.13 Modeling Perspective Showing InfoProvider's Associated Elements, Including Global Filters

The global filter modification screen has the same features as the **Filter** screen in the query designer (see Figure 7.14).

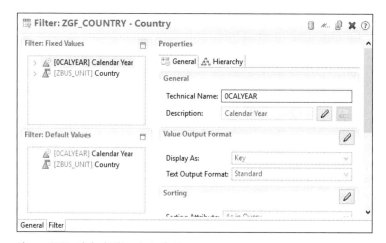

Figure 7.14 Global Filter Details Screen

Using the same process, you can create global filters by right-clicking an InfoProvider and choosing **New... • Global Filter...**.

7.1.4   Variables

Variables are used as query parameters for different types of query elements. Unlike fixed-value filters, a variable is filled with values only once the query is executed.

Query elements are often associated with InfoObjects in SAP BW/4HANA; therefore, each InfoObject type restricts the variable types that can be used. When the variables are linked to InfoObjects, these variables become available for use in all queries linked to InfoProviders which contain these InfoObjects.

The following subsections describe the process of creating variables and variable exits (SAP exit, customer exit, and SAP HANA exit) to be used in SAP BW/4HANA queries.

Creating Variables

You can create a variable either via the menu path **File • New • Variable** or by right-clicking a characteristic, key figure, time, unit info object, or query node and selecting **New • Variable**.

The **New BW Variable** screen shown in Figure 7.15 allows you to enter the properties of this new variable.

Figure 7.15 SAP BW/4HANA: New Variable Properties Screen

When you create a variable, you must select a variable type and processing type, as follows:

- The *variable type* (**Type of Variable**) indicates for which types of objects the variable can be used. The supported variable types are as follows:
  - **Characteristic Value**
    Contains or restricts SAP BW/4HANA characteristics values—for example, current date in date-type characteristics.
  - **Hierarchy**
    Contains or restricts hierarchy names—for example, cost center hierarchies that define different groupings for cost center analysis, which may share the same cost centers.
  - **Hierarchy Nodes**
    Contains or restricts hierarchy nodes relevant for the query execution—for example, specific cost centers.
  - **Text**
    Contains a text that can be used in query elements descriptions—for example, in formula descriptions.
  - **Formula**
    Contains numeric values that can be used in formulas, exceptions, and conditions. For example, you can create a formula variable for currency exchange rates that will be processed after you've executed the query.
- The *processing type* (**Processing By**) indicates the method the variable is filled with values during the query runtime. The supported processing types are as follows:
  - **Manual Input/Default Value**
    Allows you to manually enter values in variables when executing the query. You can also enter default values in variables using this processing type on the **Default Values** tab in the variables editor. Default values are shown in input fields associated with the variables in the query selection screen during the query runtime for ready-for-input variables. For variables not input-ready, the default value is used as defined in the variable.
  - **Replacement Path**
    Allows you to specify a value or a reference characteristic that automatically replaces the variable when executing the query. For example, you have dynamic

columns for last 12 months depending on the current month and you can use replacement path to set the month names used.

- **Authorization**
  Allows you to make SAP BW/4HANA populate variables of this process type with values defined in the user authorization objects generated when selecting the property **Authorization-Relevant** in the characteristic linked to the variable. It can be used with characteristic and hierarchy node variables.

- **Variable Exits**
  Allows you to set up complex rules and logic to determine the final values of a variable to be used in a query at runtime. The types of variable exits are **Customer Exit**, **SAP Exit**, and **SAP HANA Exit**.

- **Ref. Characteristic**
  The InfoObject technical name associated with the variable. When creating the variable via the InfoObject context menu, this field is prepopulated with the InfoObject's technical name.

- **Var. Represents**
  Depending on the type of variable selected, this option allows you to set the variable to represent a single value, multiple single values, an interval, or **Selection-Options** (a group of complex conditions involving single values and intervals).

Variable Exits: SAP Exits

SAP exits are variables delivered by SAP within **BI Content** that contain predefined sets of the most commonly used rules associated with different types of InfoObjects. You can use them according to your needs, but you may need to import them from the **BI Content** and activate them to be used in queries.

> **Tip**
> You can find the variables provided by SAP by searching for them using object type ELEM with subtype VAR. The technical names of SAP-delivered objects always begin with a number. For example, to retrieve the current calendar month/year, you can use the SAP-delivered variable **Current Month** (technical name: OCMONTH), which is referenced to the characteristic **Calendar Year/Month** (technical name: OCALMONTH) in the query filter.

> **Restriction**
>
> Note that the SAP exit processing type can't be used with external SAP HANA views. The SAP HANA exit processing type must be used instead when the query is created with the **External SAP Hana View** setting.

Variable Exits: Custom Exits

You can create variables with specific coding to meet your requirements' rules and complexity. *Custom exits* allow you to generate default values, populate variable values automatically, and perform validations on all variables after they're populated.

To use a custom exit variable, you need to create a *Business Add-In (BAdI)* enhancement implementation for the enhancement spot RSROA_VARIABLES_EXIT; it must include the BAdI definition RSROA_VARIABLES_EXIT_BADI. You can find this enhancement spot in the ABAP package RSROA_VAR either via the ABAP Development Tools perspective in Eclipse or via Transaction SE80. The RSROA_VARIABLES_EXIT_BADI enhancement spot is called several times when the query is executed, and the I_STEP parameter identifies the event processed. Table 7.1 lists the purposes of and actions performed in each step.

Step	Description
I_STEP = 0	The step isn't called from the variables screen, but from the authorization check or query monitor.
I_STEP = 1	The step is called before the variables screen is shown.
I_STEP = 2	This step is only used for non-input-ready variables and triggered after proceeding from the variables screen.
I_STEP = 3	The step is called after proceeding from the variables screen. If any exception is triggered, the variables screen appears again.

Table 7.1 Custom Exit Processing Steps and Their Triggering Events

If a query contains multiple variables with customer exits, when the enhancement spot is called, the system passes all variables values in the internal table I_T_VAR_RANGE, allowing you to create complex logic combining values from several variables of the query.

Variable Exits: SAP HANA Exits

This processing type is used when you need to implement complex rules in variables and you also want to generate an SAP HANA calculation view linked to the query. The creation of an SAP HANA view is possible because this processing type allows you to use an *ABAP-Managed Database Procedures (AMDP)* class implementation to determine values for variables.

You can use this processing type with characteristic value variables and formula variables. For formula variables, the variable **Entry Type** must be set to mandatory.

Unlike customer variables, which allow multiple values and intervals on the variable, SAP HANA exit variables always represent a *single value*.

The enhancement implementation of an SAP HANA exit is executed during the query runtime and it is either called before the selection screen is shown for processing and populating the input-ready variables, or after proceeding the query execution from the selection screen for processing non-input-ready variables.

Note

You can read up to 20 variable contents from the other variables on the screen if you need to reference their contents during processing.

Since this processing type has SAP HANA database procedures associated with its implementation, you can only create the enhancement implementation for the enhancement spot RSROA_VARIABLES_HANA_EXIT in the ABAP Development Tools perspective in Eclipse.

The RSROA_VARIABLES_HANA_EXIT enhancement spot is also contained in the package RSROA_VAR. The BADI implementation class requires an AMDP class and must contain the following interfaces: IF_BADI_INTERFACE, IF_AMDP_MARKER_HDB, and IF_RSROA_VAR_HANA_EXIT.

Figure 7.16 shows the enhancement spot for the SAP HANA exit variable implementation with the methods to be used: GET_PROPERTIES and PROCESS. After the method name, you must enter the addition by database procedure for hdb language SQLSCRIPT and your code must comply with *SQLScript* syntax.

Object Name	Description
▾ 🗁 RSROA_VAR	OLAP Variables
▸ 🗀 Dictionary Objects	
▸ 🗀 Class Library	
▾ 🗁 Enhancements	
▸ 🗀 Enhancement Implementations	
▾ 🗁 Enhancement Spots	
▸ 🗀 RSROA_VARIABLES_EXIT	OLAP Variables Exit
▾ 🗁 RSROA_VARIABLES_HANA_EXIT	OLAP variables HANA exit
▾ 🖳 RSROA_VAR_HANA_EXIT_BADI	OLAP variables HANA exit
▾ 🔲 IF_RSROA_VAR_HANA_EXIT	Inferface for BAdI: RSROA_VARIABLES_HANA_EXIT
▾ 🗁 Implementing Classes	
▾ 🗁 CL_RSROA_HANA_EXIT_FALLBACK	Fallback class for BAdI: RSROA_VAR_HANA_EXIT_BADI
▸ 🗀 Interfaces	
▸ 🗀 Attribute	
▾ 🗁 Methods	
▾ 🗁 IF_RSROA_VAR_HANA_EXIT	Inferface for BAdI: RSROA_VARIABLES_HANA_EXIT
• 🔲 GET_PROPERTIES	
• 🔲 PROCESS	
▸ 🗀 Types	

Figure 7.16 Enhancement Spot in Package RSROA_VAR for SAP HANA Exit

There are two methods to consider, as follows:

- IF_RSROA_VAR_HANA_EXIT~GET_PROPERTIES
  Use this method to setup the mapping from variables and their values to the input parameters of the method IF_RSROA_VAR_HANA_EXIT~PROCESS. For this to be possible, the parameter C_IS_ACTIVE must be set to "X". This mapping is stored in the C_TS_VNAM_INDEX parameter, which maps each variable value from the query to the parameter I_VAR_VALUE_<n>. For example, the {OCYEAR, 1} record in the C_TS_VNAM_INDEX parameter indicates that the value of the variable OCYEAR is assigned to the parameter I_VAR_VALUE_1.

- IF_RSROA_VAR_HANA_EXIT~PROCESS
  You can use this method to set the new value of the variable. The C_VALUE parameter is used to receive the new value of the variable. Also, you can use the I_VAR_VALUE_1 to I_VAR_VALUE_20 parameters collections to retrieve any content from other variables from the variables screen for this process.

> **Tip**
>
> The CL_RSROA_HANA_EXIT_FALLBACK class can be used as a template to create the customized class for this enhancement spot. It has all the methods and interfaces defined according to the prerequisites listed previously.

Once the implementation is active, as shown in Figure 7.17, access the ABAP Development Tools perspective in SAP HANA Studio via the menu path **Window • Open Perspective • Others...**.

Figure 7.17 ABAP Development Tools Perspective Icon in List of Available Perspectives

Once the ABAP Development Tools perspective is connected to SAP BW/4HANA via a project, you can search for your class and open it in SAP HANA Studio, as shown in Figure 7.18.

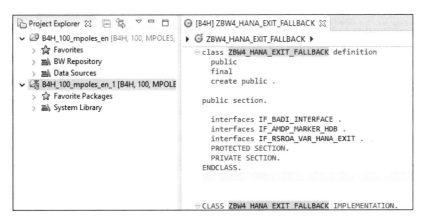

Figure 7.18 Coding for AMDP Class in SAP HANA Studio

This code processes variables at the moment the query is executed before displaying the variables screen. Then, default values are shown as filter suggestions for the query data selection (see Figure 7.19).

Figure 7.19 Query Execution Showing Prompt Screen, with Reporting Year Populated with Last Year per Rule

7.1.5   Query Sheet Definition

Use the **Sheet Definition** tab shown in Figure 7.20 to create the structure of your query. Add collections of characteristics, key figures, formulas, structures, and restrictions to help you navigate in the report, perform different analyses, and create significant information for your business. These elements can be placed in **Rows** or **Columns**, or be set as **Free characteristics**.

Free characteristics are objects that won't be shown in the default view of the report immediately after executing it. They're available in the report to be added during runtime, helping you create dynamic analyses.

Figure 7.20 Query Sheet Definition Tab

The object types available to be added to the query are defined as follows:

- **Characteristics**

  These are InfoObjects or fields available in the InfoProvider that give context to the amounts and results on the report. These characteristics can be of the following types:

  - *Time characteristics* are characteristics with references in time format, such as date, month, fiscal year, fiscal period.

  - *Master data characteristics* are characteristics that may contain master data attributes, texts, and hierarchies. Master data is data that doesn't change frequently and it isn't present physically in a transaction but referenced via a pointer called SID (Surrogate ID).

  - *Hierarchy characteristics* are characteristics that represent the master data in a tree structure contained in the InfoObject it references—for example, a product hierarchy.

  - *Unit characteristics* are master data characteristics with currencies or units of measure. They're frequently associated/linked to key figures to give context to the amount the key figure represents.

  - *Non-master data characteristics* are attributes within the transaction data itself—for example, sales order number.

- **Basic key figures**

  These are InfoObjects that usually represent numbers. They may be associated with a unit type characteristic in cases of currency amounts or quantities.

- **Calculated key figures**

  These are reusable elements; they're created with an association to an InfoProvider and can be used in multiple queries that share the same InfoProvider. With calculated key figures, you can define formulas and aggregations. If you need a special calculation in a query, you can create a local element in the query referenced to the calculated key figure definition and apply the changes to this new element.

- **Restricted key figures**

  These, like calculated key figures, are reusable elements. With restricted key figures, you can define filter selections to further restrict the records that will be used for the key figure. For example, in an InfoProvider with planned and actual amounts in the same basic key figure, you may want to create two separate restricted key figures to show the planned and actual amounts split in the report into two columns, without adding a navigation level to your report that might contain many characteristics.

- **Structures**
  These are groups of characteristics or key figures that allow a restriction to be applied for multiple elements with a central rule. You can create a maximum of two structures per query, and only one of these can contain key figures. You can use these structures in either rows or columns in the query.

- **Global structures**
  These are structures that were created linked to an InfoProvider directly and can be reused in multiple queries that share the same InfoProvider; changes to these structures are replicated to those queries.

You can add objects in each section of the report sheet by right-clicking the area in which you want to add the objects and selecting the desired option from the context menu, as shown in Figure 7.21.

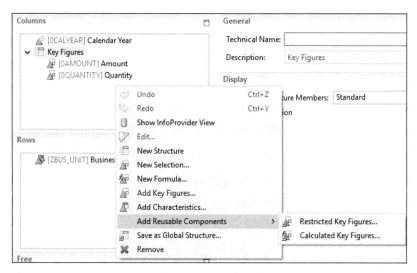

Figure 7.21 Context Menu with Options to Add Objects to Report Sheet

7.1.6   Query Elements

Query elements are objects added to the query sheet definition to form the structure of the query. The following subsections will describe the properties and use of characteristics, key figures, and formulas.

Characteristics

When you add characteristics to the query sheet definition, they inherit properties defined in the InfoObject as default settings for reporting. However, you can override some of them for the specific needs of your query, along with adding extra options.

Figure 7.22 shows the options you can specify for query characteristics. All properties that you can override have a **Toggle Default Value/Manual Entry** button (pencil icon) beside them; the ones for which you can use variables to determine their contents during query execution have an **Add Text Variable** button icon ⚎ beside them.

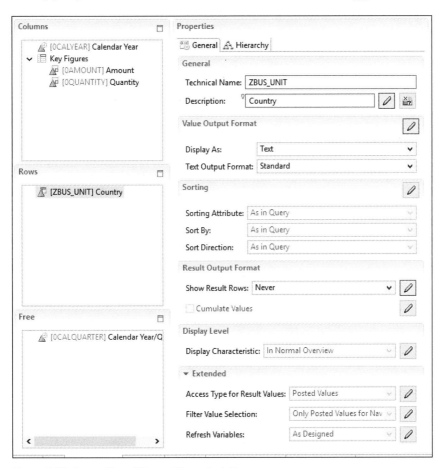

Figure 7.22 Properties of Query Characteristics

Let's examine these properties and some important details of each:

- **General: Description**
  Shows the description defined in the InfoObject or InfoProvider field by default. You can change the description for this query as shown in Figure 7.22, in which the description was changed to **Country** for the InfoObject **Business Unit** (ZBUS_UNIT).

- **Value Output Format**
  For an InfoObject that contains text master data, this property allows you to show the key (code associated with the transaction data) and/or text (associated with the code via master data). For example, as shown in Figure 7.22, we configured to display only the text in the property **Display As** for the country object. In the property **Text Output Format**, you can also choose the size of the text you want to display in case you have different text sizes (short, medium, or large) stored in the master data texts of the InfoObject.

- **Sorting**
  Allows you to define the default sorting for this characteristic when shown in the report.

- **Result Output Format**
  Allows you to define the how the result rows are displayed for the data grouped by this characteristic. As shown in Figure 7.22, we selected to **Never** display the subtotals to make this query a single list of values.

- **Display Level**
  Allows you to create tailored views of your query for certain groups of end-users. If you have filters created on characteristics in your query, you can set such filters to **In Detailed Overview Only** and they'll only be shown to end users when the detailed view is selected in the frontend. When **In Normal Overview** is selected, as in Figure 7.22, the filter will be shown in both normal and detailed query views.

- **Extended: Access Type for Result Values**
  Allows you to define data access options for the query results:
  - **Master data**
    Always displays a row of data even without transaction data if values for this characteristic are maintained in the master data.
  - **Posted Values**
    Only shows data rows when transaction data is present for the selected characteristic values.
  - **Characteristic Relationships**
    Restricts the posted data to be shown only for allowed combinations of the

characteristics with this attribute—for example, compounded characteristics, hierarchies, or in planning areas.

- **Extended: Filter Value Selection**
Allows you to define how filter values are selected and displayed during query execution. With this option, you can set the filter values to come from the master data table so that the user can select values applicable to the query execution, instead of coming from the transactional data, which may provide better filter performance.

- **Extended: Refresh Variables**
Allows you to define how variables that you use in default values or for a hierarchy's presentation behave:

  - **Dynamically**
  Uses the current settings of the navigation view during query runtime.

  - **As Designed**
  Uses the query filter and hierarchy definition settings for refreshing these variables.

If your characteristic has hierarchies associated with it, the **Hierarchy** tab allows you to select specific hierarchies and levels to be used in the query, as shown in Figure 7.23.

Figure 7.23 Hierarchy Properties for Characteristics in Query Design

The hierarchy properties are as follows:

- **General**

  In this section, you can enable the use of a hierarchy for navigating and drilling down through data in the query runtime and for selecting filter values to be used for data selection. You can also use variables to determine the name of the hierarchy to be used via automatic calculation or via input from the user in the prompt screen for selection variables.

- **Display Nodes**

  Allows you to define how the nodes will be displayed in the report and up to what level of the hierarchy the data will be selected and displayed when the hierarchy is expanded.

- **Sorting**

  Defines the sorting method for the hierarchy. It can be based on the key or text of nodes.

Key Figures

Key figures also have specific properties that can be customized for specific query needs. Figure 7.24 shows the following general properties:

- **General: Description**

  Shows the description defined in the InfoObject or InfoProvider field by default. You can change it for this query via clicking the **Toggle Default Value/Manual Entry** button (pencil icon) and you can define a text variable to determine its value.

- **Constant Selection**

  When this option is selected, it ignores the query filters and navigation during runtime by setting a constant filter in a characteristic or structure of your report. This helps you create comparison of key-figures in different granularities. For example, a plan and actual comparison, when you have yearly plan amounts and monthly actuals amounts.

- **Display**

  Allows you set how the key figure is displayed during query execution. You can define the scaling factor, sign position, decimal places displayed, a highlight or normal display, and whether it's permanently hidden during query execution.

- **Selection Details**

  Allows you to define additional restrictions to the key figure. For example, in an InfoProvider with both planned and actual data stored or calculated in the same key figure, you can add to the **Selection Details** panel of that specific key figure the characteristic that defines actual or planned and add a restriction to it to filter the data to the specific key figure that needs to be displayed.

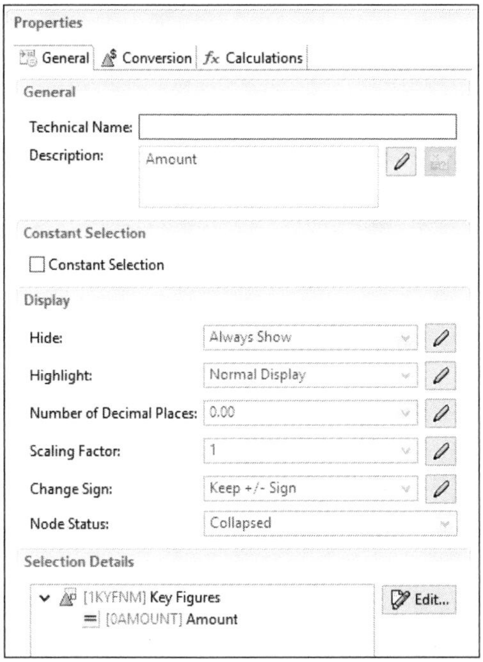

Figure 7.24 Properties of Key Figures in Query Designer

- **Unit and Currency Conversions**
  You can also perform conversions of currency and quantity units. The **Conversion** tab, shown in Figure 7.25, contains the parameters you need to enter to perform these conversions. As an example, we set a currency conversion from USD to EUR.

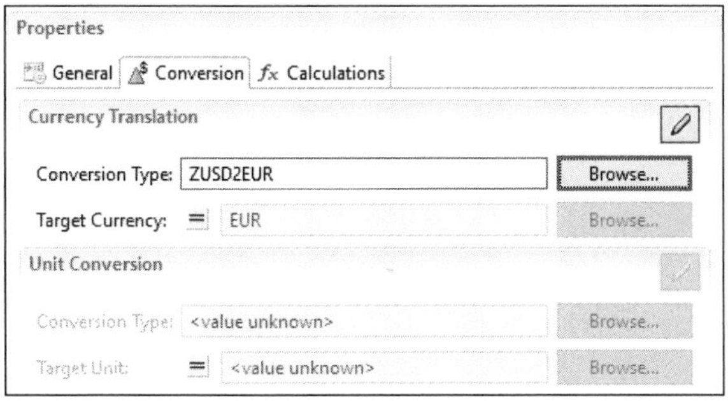

Figure 7.25 Conversion Properties in Query Designer

- **Conversion Type**
  This is an SAP BW/4HANA modeling object that defines how the conversion is performed. You must create the conversion types beforehand in SAP BW/4HANA using Transaction RSUOM for unit conversion and Transaction RSCUR for currency conversion.

- **Variables in Conversion Types**
  If you want to use variables in the currency translation type, you must create them beforehand. You can create these variables in the Eclipse modeling perspective by right-clicking the InfoObject in which you need the variable created and choosing **New... • Variable....**

- **InfoObject Types for Variables**
  You can use the following object types for variable creation, depending on the conversion type, as follows:

  - **Currency Conversion**: **Exchange Rate Type** (example: ORTYPE), **Currency** (example: OCURRENCY), or **Date** (example: ODATE).

  - **Unit Conversion**: **Unit** (example: OUNIT).

- **Local Calculations**
  You can predefine local calculations for a formula or key figure as shown in Figure 7.26. These calculations are performed on the frontend tool and they only change how the values are displayed. If you have other calculations or formulas that use these values, the frontend tool uses the original value provided by the SAP BW/4HANA system. The options available to customize the local calculations are as follows:

  - **Calculate Result As**
    Allows you to select a rule to be used to recalculate the results of a report locally—for example, to calculate results based on values displayed rather than from original values.

  - **Calculate Single Value As**
    Allows you to select a rule to be used to recalculate individual values of a report locally—for example, to display the rank position instead of the amount.

  - **Calculation Direction**
    Always from the top towards the drilldown direction. For example, if characteristics are in rows and key figures in columns, you can choose the calculation direction to be from top to bottom.

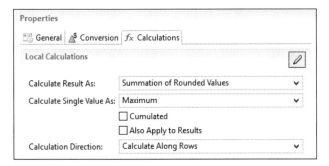

Figure 7.26 Local Calculation Properties in Query Designer

Recommendation

Because local calculations are performed on the client side, for large datasets, these local calculations may significantly affect the performance of the query. Therefore, we recommend using exception aggregations or calculated key figures, because they're pushed down to be executed on the SAP HANA database instead.

Formulas

You can create specific calculations using key figures in a structure in the query by using a formula. You can include basic key figures, restricted key figures, calculated key figures, reusable key figures, and variables in the formula definition.

To add a formula, open the context menu of the structure that contains the key figures and select **New Formula…**. Figure 7.27 shows the formula definition screen in which you define your formula. The properties shown are as follows:

- **Technical Name**
  Define a technical name for the formula.

- **Description**
  Edit the description of the formula, or use variables to define the description at runtime.

- **Formula**
  This is where you define your formula. You can use the calculator buttons and available formula elements arranged in groups. These groups and formula elements are accessible in the panels at the bottom of the screen.

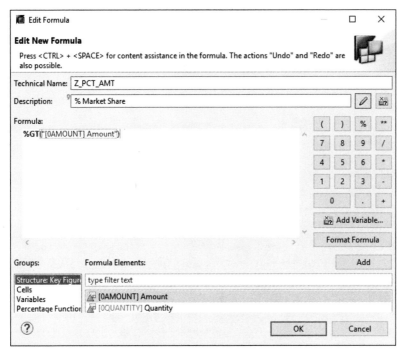

Figure 7.27 Formula Definition Screen in Query Editor

> **Note**
>
> Some operations, such as **% of the Grand Total**, aren't available in SAP HANA views. For such operations, you should develop these calculations on the frontend tool for which the SAP HANA view is used as the source of data.

7.1.7   Query Conditions

You can use query conditions to formulate different sets of rules to narrow down your analysis and filter the query data so that only part of the data retrieved is displayed in the query results—for example, to display only the top 10 countries with the largest volumes of sales items delivered.

On the **General** tab (see Figure 7.28), you can define the following:

- **Description**
  Stores a short description of the condition.

- **Active**
  Marks whether the condition is active or not.

- **Condition Parameters**
  The rules defined to filter the data to be displayed. They can be of two types:

  - **Threshold Value**
    Limits the data displayed according to range of values of a key figure—for example, to limit quantity delivered to greater than 100,000 units.

  - **Ranked List**
    Limits the data displayed according to certain ranking options—for example, to show the top five countries in revenue.

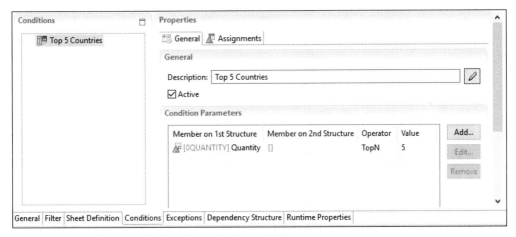

Figure 7.28 Conditions Definition Screen in Query Editor

On the **Assignments** tab, you can define characteristics that will be used to apply the conditions. You can apply the conditions independently on each characteristic or on the most detailed characteristic used in the drill-down.

> **Note**
>
> You can add more than one condition parameter and more than one active conditions. When you have multiple active conditions rules, the system displays only data that satisfies all conditions rules.
>
> However, if you have multiple condition parameters in one condition rule, the system shows a union of the data retrieved using each of the condition parameters.

7.1.8   Query Exceptions

Query exceptions allow you to define different limits for query results. Deviations from these limits are highlighted in different colors, which helps you quickly identify areas that require attention. In the **General** tab shown in Figure 7.29, you can define the following:

- **Description**
  Stores a short description of the exception.

- **Active**
  Marks whether the condition is active.

- **Exception Parameters**
  Define the ranges, colors, and intensities of the colors. There are three colors available, with three intensity levels for each.

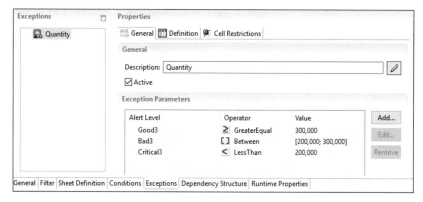

Figure 7.29 Exceptions: General Tab in Query Editor

In the **Definition** tab, you can define in which cells or group of cells the alerts will be displayed. For example, in Figure 7.30, we set the alerts defined on the quantity column, performing the evaluation of the amounts before list calculation, and display the alerts in data cells of quantity column and also display in characteristics cells on the row linked to the quantity amount being alerted.

In the **Cell Restrictions** tab, you can define restrictions to apply to alerts. For example, in Figure 7.31, we selected to show alerts on individual rows but not on result cells.

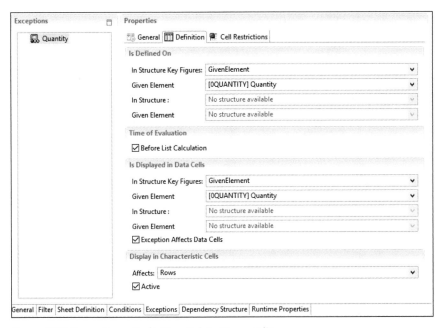

Figure 7.30 Exceptions: Definition Tab in Query Editor

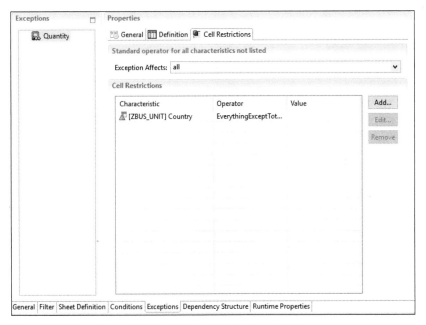

Figure 7.31 Exceptions: Cell Restrictions Tab in Query Editor

A visual example of the alerts settings described in the previous paragraphs is shown in Figure 7.32. There, we can see that the **Quantity** column and the characteristics present in the report have different alerts; the totals remain set in their standard colors.

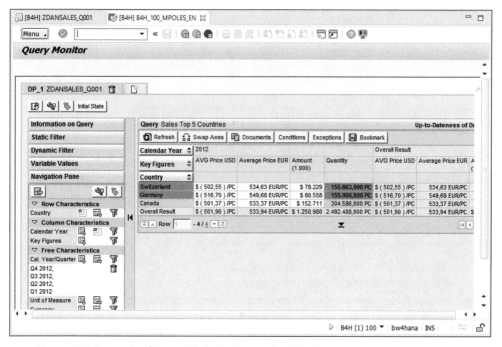

Figure 7.32 Example of Query Alerts in Transaction RSRT

Note

Alerts aren't transferred to the SAP HANA views associated with the SAP BW/4HANA query. Therefore, you can see alert colors by using an ABAP BICS interface via Transaction RSRT or in a frontend tool such as SAP Lumira Designer.

7.1.9   Query Transport

When queries or other SAP BW/4HANA objects will be transported to an environment for quality testing and then to a productive environment, best practice is to create these queries under a package that requires a transport request to collect all the query elements, ensuring that you transport the intended version of all developments to the upper environments.

When creating a query, as described in the Section 7.1.1, you had to link the query to a package. In SAP BW/4HANA, we have a package with the technical name $TMP for local developments, package delivered by SAP, and custom client development packages. If you enter a package name other than $TMP, a new pop-up window will open, asking for the transport request to be used (see Figure 7.33).

In the **Selection of Transport Request** window, you can do one of the following:

- Select a transport request from the **list of open transports you are involved** you're assigned to (**Choose from requests in which I am involved**)
- **Create a New Request**, in which case you must enter a brief description of the transport request in the **Request Description** field
- Directly **Enter a Request Number**

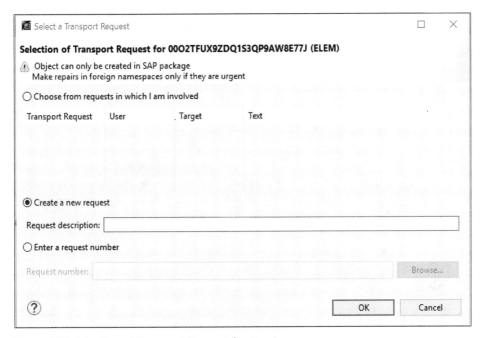

Figure 7.33 Selection of Transport Request for Queries

Note

You can access transport requests associated with your user via **ADT Perspective • Transports** or via Transaction SE09.

To help organize the transport list and verify that the dependent objects for the query are selected, go to the **Dependency Structure** tab of the SAP BW/4HANA query editor. This tab shows all global elements associated with and used in the query. As shown in Figure 7.34, the **Dependency Structure** tab shows that the calculated key figure **ZCK_PRICEAVG** is used in the selected query.

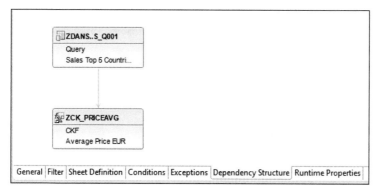

Figure 7.34 Dependency Structure Tab in Query Editor

7.2   Interfaces for Analysis

SAP BW/4HANA integrates with several frontend tools for query analysis. You can use the open analysis interfaces available in the analytic manager, which include multidimensional interfaces and lightweight consumption interfaces. We'll discuss each interface type next.

7.2.1   Multidimensional Interfaces

Multidimensional interfaces are based on the Multidimensional Expressions (MDX) query language. The main characteristic of the MDX is the ability to send data to different frontend tools in a generic format, allowing you to carry complex objects such as hierarchies.

Different technical protocols for communication with these front-end tools are as follows:

- **OLE DB for OLAP (ODBO)**
  Uses *Component Object Model* (COM) protocol and is only used on the Microsoft Windows platform. It requires driver installation on local machines.

- **OLAP BAPI**
  Uses RFC protocol and is used on every platform supported by SAP.

- **XML for Analysis**
  Uses HTTP/SOAP protocol; the SOAP client proxy must be generated on the client side using Web Service Definition Language (WSDL).

The communication between the frontend and the SAP BW/4HANA are handled by a component called MDX processor. It is, therefore, an agent between the OLAP processor and the frontend tool. The MDX processor receives the query requests from the front-end tools using these protocols and forwards the request to the OLAP processor for processing.

7.2.2   Lightweight Consumption Interfaces

Lightweight consumption interfaces are used in simple scenarios to send SAP BW/4HANA query requests directly to the OLAP processor by using the OData communication method. With the increasing demand for reporting and dashboards to be available in mobile devices such as smartphones, tablets, and digital signage, it's now important to make SAP BW/4HANA data providers available as OData services. This is possible due to the intrinsic integration of SAP BW/4HANA with SAP Gateway services.

When you define a query with the **By OData** property selected, the system creates the objects for OData services. However, you need to release the query for access via OData protocol via the maintenance service Transaction /IWFND/MAINT_SERVICE. Figure 7.35 shows an OData service created and active.

Use the same transaction to delete the service if you want to remove the access to the OData service.

> **Note**
>
> If a query has the **By OData** property and the OData service was released in SAP Gateway, then the service will still be available even if the **By OData** property is removed. The service is only deleted automatically by deleting the query.

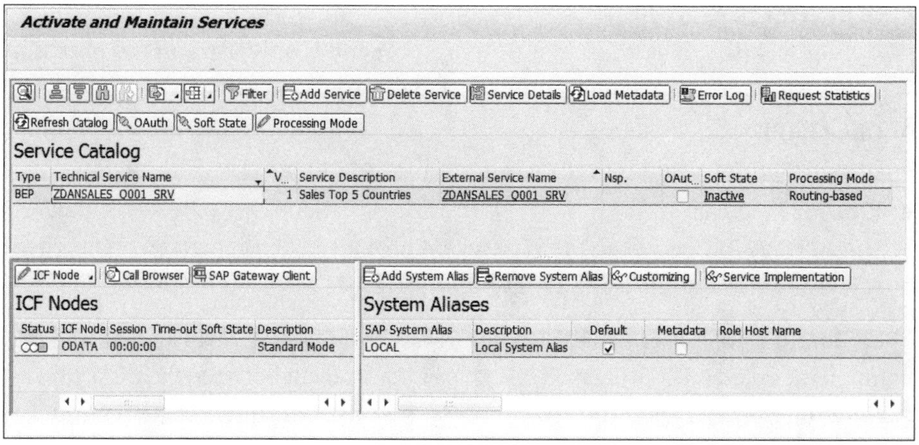

Figure 7.35 OData Service Created and Active

The structure of the URL for a service delivered in the OData namespace is as follows:

<Protocol>://<Server>:<Port>/sap/<Service>

For example:

http://sapserver.com:8000/sap/opu/odata/sap/ZDANSALES_Q001_SRV

Tip

You can get the URL prefix and server using the function module RSBB_URL_PREFIX_GET via Transaction SE37 with the import parameter. For the I_HANDLERCLASS import parameter, enter the name of the ICF handler (HTTP request handler) for the required service—for example, CL_RSR_WWW_HTTP.

After entering the parameters, click **Execute** and the export parameter E_URL_PREFIX will contain the generated URL prefix.

The important parameters for OData queries are as follows:

- **$metadata**
  Displays the query metadata—for example:

  http://sapserver.com:8000/sap/opu/odata/sap/ZDANSALES_Q001_SRV/$metadata

- **$format=<format name>**

  Displays the result in the specified format—for example, to retrieve the data of the query in XML format:

  http://sapserver.com:8000/sap/opu/odata/sap/ZDANSALES_Q001_SRV/ ZDANSALES_Q001Results/?$format=xml

- **.../QerynameResults**

  Displays the result set without passing parameters to the query—for example:

  http://sapserver.com:8000/sap/opu/odata/sap/ZDANSALES_Q001_SRV/ ZDANSALES_Q001Results/?$format=xml

- **$top=3**

  Displays the top three results—for example:

  http://sapserver.com:8000/sap/opu/odata/sap/ZDANSALES_Q001_SRV/ ZDANSALES_Q001Results/?$top=3&?$format=xml

- **$orderby=<field name>%20asc|desc**

  Displays the results sorted ascending or descending by <field name>. For ascending results, use asc (or nothing). For example, using descending:

  http://sapserver.com:8000/sap/opu/odata/sap/ZDANSALES_Q001_SRV/ ZDANSALES_Q001Results/$orderby=ZBUS_UNIT%20desc&?$format=xml

For example, say you want to retrieve the country with the largest sales quantity. From the metadata, we discover that the quantity is stored in the *A00O2TFUX9ZDQ1 T6UGAZC7BRCN* field. The URL to use then is as follows:

http://sapserver.com:8000/sap/opu/odata/sap/ZDANSALES_Q001_SRV/ ZDANSALES_Q001Results/?$format=xml&$top=1&$orderby=A00O2TFUX9ZDQ1T6UG AZC7BRCN%20desc

You can use other parameters to retrieve the desired result from the query.

Note

The $ sign on the parameters and the %20 (space character) are required in the OData URL to execute in browsers; however in tools such as Microsoft Excel, the $ and the %20 signs must be removed. So, the last example seen above should be executed in Microsoft Excel as follows:

http://sapserver.com:8000/sap/opu/odata/sap/ZDANSALES_Q001_SRV/ZDANSALES_ Q001Results/?format=xml&top=1&orderby=A00O2TFUX9ZDQ1T6UGAZC7BRCN desc

You're now familiar with the available communication protocols from SAP BW/4HANA to be used with various reporting frontend tools. The next sections will describe different methods for connecting these frontend tools to your query in SAP BW/4HANA.

7.3   SAP BusinessObjects Tools

SAP BusinessObjects includes several tools that integrate with various SAP systems. In this section, we'll focus on the integration points between SAP BusinessObjects version 4.2 and SAP BW/4HANA.

The first part of this integration is the connection. In SAP BusinessObjects, connections are managed in the administrative component called the *Central Management Console (CMC)*. To access the CMC, use the following URL structure: *<protocol>://<server>:port/BOE/CMC*, where <protocol> is either HTTP or HTTPS (for secure connections) according to your installation.

In the CMC, you'll see two connection types:

- **Relational Connection**
  Used when the tool uses SQL to process the data.

- **OLAP Connections**
  Used when the tool uses MDX to process the data. Various system providers can be selected with this connection type, as shown in Figure 7.36, which shows the **Provider** dropdown options.

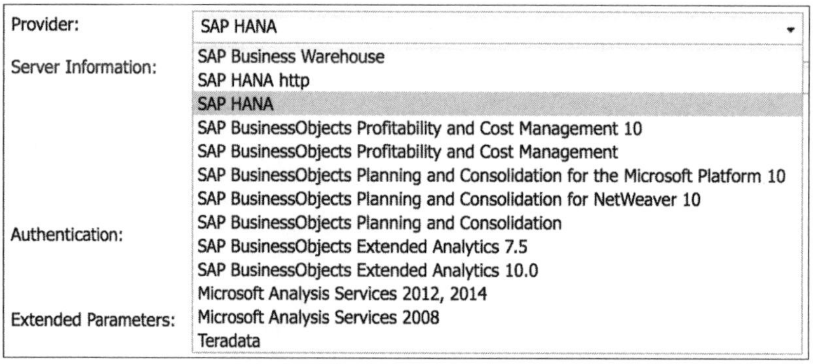

Provider:	SAP HANA ▾
Server Information:	SAP Business Warehouse
	SAP HANA http
	SAP HANA
	SAP BusinessObjects Profitability and Cost Management 10
	SAP BusinessObjects Profitability and Cost Management
	SAP BusinessObjects Planning and Consolidation for the Microsoft Platform 10
	SAP BusinessObjects Planning and Consolidation for NetWeaver 10
Authentication:	SAP BusinessObjects Planning and Consolidation
	SAP BusinessObjects Extended Analytics 7.5
	SAP BusinessObjects Extended Analytics 10.0
	Microsoft Analysis Services 2012, 2014
Extended Parameters:	Microsoft Analysis Services 2008
	Teradata

Figure 7.36 Available Provider Systems for OLAP Connections

Depending on the SAP BusinessObjects tool you're using, you'll have different data source options when using the connection types described previously. In the following sections, we'll cover the four most common data sources used: universes, SAP HANA, SAP HANA: Online, and SAP BEx.

7.3.1   Universes

Universes are well-known tools used to bridge the connection from the frontend tools to SAP HANA views. In this method, part of the processing is performed in the SAP BusinessObjects servers, and the query result is sent to the frontend.

> **Tip**
> For multiple SAP HANA views using universe joins, you can optimize the SAP HANA processing by setting the `JOIN_BY_SQL` parameter in the properties of the data foundation in the universe definition.

Currently, SAP BusinessObjects tools allow you to connect directly to SAP HANA views, removing this extra layer of processing between the frontend tools and the SAP HANA database.

7.3.2   SAP HANA

The SAP HANA data source allows you to connect directly to the SAP HANA views created.

In SAP BW/4HANA, you can make use of this connection type by selecting the **General** property **External SPA HANA View** in the **Remote Access** panel. With this option, an SAP HANA view will be created with the same name as the query.

When you use this data source, you can choose either the relational or OLAP connection type. Once you select the connection type to be used, the connection assistant shows the available objects that can be used as a source for your query.

Figure 7.37 shows an example using an OLAP connection in SAP HANA to directly access the SAP HANA view created by the `ZDANSALES_Q001` query inside the SAP HANA `system-local.bw.bw2hana.query.zdansales` package.

Note that the last node of the package tree is the name of the InfoProvider associated with the query.

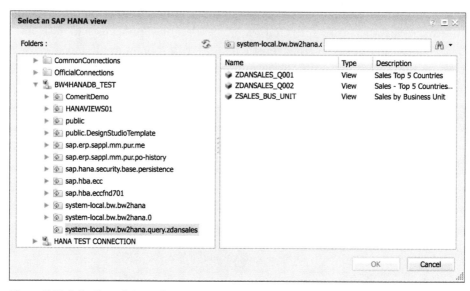

Figure 7.37 Selection of Query in SAP HANA Data Source with OLAP Connection

Figure 7.38 shows the **Query Panel** for the data source to use to create the microcube in the frontend, thus speeding the drill-down analysis.

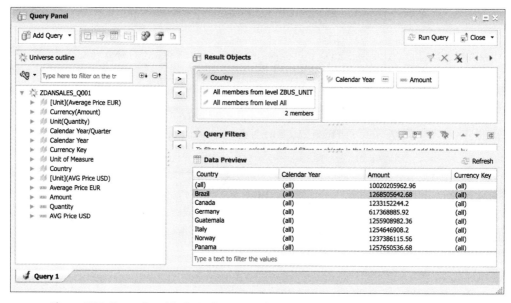

Figure 7.38 Query Panel in Data Source Assistant

Note

As seen in Figure 7.38, when creating the data source query in SAP BusinessObjects Web Intelligence using a universe connected via SAP HANA OLAP connection type, hierarchy members are assigned to each of the characteristics used in the query data source. Depending on the report you are building you have 3 options:

- Select the hierarchy member: **All**, to display only aggregated total lines for the characteristics linked to this hierarchy member selected..
- Select the hierarchy member with the characteristic name to show data with individual values.

You need to select at least one hierarchy level for each characteristic used in the report.

Once the design of the data source query is complete and you click the **Run Query** button, the objects are transferred to the frontend tool for building the report or graphical analysis.

For example, Figure 7.39 contains both analytical and graphical elements based on the query created with the microcube from Figure 7.38.

Figure 7.39 Example Report with Graphical Elements in SAP BusinessObjects Web Intelligence

SAP BusinessObjects Web Intelligence, SAP BusinessObjects Analysis for Microsoft Office, SAP Crystal Reports, SAP Lumira Desiger, and SAP Lumira Discovery are commonly used frontend tools from the SAP BusinessObjects suite.

SAP Lumira

SAP Lumira is a self-service data visualization tool for business users. It allows for powerful data visualizations including the possibility to combine them to create a story with multiple elements. It also allows you to send active data or saved visualizations by email or PDF.

With SAP Lumira as your frontend tool, you can use the SAP HANA OLAP connection type. SAP Lumira also has the same functionality for creating a microcube for fast drill-down processing, but it doesn't automatically create hierarchy members for the characteristics as seen in SAP BusinessObjects Web Intelligence. However, the hierarchy levels are available to be used when activated in the SAP BW/4HANA query.

Figure 7.40 shows an example of a report developed in SAP Lumira with an SAP BW/4HANA view.

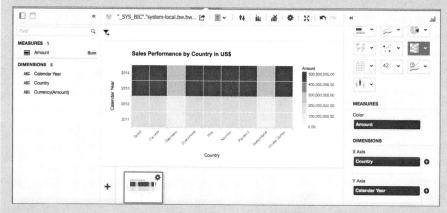

Figure 7.40 Report Developed in SAP Lumira Using SAP BW/4HANA View

---

7.3.3   SAP HANA: Online

SAP HANA: Online is a data source available in SAP BusinessObjects version 4.2. This data source only allows you to use relational connection types. This means that multidimensional elements, such as hierarchies, aren't fully available.

This data source also doesn't create a microcube for the frontend. The moment you select your query, the report design sheet is presented with all the available objects from the query, as shown in Figure 7.41.

Figure 7.41 SAP BusinessObjects Web Intelligence Report Design Sheet Using SAP HANA Online

For an SAP HANA: Online connection, an **SAP HANA** subtab is available within the **Data Access** tab, with options to connect to/disconnect from the SAP HANA system, to limit the size of the result set, and to limit the execution time.

7.3.4   SAP BEx

SAP BW/4HANA queries are created in the Eclipse-based editor and saved in the backend of the SAP BW/4HANA system. These queries also can be accessed and executed via Transaction RSRT.

Within SAP BusinessObjects, you can access these queries using the SAP BEx data source.

> **Note**
>
> Most commonly, SAP BusinessObjects reporting is connected to an SAP BW system using a BEx query as the source of the data. This connection type was preserved in SAP BW/4HANA, facilitating SAP BW migration to SAP BW/4HANA. Once BEx queries are transferred to SAP BW/4HANA queries, they require a manual step of entering in each query, resolving inconsistencies, and saving it.

When you select the SAP BEx data source, the selection of the query isn't performed via SAP HANA content packages but is based on SAP BW/4HANA InfoAreas and Info-Providers, as shown in Figure 7.42.

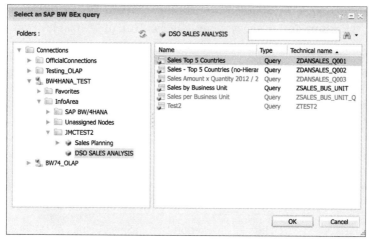

Figure 7.42 Query Selection Using SAP BEx Data Source

Comparing the SAP BEx and SAP HANA OLAP connection types, when creating a report in SAP BusinessObjects Web Intelligence, the SAP BEx connection doesn't create hierarchy members to all characteristics selected for reporting in the data source, but only active hierarchies defined for the characteristics in SAP BW/4HANA are shown in the query builder.

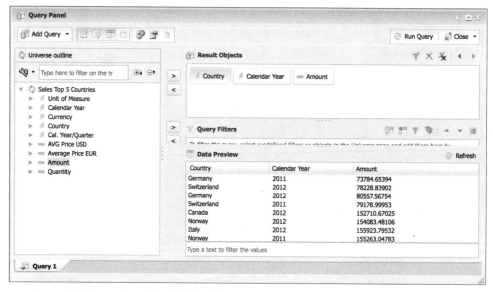

Figure 7.43 Query Panel for SAP BEx Data Source

After running the query, the elements chosen are transferred to the report definition design to be used for building the final report, as shown in Figure 7.43.

Now that you are familiar with the integration of SAP BusinessObjects with SAP BW/4HANA, the next section discuss the integration methods with third-party tools.

7.4   Third-Party Business Intelligence Tools

SAP HANA offers the ability to work with third-party tools via standard ODBC, JBDC, or ODATA data sources or by using SAP connectors or third-party connectors developed specifically for SAP HANA.

In this section, we'll discuss using ODBC, ODATA, and OLE DB connectors.

> **Prerequisite**
>
> As a prerequisite to work with the standard connectors, such as ODBC, you must have the SAP HANA Client installed, which contains several drivers, such as SAP *HANA Database ODBC (HDBODBC)*, which are required to configure and establish these connections.

7.4.1   ODBC Data Source

To use ODBC as a source for the frontend tools, we need to establish a connection from the ODBC data source to the SAP HANA database.

Depending on the OS you're using, the procedure varies. We'll describe the procedure to create the connection for a Microsoft Windows platform:

1. Access the **Control Panel**, then click **Administrative Tools**.

2. Click **ODBC Data Sources (32-bit)** or **(64-bit)**

3. Click the **System DSN** tab, then click **Add....**

4. In the pop-up, select **HDBODBC**, then click **Finish**.

5. Fill in the following fields:
   - **Data Source Name**
     A name for the data source you're creating
   - **Description**
     An optional description

  - **Server and Port**
    In the format *<HANA DB server name>:<port>*
  - **Settings...**
    Optional settings depending on the server configuration, such as SSL connection parameters

6. Once you've finished filling in all the necessary information, click **OK**.

The data source created will appear in the list in the **System DSN** tab when connecting the frontend tool to the SAP HANA database via an OBDC connector.

> **Note**
>
> SAP Note 2077827 provides information about supported third-party client tools certified for SAP HANA.

To provide a concrete example of using an OBDC connection with a frontend tool, let's look at using an OBDC connection with Qlik Sense Desktop, a tool created by Qlik, which delivers intuitive platform solutions for self-service data visualization, guided analytics applications, and embedded analytics and reporting.

Figure 7.44 shows the Qlik Sense Desktop initial screen with the reports and dashboards developed. These are called *apps* in the Qlik frontend.

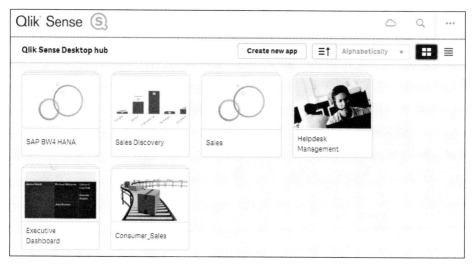

Figure 7.44 Qlik Initial Screen

You can create a new app by clicking the **Create New App** button. A pop-up screen will open, and you can enter a **Name** and the **Description** of the app.

As shown in Figure 7.45, you will see a screen to set the data source for the report; the screen offers two options:

- **Add Data**
  For direct connection to the source

- **Data Load Editor**
  For using scripting logic to transform the data received from the data source

Figure 7.45 Data Source Selection in Qlik Sense Desktop

For this example, we'll select **Add Data**. You'll see a list of available data sources for this tool, as shown in Figure 7.46.

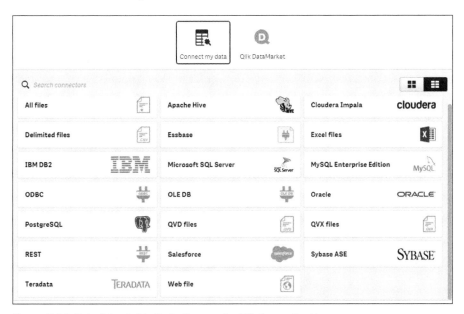

Figure 7.46 List of Available Data Sources in Qlik Sense Desktop

For this example, we'll connect to SAP BW/4HANA via an ODBC data source.

After you select **ODBC**, a screen with available OBDC data sources will display. Select the data source that was created with a connection to the desired SAP HANA system, as shown in Figure 7.47.

Figure 7.47 OBDC Data Source Selection

Once you select the desired OBDC connection, enter the login details for that connection and click **Continue**.

Note

The SAP BW/4HANA queries are available under the system owner _SYS_BIC.

Figure 7.48 shows an example of a query selected with its metadata. You can complete the query selection by clicking the **Load Data and Finish** button.

You can drag and drop elements into the sheet as shown in Figure 7.49 to create your dashboard or report.

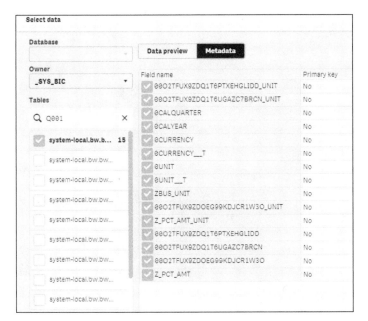

Figure 7.48 Query Selection Screen in Qlik Sense Desktop

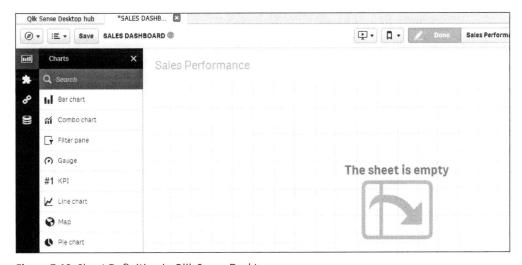

Figure 7.49 Sheet Definition in Qlik Sense Desktop

Figure 7.50 shows the sales performance report divided with different regions and with a gauge to measure the net price average for the company based on the SAP BW/4HANA query.

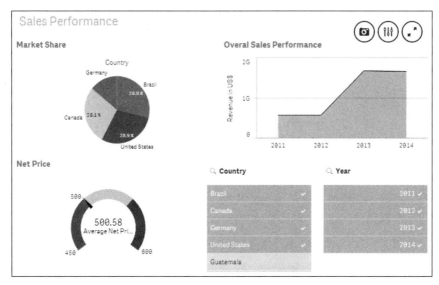

Figure 7.50 Example of Dashboard in Qlik Sense Desktop

7.4.2   OData Data Source

You can use OData as a data source for your reporting if you've enabled the OData service for the SAP BW/4HANA query and set the **General** property **Remote Access** to **By OData**.

In the Qlik view, use the REST data source shown in Figure 7.51 to access the data feed.

Figure 7.51 OData Request Panel in REST Data Source

In the request, enter the URL for your query results—here, for example:

http://sapserver.com:8000/sap/opu/odata/sap/ZDANSALES_Q001_SRV/ZDANSALES_Q001Results

We entered additional parameters in the **Query Parameters** panel, as shown in Figure 7.52.

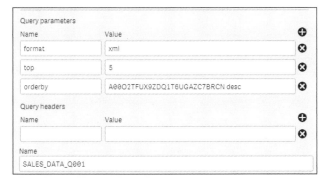

Figure 7.52 OData Query Parameters and Connection Name

The next step is to select the final query structure to be used in the report. SAP BW/4HANA sends the report feed to the OData data source via XML. The content of the query is available by following the menu path **Feed • Entry • Content**. Figure 7.53 shows an example of the query fields selected to be sent to the frontend report editor.

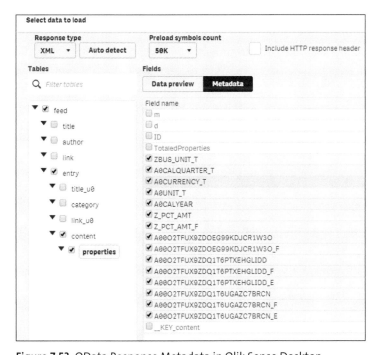

Figure 7.53 OData Response Metadata in Qlik Sense Desktop

After completing the data source creation and the query structure selection, you're sent to the sheet designer. The pivot table in Figure 7.54 was created using the OData query used as an example in this section.

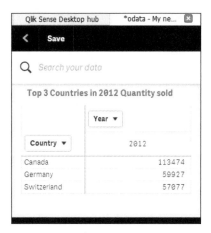

Figure 7.54 Pivot Table Example with OData Query in Qlik Sense Desktop

7.4.3   OLEDB Data Source

After installing the SAP HANA client, the SAP HANA MDX option will appear in the list of possible OLE/DB providers to be used in third-party tools. For this option, we will use the *Microsoft Excel (MS-Excel)* to connect to SAP BW/4HANA query via OLEDB data source.

In Excel, select the **Data** tab, then go to **Get External Data**. Select **From Other Sources**, then **From Data Connection Wizard**, as shown in Figure 7.55.

A pop-up window will open with available data sources for this tool. Select **Other/ Advanced** and click **Next**. Select the **SAP HANA MDX Provider** option shown in the list and click **Next**.

Now, the configuration screen will be open. Here, enter the SAP HANA DB connection details and proceed by clicking **Next**.

The next step is to select the query. Figure 7.56 shows the available options to select the query:

- **Database**
  This dropdown list contains the SAP HANA content packages that can be found in the SAP HANA modeling perspective.

■ **Connect to a Specific Cube**
   Allows you to connect to a specific InfoProvider, selected here, that contains the list of queries available for reporting.

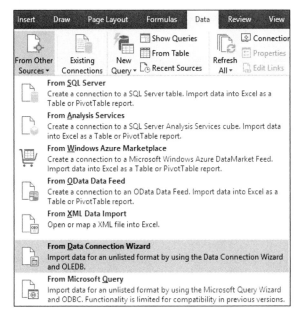

Figure 7.55 Get External Data Sources Options in Other Sources

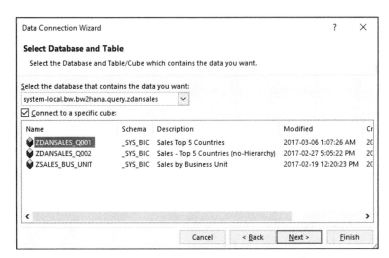

Figure 7.56 Query Selection Using SAP HANA MDX Provider

Selecting the SAP BW/4HANA query is the final step, after which the data is selected and transferred to Excel for you to format your report.

In the example shown in Figure 7.57, we created a pivot chart.

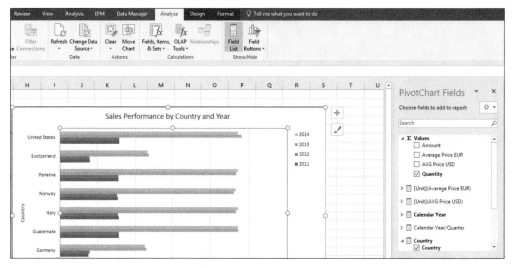

Figure 7.57 Pivot Chart Created Using SAP HANA MDX Data Source

The query elements using the SAP HANA MDX connection come with multidimensional elements defined in SAP BW/4HANA and thus requires less effort to maintain in report creation.

7.5 Summary

SAP BW/4HANA brings significant advancements in reporting and analytics capabilities and integration with external frontend tools. In this chapter, we discussed SAP BW/4HANA as the central repository of data modeled and harmonized for analytical reporting.

The following reporting capabilities and integration with external tools were described in detail:

- SAP BW/4HANA query properties, elements, and settings
- Integration with SAP HANA and SAP BW
- Differences between SAP BW/4HANA and SAP BEx queries in older versions of SAP BW

- Protocols for external access to SAP BW/4HANA queries
- Methods to connect with different SAP BusinessObjects tools and third-party tools, including SAP Lumira, Qlik, and Excel

With the review of SAP BW/4HANA reporting capabilities and integration with different frontend tools in this chapter, you can now identify and implement different reporting and analytics solutions applicable to your platform, visualization, and business reporting requirements. The next chapter discuss the SAP HANA tools provided by SAP to connect SAP BW/4HANA with different third-party source systems.

Chapter 8
Integrating External Data

Because companies might use non-SAP databases to store their data, integrating SAP and non-SAP data is critical for enterprise reports. In this chapter, we discuss SDA and SDI in SAP BW/4HANA, which make accessing external data more efficient and cost-effective.

Companies often replicate or load data from other systems into an SAP BW/4HANA system and then perform analysis and processing in SAP BW/4HANA. However, not only does data loading or replication consume a lot of time and system resources (i.e., CPU and memory), but also, it can be difficult to manage delta loading from source systems to SAP BW/4HANA.

In this chapter, we'll look at how SAP HANA smart data access (SDA) and SAP HANA smart data integration (SDI) can help you load your data into the SAP BW/4HANA system. We'll then discuss the options for integrating data with the SAP BW/4HANA system, including combining data under a BW schema or via Open ODS views.

8.1 SAP HANA Smart Data Access

SDA enables remote data to be accessed via SAP HANA SQL queries as if they're local tables in SAP HANA, without copying the data into the SAP HANA database. With SDA, data can be combined from heterogeneous remote source systems—such Microsoft SQL Server, Oracle, DB2, Microsoft Excel, Teradata, Sybase IQ, and Hadoop—into EDW landscapes. SDA makes it possible to access remote data without having to replicate the data into the SAP HANA database. The following are some use cases for which to consider using SDA:

- Making other data warehouses transparent for SAP BW/4HANA. Previously, you needed to set up a DB connection to load data into SAP BW/4HANA.
- Consolidating your data warehouse landscape.

- Consuming remote data from multiple connected remote databases in SAP BW/4HANA.

SDA not only provides operational and cost benefits, but also supports the development and deployment of the next generation of analytical applications, which require the ability to access and integrate data from multiple systems in real time regardless of where the data is located or which system is generating it.

SDA is based on local virtual tables that map to existing remote tables in the remote database. Data required from remote sources will be visible in virtual tables in SAP HANA. SDA will enable remote access (smart access) to data regardless of where the data is located.

SAP HANA developers can then create SAP HANA views on top of the virtual tables or combine data from virtual tables and internal SAP HANA tables in SAP HANA Studio. The SAP HANA query processor optimizes these queries and executes the relevant parts of the queries in the remote database, returns the results of the query to SAP HANA, and completes the query.

Not only can an SAP HANA developer select data in a virtual table and pull data from a remote data source into an SAP HANA table, but SDA even supports INSERT/UPDATE/DELETE statements executed against the virtual table. The data in a virtual table can be modified (i.e., via insert, update, and delete operations) and then written back to the remote table in a remote data source.

Before you create remote connections to external databases, it's a good idea to examine if your databases are supported by SDA or SDI in SAP BW/4HANA, as we'll discuss in the following section. We'll then briefly look at the steps to configure SDA and how to create remote sources.

8.1.1   Supported Remote Sources

As of SAP HANA SPS 11, the following remote sources are supported by SDA (refer to SAP Note 1868209 for more information):

- Oracle 12c
- Microsoft SQL Server 2008, 2012
- SAP HANA (SAP BW powered by SAP HANA, SAP Business Suite on SAP HANA)
- SAP ERP and SAP BW
- Hadoop

- Excel worksheets
- Text files
- Teradata
- DB2
- Sybase IQ
- Apache Hive 0.9.0 or higher and Simba Hive ODBC driver

8.1.2   Configure SAP HANA Smart Data Access

The steps to configure are as follows:

1. Download and install the Unix ODBC driver manager (2.3.0 or above) from *http://www.unixodbc.org/* and use it to test the connection to external databases in the Linux box on the SAP HANA server. Because you need administrator rights, you may need to get help from your SAP Basis team to install the driver manager. For more information, see the SAP HANA Administration Guide at *https://help.sap.com/hana/SAP_HANA_Administration_Guide_en.pdf*.

2. Download and install the Unix ODBC drivers for external databases from each database provider's website. Because installing Unix ODBC drivers requires administrator rights, you may need to get help from your SAP Basis team. For more information, see the SAP HANA Administration Guide.

3. To start the process to create the odbc.ini file (which SAP HANA requires to communicate with remote databases) in $HOME directory in the SAP HANA Linux server, log in with the admin user and create odbc.ini file.

4. Create a DSN for external databases. You will perform the following:
   - Configure SQL server in the *odbc.ini* file as follows:
   ```
   [DSN]
   SERVER = <your server>, <port number>
   Driver = <Location of the MS SQL Server ODBC driver>
   Database = <your database name>
   ```
   - Configure the Hadoop system in the *odbc.ini* file as follows:
   ```
   [HIVE]
   Driver = <Location of the Hive ODBC driver>
   HOST = <Hadoop host name>
   Port = <port number>
   ```

> **Note**
>
> For SQL server, the default port number is 1433. To find the SQL server port being used, open the SQL Server Configuration Manager, then locate the TCP port (see Figure 8.1).
>
> For an SQL server, for example, the driver is /opt/microsoft/msodbcsql/lib64/libmsodbcsql-13.0.so.0.0
>
> For Hadoop, the driver is /simba/hiveodbc/lib/64/libsimbahiveodbc64.so
>
> For database, enter the name of database you want to connect to; if the database isn't specified, the system will connect to the default database of the connected server.

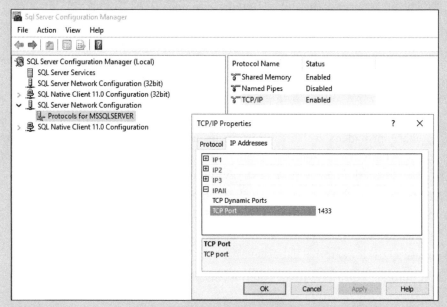

Figure 8.1 Locate TCP Port in SQL Server Configuration Manager

5. Restart SAP HANA.

6. Test the ODBC connection in the Linux box. Before you create remote sources for SAP HANA Studio, you should test the ODBC connection in the Linux box to ensure the connection has been set up correctly. In the Linux server, you can use the following command to test the connection:

```
isql -v <DSN> <user name> <password>
```

7. Provide the following parameters to connect to the database:

   - DSN: Enter the data source name defined in *odbc.ini* file.

   - Enter the user name and password.

8. If the Unix ODBC connection has been set up correctly, the result should look something like Figure 8.2.

```
+-------------------------------------------+
| Connected!                                |
|                                           |
| sql-statement                             |
| help [tablename]                          |
| quit                                      |
|                                           |
+-------------------------------------------+
SQL> █
```

Figure 8.2 Testing ODBC Connection

8.1.3 Create Remote Source via Smart Data Access Adapter

The following privileges are required in SAP HANA to manage the agent and adapters and to create remote sources and virtual tables in SAP HANA Studio:

- System privileges:
  - AGENT ADMIN ADAPTER ADMIN
  - CREATE REMOTE SOURCE
- SQL object privileges on the remote source:
  - CREATE VIRTUAL TABLE
  - DROP

Once the SAP HANA administrator has granted those roles to you, you can create remote sources in SAP HANA Studio to connect the external databases defined in odbc.ini in the Linux box, as in Section 8.1.2.

Log on to SAP HANA Studio, as shown in Figure 8.3, and go to **Provisioning • Remote Sources**. Right-click **Remote Sources** and select **New Remote Source**.

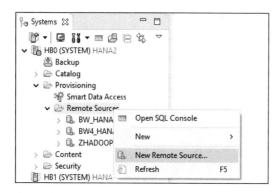

Figure 8.3 Create New Remote Source

A new screen will open, which should look something like Figure 8.4 and should include the following parameters:

- **Source Name**
  Specify the name of the remote source.

- **Adapter Name**
  Choose an adapter from the predefined adapter list, as shown in Figure 8.5. SAP provides a wide range of adapters: Oracle ODBC adapter, MSSQL ODBC adapter, HADOOP adapter, and so on.

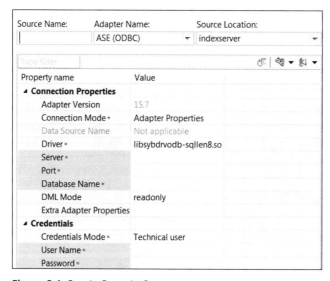

Figure 8.4 Create Remote Source

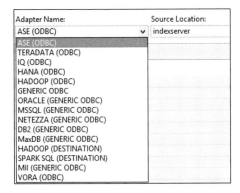

Figure 8.5 List of Adapters

- **Source Location**
  For an SDA adapter, the only option is **indexserver**.

The other parameters will change according to the adapter selected, which will be explained in more detail in the next few sections.

Create Remote Source Connection to SQL Server via SDA Adapter

With an SDA adapter, a remote source can be created to connect to the SQL Server 2012 database. The MSSQL (GENERIC ODBC) adapter is an SDA adapter and will be used to connect to the SQL Server database. The properties shown in Figure 8.6 need to be populated as follows:

- **Source Name**
  Enter the source name for your remote source.

- **Adapter Name**
  Choose **MSSQL (GENERIC ODBC)** from the predefined adapter list.

- **Source Location**
  The **indexserver** option will be used for an SDA adapter.

- **Adapter Version**
  Select **SQL Server 2012**.

- **Connection Mode**
  For MSSQL (GENERIC ODBC), a developer can only choose **Data Source Name**; for other adapters, more modes might be available.

- **Data Source Name**
  Provide the data source name defined in *odbc.ini*.

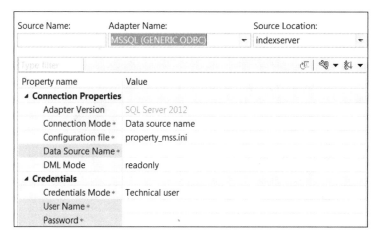

Figure 8.6 Properties to Create SQL Server Remote Source

- **DML Mode**:
  - **Read-only**
    Will only allow you to read into SAP HANA.
  - **Read-write**
    Will allow you to write changes in virtual tables back to the original database.
- **Credential Mode**
  Choose **Technical user**.
- **User Name** and **Password**
  Provide the user name and password of the remote SQL Server system for logon.

> **Note**
>
> If the database name isn't specified in odbc.ini, only the default database will be available under the **Provisioning** folder in SAP HANA Studio.

You can follow Figure 8.6 to create remote sources using the graphic method, but you can also create remote source connections to remote databases with SQLScript. Listing 8.1 provides a template for SQLScript to create remote sources for SQL server; it's been tested in SAP HANA SPS 11. You can copy the script to the SQL console, change the parameters accordingly, and execute the script to create the remote source connection to SQL server.

```
CREATE REMOTE SOURCE <input your remote source name>
ADAPTER "odbc"
CONFIGURATION FILE 'property_mss.ini'
CONFIGURATION 'DSN=<input DSN>'
WITH CREDENTIAL TYPE 'PASSWORD'
USING 'user=<Input username>; password=<Input the password>';
```

Listing 8.1 Create Remote Source for MS SQL Server

Create Remote Source Connection to Hadoop

SDA can support access to Hadoop remotely. To connect to a Hadoop system, the Simba ODBC driver needs to be installed in the Linux box on the SAP HANA server; the driver can be downloaded from *http://startupfocus.saphana.com/spark/spark-sap-hana-integration/*.

Figure 8.7 illustrates the role that ODBC drivers play in the communication between SAP HANA and a Hadoop cluster.

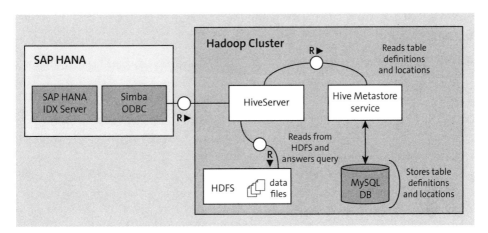

Figure 8.7 Connect Hadoop via ODBC

In this case, choose **HADOOP (ODBC)** for **Adapter Name**, select **ATA Source Name** for **Connection Mode**, specify the **Data Source Name** as defined in odbc.ini, and provide the **User Name** and **Password** to connect the Hadoop system from SAP HANA Studio.

You can also choose the SPARK SQL adapter to create the remote source. See Chapter 9, Section 9.3.2 on NLS configuration for more details.

Figure 8.8 shows the properties to create a Hadoop remote source.

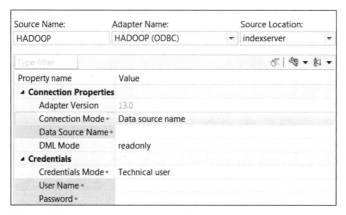

Source Name:	Adapter Name:		Source Location:	
HADOOP	HADOOP (ODBC)	▾	indexserver	▾

Type filter		⌕ | ⌖ ▾ 丿 ▾
Property name	Value	
⊿ **Connection Properties**		
Adapter Version	13.0	
Connection Mode ∗	Data source name	
Data Source Name ∗		
DML Mode	readonly	
⊿ **Credentials**		
Credentials Mode ∗	Technical user	
User Name ∗		
Password ∗		

Figure 8.8 Properties to Create Hadoop Remote Source

You can also create remote source connection to a remote Hadoop system with SQLScript. Listing 8.2 provides an SAP HANA SQL script template to create a remote source for Hadoop; it's been tested in SAP HANA SPS 11. You can copy the script to the SAP HANA SQL console, change the parameters accordingly, and execute it to create the remote source connection for Hadoop.

```
CREATE REMOTE SOURCE <input your remote source name for hadoop>
ADAPTER "hiveodbc"
CONFIGURATION 'DSN=<specify DSN defined in odbc.ini file>'
WITH CREDENTIAL TYPE 'PASSWORD'
USING 'user=<provide the username>; password=<provide the password>';
```

Listing 8.2 Create Remote Source for Hadoop

8.2   SAP HANA Smart Data Integration

SDA functionality has been further enhanced in SDI to provide virtual access for non-critical data for SAP BW/4HANA. Real-time data replication is also possible for some data source types. Moreover, processing occurs in a new SAP HANA service called the *Data Provisioning Server*, which enhances the stability of core SAP HANA processes.

SDI enhances, cleanses, and transforms data to make it more accurate and useful. With the speed advantages of SAP HANA, SDI can connect with any remote source, provision and cleanse data, and load data into SAP BW/4HANA on-premise or in the cloud.

Launched in SAP HANA SPS 09 and further enhanced in SAP HANA SPS 10, the native integration capabilities of SDI are designed for on-premise, cloud, or hybrid deployments and support all styles of data delivery, including the following:

- Federated
- Batch
- Real time (for some data sources)

In addition, the architecture benefits in-memory processing in SAP HANA, which gets a massive performance boost along with an open framework and SDK. All of this enables you to build custom adapters to integrate any data sources you can imagine to get data into SAP HANA.

Some key differences between SDI and SDA are as follows:

- Data processing occurs in the Data Provisioning Server with SDI, which enhances the stability of core SAP HANA processes.
- With SDA using Unix ODBC drivers, you need to maintain DSNs for each database in the Linux box on the SAP HANA server; SDI instead uses JDBC drivers.

In the following sections, we'll explain how to create a remote source via SDI step by step.

8.2.1   Configure SAP HANA Smart Data Integration

The following list provides the high-level overview of steps required to access data residing in external databases via SDI:

1. Enable the data provisioning server in SAP HANA Studio.
2. Import data provisioning delivery units in SAP HANA Studio.
3. Install the Data Provisioning Agent.
4. Connect the Data Provisioning Agent to SAP HANA.
5. Register an adapter.
6. Create a remote source in SAP HANA Studio.
7. Create a virtual table in SAP HANA Studio.

We'll discuss each high-level step in more detail in the following subsections.

Enable the Data Provisioning Server

The data provisioning server can be enabled in the administration console in SAP HANA Studio, as follows:

1. Right-click the SAP HANA system and select **Configuration and Monitoring • Open Administration**.

2. In the administration console, go to the **Configuration** tab (see Figure 8.9).

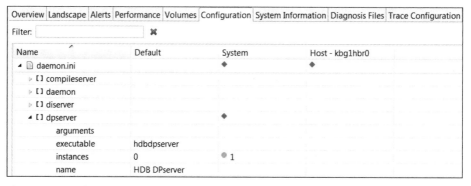

Figure 8.9 Configuration Tab for Data Provisioning Server

3. Expand the **daemon.ini** configuration file.

4. Expand **dpserver**.

5. Figure 8.10 shows the default value is 0. Right-click **instances** and choose **Change...** to open a new window in which you can change the configuration value.

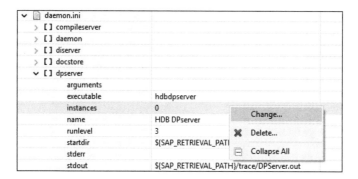

Figure 8.10 Change Instance

6. Here, in the **Change Configuration Value** screen, you can again see that the **Default Value** is **0**. Set the **New Value** to **1** (see Figure 8.11).

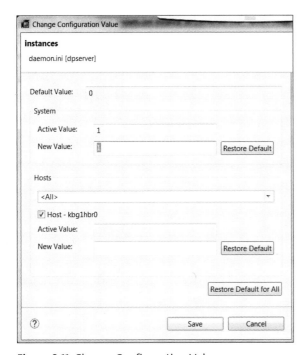

Figure 8.11 Change Configuration Value

7. Click **Save** to save your changes and close the **Change Configuration Value** screen. The new value of 1 shows a green indicator to the left (see Figure 8.12).

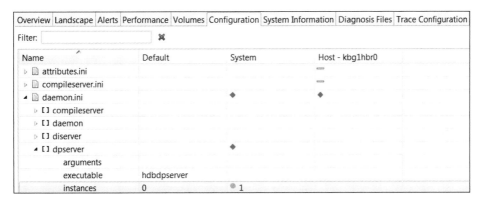

Figure 8.12 Enable Data Provisioning Server

Figure 8.13 shows **dpserver** with a green status indicator in the **Active** column in the **Landscape** tab; this means the Data Provisioning Server is active and ready for use.

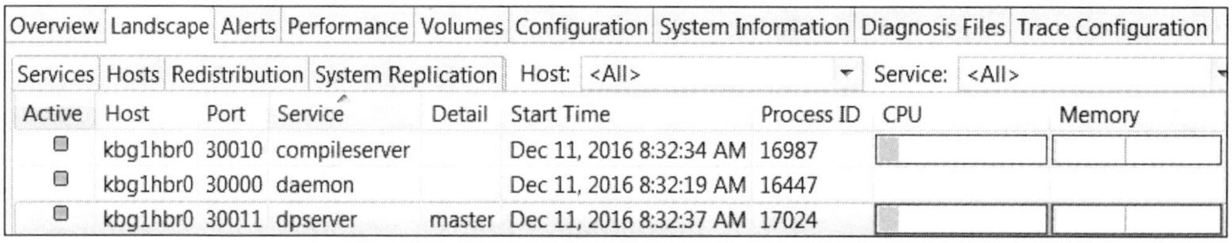

Overview	Landscape	Alerts	Performance	Volumes	Configuration	System Information	Diagnosis Files	Trace Configuration

Services	Hosts	Redistribution	System Replication	Host:	<All>	▼	Service:	<All>	▼

Active	Host	Port	Service	Detail	Start Time	Process ID	CPU	Memory
▣	kbg1hbr0	30010	compileserver		Dec 11, 2016 8:32:34 AM	16987		
▣	kbg1hbr0	30000	daemon		Dec 11, 2016 8:32:19 AM	16447		
▣	kbg1hbr0	30011	dpserver	master	Dec 11, 2016 8:32:37 AM	17024		

Figure 8.13 Status of Data Provisioning Server

Download and Import Data Provisioning Delivery Unit

Download SDI from the SAP Software Download Center and import a data provisioning delivery unit into SAP HANA Studio, which can be used to monitor the replication task status if you want to move data into SAP BW/4HANA system. You will need to take two further steps, as follows:

1. **Grant the data provisioning monitor privilege to the SYSTEM user**
   Log on to SAP HANA Studio using SYSTEM and execute the following code in the SQL console:

   ```
   CALL GRANT_ACTIVATED_ROLE ('sap.hana.uis.db::SITE_DESIGNER','SYSTEM');
   CALL GRANT_ACTIVATED_ROLE ('sap.hana.im.dp.monitor.roles::Monitoring','SYSTEM');
   ```

2. **Test the DP monitor cockpit using the following URLs**
   Now, you should be able to access the UI of the data provisioning delivery unit via the following URLs:

   - *http://<HANA host name>:<HANA port number>/sap/hana/im/dp/monitor/?view=DPAgentMonitor*
   - *http://<HANA host name>:<HANA port number>/sap/hana/im/dp/monitor/?view=DPSubscriptionMonitor*
   - *http://<HANA host name>:<HANA port number>/sap/hana/im/dp/monitor/?view=IMTaskMonitor*

Install Data Provisioning Agent

The Data Provisioning Agent installation package, SAP HANA SDI 1.0, is available as an optional component from the SAP Software Download Center. You can install the agent on a separate server from your SAP HANA server.

SAP provides Data Provisioning Agent installers for Windows and Linux servers.

To install on Windows, follow these steps:

1. Right-click **hdbsetup.exe** and choose **Run as Administrator**. The first installation screen, **Define dataprovagent Properties**, will appear. As shown in Figure 8.14, you can choose to update or install SAP HANA Data Provisioning Agent; here, we'll choose to install.

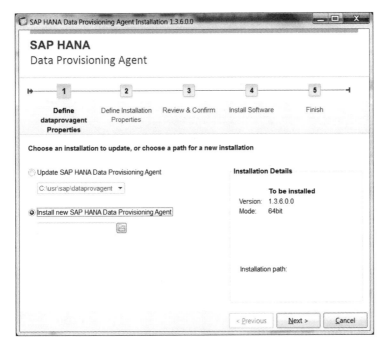

Figure 8.14 Install SAP HANA Data Provisioning Agent

2. In Step 2 (Figure 8.15), the following parameters need to be specified:
   - **Installation Path**
     Specify the directory for the installation, such as */usr/sap/dpagent*.

- **Domain\Username**
  Specify the domain and user name for a user with administrator rights.
- **Password**
  Enter the user's password.
- **Agent Listener port**
  By default, 5050.
- **Agent Administrator port**
  By default, 5051.

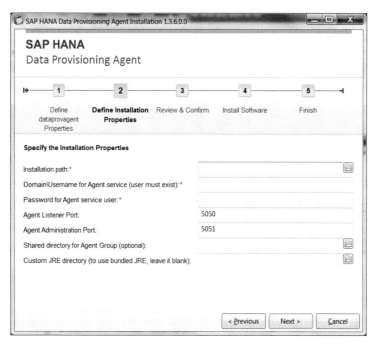

Figure 8.15 Specify Installation Properties

The rest can be left set to their default settings.

Start Data Provisioning Agent and Connect to SAP HANA

By default, the Data Provisioning Agent is installed under *C:\usr\sap\dataprovagent* in Windows. You can execute dpagentconfigtool.exe under *C:\usr\sap\dataprov-agent\configTool* to launch the SAP HANA Data Provisioning Agent configuration tool, and then you can perform the following steps:

1. **Connect to SAP HANA**

   Click the **Connect to HANA** button (see Figure 8.16), then enter SAP HANA server connection information.

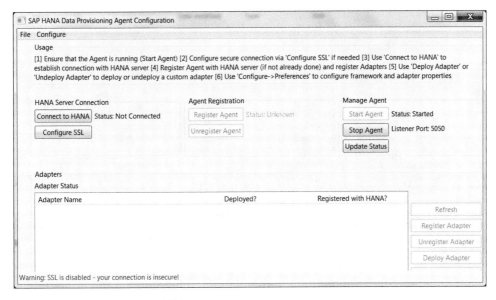

Figure 8.16 Connect to SAP HANA

2. Figure 8.17 to connect to the SAP HANA server, as follows (see Figure 8.17):

   - **HANA Hostname**
     Specify the SAP HANA server to which you want to connect.

   - **HANA Port**
     Specify the SAP HANA port number; the default port number is 30015.

Figure 8.17 Enter SAP HANA Server Connection Information

- **HANA Admin User**
  Provide an SAP HANA user with administrator rights.

- **HANA Admin Password**
  Provide the password corresponding to the SAP HANA admin user entered.

3. Once you've connected to the SAP HANA server successfully, you should see a screen like that in Figure 8.18.

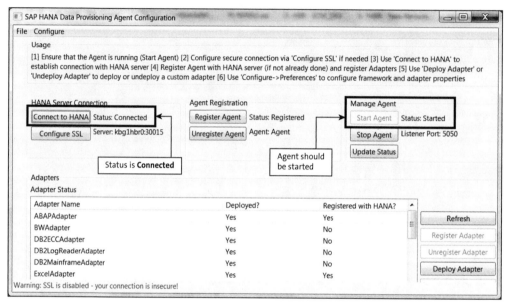

Figure 8.18 Connected to SAP HANA Server

The screen should appear as follows:

- **HANA Server Connection**
  - **Status: Connected**
  - **Server:** Showing the HANA hostname and port number
- **Manage Agent: Status: Started** (If **Status** isn't **Started**, click **Start Agent**.)
- **Adapter Status**: List of deployed adapters appears at bottom of dialog

4. The first time you start the agent, if the agent **Status** is **Unknown**, you need to register the agent, as shown in Figure 8.19. The agent can be used in SAP HANA Studio later. Click the **Register Agent** button, and enter the following:

- **Agent Name**: Enter "myAgent" (or use your own name instead).
- **Agent Hostname**: The computer name will be displayed by default.

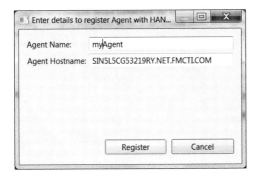

Figure 8.19 Register Agent

5. Click **Register**. If the agent has been registered successfully, the **Agent Registration Status** should change to **Registered**, as shown in Figure 8.20.

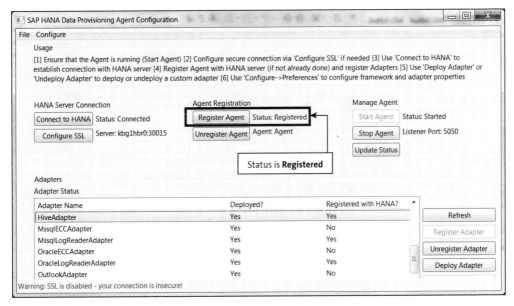

Figure 8.20 Registered Agent Status

6. Once the agent is registered successfully, you'll see a list of adapters delivered by SAP displayed at the bottom of the configuration dialog, as shown in Figure 8.21. The **Registered with HANA?** column should read **No** by default. To make the adapters visible when creating a remote source in SAP HANA Studio, the next step is to register them. Highlight an adapter and click the **Register Adapter** button.

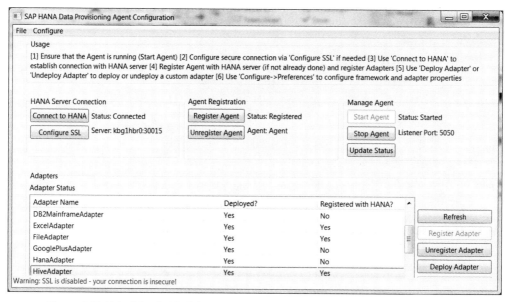

Figure 8.21 List of Available Adapers

7. The **Registered with HANA?** column should now read **Yes** for the adapter you selected.

Configure SQL Server Adapter

The adapter itself is part of the Data Provisioning Agent installer, but for SQL server, Oracle, and Hive, the JDBC drivers are missing because SAP can't distribute software components owned by other companies. Therefore, the JDBC drivers need to be downloaded from the providers' websites and installed on the server on which you installed the Data Provisioning Agent. Before downloading the JDBC driver, we need to check the PAM for SDI to make sure we download the correct version, as follows:

1. Check the PAM for SDI for the supported client library; version 4 of the SQL server JDBC driver is required. The JDBC driver for the SQL server database can be downloaded from Microsoft's download center. From the following website, select version 4.0 and download to a local machine: *https://www.microsoft.com/en-us/download/details.aspx?id=11774*.

2. Once the .exe file is available locally, the content can be extracted; Locate the sql-jdbc4.jar file and copy it into the *lib* folder in the location where the Data Provisioning Agent was installed, as shown in Figure 8.22; by default, the path should be *\usr\sap\dataprovagent\lib*.

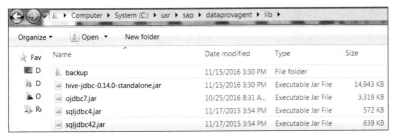

Figure 8.22 Installation of JDBS Driver for SQL Server

3. Deploy the adaptor via the Data Provisioning Agent configuration tool. Highlight **MssqlLogreaderAdapter** and click the **Deploy Adapter** button as shown in Figure 8.23 to deploy the adapter for the SQL Server database.

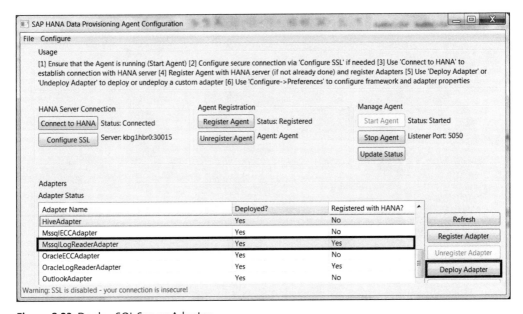

Figure 8.23 Deploy SQL Server Adapter

Configure Hive Adapter

Now, let's configure the Hive adapter for Hadoop. Like the SQL server adapter, the Hive JDBC needs to be downloaded from the Hive website and installed on the server on which you installed the Data Provisioning Agent. We need to check the PAM for SDI to make sure we download the correct version. First, however, we need make sure we download the supported HIVE JDBC driver version, as follows:

1. Check the PAM for SDI for for the supported client library; as of May 2017, version of 0.12.0, 0.13.0, or 0.13.1 JDBC drivers are supported. Download version 0.12.0, 0.13.0, 0.13.1, or 0.14 of the Hive JDBC driver from *https://hive.apache.org/downloads.html*. For the purposes of this example, we've downloaded to the local machine. Locate the hive-jdbc-0.14.0-standalone.jar file and copy it into the *lib* folder of the location in which the Data Provisioning Agent was been installed; by default, that would be *\usr\sap\dataprovagent\lib*.

2. Figure 8.24 shows how to deploy the Hive adaptor via the configuration tool: Select **HiveAdapter** from the list of adapters and click the **Deploy Adapter** button.

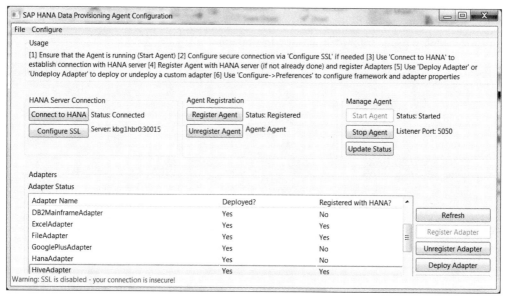

Figure 8.24 Deploy Hive Adapter

Once the Hive adapter has been deployed and registered, the Hive adapter will be available in the list of adapters when you create a remote source in SAP HANA Studio.

Configure Oracle Adapter

Like the MS SQL Server adapter and Hive adapter, follow the same steps to download the Oracle JDBC driver (ojdbc7.jar), copy the JAR file to *\usr\sap\dataprovagent\lib*, and then deploy and register the Oracle adapter. Now you can create a remote source to connect to the Oracle database with the Oracle SDI adapter.

8.2.2   Create Remote Source with Smart Data Integration Adapter

Once the required SDI adapters have been registered and deployed, you can create corresponding remote sources in SAP HANA Studio. You should use the SYSTEM account to create remote sources to avoid any access issues when other SAP HANA users want to access the created remote sources later.

Use the SYSTEM account to log on to SAP HANA and create one new remote source to point to the SQL Server 2008 or 2012 database through the Data Provisioning Agent. We'll choose the MssqlLogReader adapter here, instead of the MS ODBC driver, which is used for SDA. The MssqlLogReader adapter is used to read and load data from the SQL Server database and supports batch and real-time data replication. It's based on Sybase RepAgent for real-time capture of changes.

Figure 8.25 shows how to create remote source objects in SAP HANA Studio. You need to provide the SQL server database's **Hostname** and **Port Number**, **Database Name**, and login credentials, the same parameters entered when connecting to a SQL server database using SQL Server Management Studio.

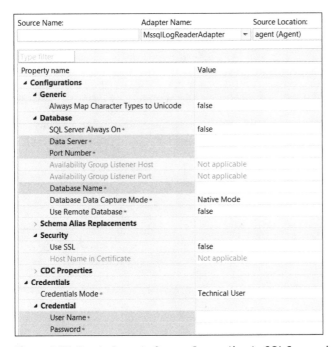

Figure 8.25 Create Remote Source Connection to SQL Server via SDI

The parameters on this page are as follows:

- **Source Name**
  Enter your source name here.

- **Adapter Name**
  Choose **MssqlLogreaderAdapter** from the list of adapters; we registered and deployed this adapter in the previous section.

- **Data Server**
  Specify the host name of the remote database server. The MssqlLogreaderAdapter adapter can be installed on the same server as SQL Server itself or on a different server.

- **Port Number**
  Specify the port number of the SQL Server instance. The default port number for a SQL Server instance is 1433. Depending on your company's SQL Server database installation, the port number could be something other than 1433. To find the actual port number being used, open the SQL Server Configuration Manager.

- **Database Name**
  Specify one of the existing databases you want to retrieve data from. This remote source points to only one database of the SQL Server database instance at a time.

- **Credentials Mode**
  Choose **Technical User**.

- **User Name** and **Password**
  Provide the user name and password for the remote SQL Server database to log on.

When the remote source is set up correctly and the connection tested successfully, all tables in the remote source can be browsed, as in Figure 8.26, and then virtual tables can be created.

Figure 8.26 Remote Source and Virtual Tables

It might be much easier to create a remote source connection to a remote SQL Server database with SQLScript. Note that the syntax for using SDI adapters is different than the syntax for using SDA adapters. For SDI adapters, the parameters in SQL scripts need to be wrapped in XML format. The SQLScript in Listing 8.3 is a template to create a remote source connection to the SQL Server database using Mssql-LogreaderAdapter, which has been tested in SAP HANA SPS 11 successfully. You can copy the script in Listing 8.3 into the SAP HANA SQL console, change the parameters accordingly, and execute it to create the remote source connection to the SQL server database in SAP HANA Studio.

```
CREATE REMOTE SOURCE <remote source name>
ADAPTER "MssqlLogReaderAdapter" AT LOCATION AGENT "<the registered agent name>"
CONFIGURATION
'<?xml version="1.0" encoding="UTF-8" standalone="yes"?>
<ConnectionProperties name="configurations" displayName="Configurations">
<PropertyGroup name="database">
    <PropertyEntry name="pds_server_name">remote server name</PropertyEntry>
    <PropertyEntry name="pds_port_number">port number</PropertyEntry>
    <PropertyEntry name="pds_database_name">your database name</PropertyEntry>
</PropertyGroup>
</ConnectionProperties>'
WITH CREDENTIAL TYPE 'PASSWORD' USING
'<CredentialEntry name="credential">
<user>user name</user>
<password>password</password>
</CredentialEntry>';
```

Listing 8.3 Create Remote Source Connection to SQL Server with SDI Adapter

8.2.3   Create Remote Source Connection to Oracle

Use the SYSTEM account to log on to SAP HANA Studio and create a new remote source to point to the Oracle database 12c through the Data Provisioning Agent. As shown in Figure 8.27, the OracleLogReader adapter is used to read and load Oracle database data and supports batch and real-time data replication.

Source Name:	Adapter Name:	Source Location:
BOR	OracleLogReaderAdapter ▼	agent (Agent)

Type filter	
Property name	**Value**
▲ **Configurations**	
› **Generic**	
▲ **Database**	
Multitenant Database *	false
Use Oracle TNSNAMES File *	false
Host *	kbg1bor0.kongsberg.fmcweb.com
Port Number *	1527
Database Name *	BOR
Container Database Service Name	Not applicable
Pluggable Database Service Name	Not applicable
Oracle TNSNAMES File	Not applicable
Oracle TNSNAMES Connection	Not applicable
Container Database TNSNAMES Connection	Not applicable
Pluggable Database TNSNAMES Connection	Not applicable
› **Schema Alias Replacements**	
› **Security**	
› **JDBC Connection Parameters**	
› **CDC Properties**	
▲ **Credentials**	
Credentials Mode *	Technical user
▲ **Oracle Connection Credential**	
User Name (Case Sensitive)	Not applicable
Password	Not applicable

Figure 8.27 Create Remote Source Connection to Oracle via SDI

The parameters on this page are as follows:

- **Source Name**

  Enter your source name here.

- **Adapter Name**

  Choose **OracleLogReaderAdapter** from the adapter list, instead of the Oracle ODBC driver, which is used for SDA.

- **Host**

  Enter the host name of the database server. The communication between SAP HANA and the adapter happens via the Data Provisioning Agent. When the Oracle-LogReader adapter is installed on the same computer as the Oracle database being installed, the host name will be **localhost**. When the OracleLogReader adapter has been installed on a different server, the remote server name should be specified.

- **Port Number**

  Specify the port number of the Oracle database.

- **Database Name**
  Specify one of the existing databases you want to retrieve data from. This remote source points to only one database of the Oracle database at a time.

- **Credentials Mode**
  Choose **Technical User**.

- **User Name** and **Password**
  Provide the user name and password for the remote Oracle database to log on.

With the remote source connection to the Oracle database set up correctly and tested successfully, all tables in the remote Oracle database can be browsed and all virtual tables can be created.

8.2.4 Create Remote Source Connection to Hadoop

Use the SYSTEM account to log on to SAP HANA Studio and create a new remote source to point to Hadoop through the Data Provisioning Agent. Figure 8.28 shows the Hive adapter that can be used to read and load Hadoop database data into SAP HANA.

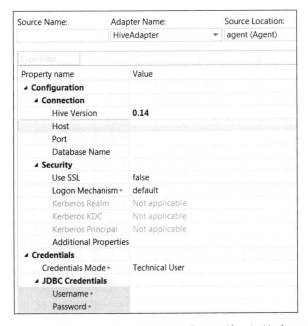

Figure 8.28 Create Remote Source Connection to Hadoop via SDI

The parameters on this page are as follows:

- **Source Name**
  Enter your own source name here.

- **Adapter Name**
  Choose **HiveAdapter** from the adapter list.

- **Source Location**
  Specify the agent name configured previously.

- **Hive Version**
  Specify the Hive version: 0.12.0, 0.13.1, or 0.14.

- **Host**
  Specify the host name of the Hadoop system.

- **Port Number**
  Specify the port number of the Hadoop system.

- **Database Name**
  Specify an existing Hadoop system you want to retrieve data from.

- **Credentials Mode**
  Choose **Technical user**.

- **User Name** and **Password**
  Provide the user name and password for the remote Oracle database to log on.

Now, save and test the connection. If the connection has been set up correctly, you should able to see your own Hive remote source under **Provisioning • Remote Sources**. All tables in the remote Hadoop database can be browsed and all the virtual tables can be created.

8.2.5   Create Virtual Tables

With the remote source connections to remote databases set up correctly and connections tested successfully, all tables in the remote databases can be browsed. Now, virtual tables can be created based on the remote tables.

Figure 8.29 shows how to add virtual tables. Right-click the remote table under the remote source created before and choose **Add as Virtual Table**.

On the screen shown in Figure 8.30, enter the virtual **Table Name** and the **Schema**. The new virtual table will be created under the specified schema. The virtual table doesn't store any data (data is kept in the external database), but will be visible to SAP HANA.

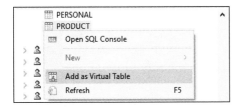

Figure 8.29 Add Virtual Table

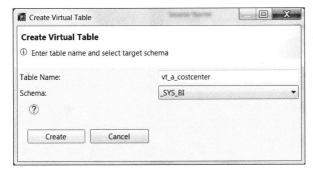

Figure 8.30 Create Virtual Table

After you click **Create**, a new virtual table will be created under the specified schema. You can right-click the virtual table to display data. A green icon next to the table means that it's virtual. You can review data from the virtual table as though the data is stored locally in SAP HANA.

8.3   Integration with SAP BW/4HANA

With SAP BW/4HANA, we either combine data from SAP HANA tables or views under the schema SAPSR3 or by integrating with InfoProviders. The next section will explain how to combine data under the schema SAPSR3. We will then discuss how to combine data via open ODS views and CompositeProviders in Section 8.3.2.

8.3.1   Combining Data under Schema SAPSR3

Figure 8.31 shows that SAP BW/4HANA objects (InfoObjects, DSOs, Cubes, and Multi-Providers) can be accessed as SAP HANA tables or views under schema SAPSR3 in SAP HANA Studio.

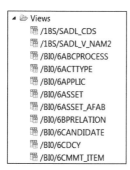

Figure 8.31 SAP HANA Views under SAPSR3 Schema

For example, as shown in Figure 8.32, the InfoObject OPROJECT has a master data view /BIO/MPROJECT, time-independent master data table /BIO/PPROJECT, time-dependent master data table /BIO/QPROJECT, and text table /BIO/TPROJECT, all of which can be accessed via the same names in SAP HANA Studio.

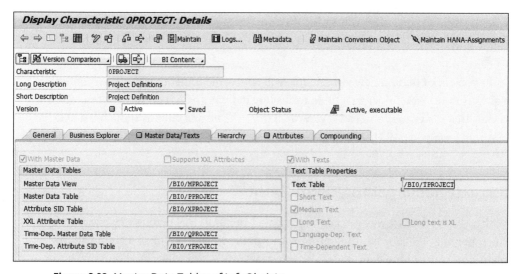

Figure 8.32 Master Data Tables of InfoObejcts

Keep in mind that the schema name SAPSR3 will be required in SQLScript if you want to select data from those tables or views.

8.3.2   Combine Data via Open ODS Views or CompositeProvider

In SAP BW/4HANA, Open ODS views and CompositeProviders are available and are based on fields of tables or views rather than InfoObjects. Prior to SAP BW 7.4, all SAP BW modeling—InfoProviders, data flows, SAP BEx queries, and even authorizations—was built on top of InfoObjects. InfoObjects are the bricks of data modeling. However, the Open ODS field-based approach makes the following possible:

- Data modeling on any table field
- Crossing the border: Open ODS function modeling on virtual tables via SDA to get data from remote sources
- Integration of field data into EDW contexts: association of InfoObjects to Open ODS views and CompositeProviders
- SAP BEx queries on top of Open ODS views or CompositeProviders
- Embedding Open ODS views into CompositeProviders

Figure 8.33 illustrates the implementation of the real time reporting solution for CO-PA (Profitability Analysis), which including the following steps:

1. Use the system landscape directory to synchronize CO-PA line item data in real time from SAP ERP to SAP HANA.
2. Generate a time dimension based on the posting date.
3. Use an Open ODS view to combine the SAP HANA view and SAP BW models to leverage existing SAP BW developments.
4. Associate the table fields with InfoObjects to get text and attributes to avoid keeping duplicate data SAP BW/4HANA system.
5. Create SAP BEx queries on top of Open ODS views.

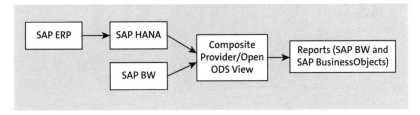

Figure 8.33 Real-Time Solution for CO-PA

In SAP HANA Studio, the analytics view ZCOPA_AV01 (see Figure 8.34) was created with the data foundation on CO-PA line table and star joins to make some additional enhancements, such as joining the generated time table to get time dimensions and converting the currency type and project formats from an internal to external format.

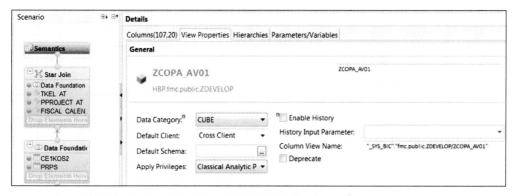

Figure 8.34 Create Analytics View in SAP HANA Studio

The following sections will illustrate how to create Open ODS views, associate them with existing InfoObjects, and turn on navigation attributes. We will also briefly touch upon compounding InfoObjects.

Create Open ODS View

In this step, we'll create an Open ODS view in SAP BW/4HANA, which will allow us to consume the SAP HANA analytics view ZCOPA_AV01 and expose the view to SAP BW/4HANA. In Figure 8.35, we need to specify the Open ODS **View Name**, **Description**, **Semantics**, **Type**, **Schema**, **Source System**, and **DB Object Name**.

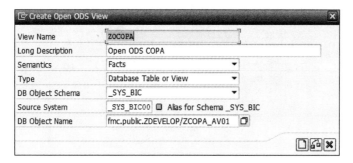

Figure 8.35 Create Open ODS View

In Figure 8.36, after clicking the **Create Proposal** icon ⊙, the source fields from the SAP HANA view will be added to the target Open ODS view. The creation of an Open ODS view is quite straightforward; after activating the Open ODS view without creating any InfoObjects, the activated Open ODS view is ready for reporting, and a developer can create SAP BEx queries using the SAP BEx query designer.

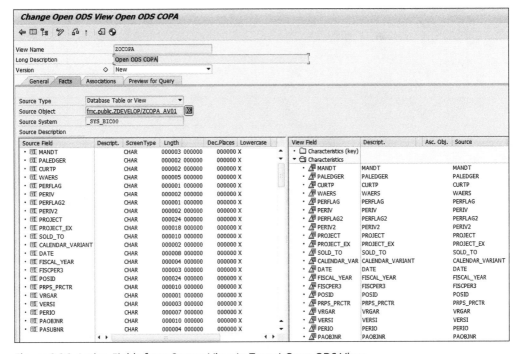

Figure 8.36 Assign Fields from Source View to Target Open ODS View

Note that it's also possible to create an Open ODS view within SAP HANA Studio, as shown in Figure 8.37, via a plug-in installed in Eclipse.

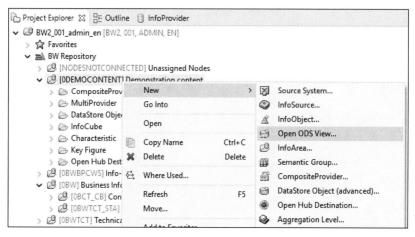

Figure 8.37 Create Open ODS View in Eclipse

Association with InfoObjects

To leverage existing SAP BW objects, models, or features offered by SAP BW/4HANA—for example, InfoObjects' navigational attributes, text, and hierarchies—it's possible to integrate with SAP BW/4HANA InfoObjects by associating fields with InfoObjects in Open ODS views or CompositeProviders. Figure 8.38 shows a table field associated to the InfoObject 0WBS_ELEMT.

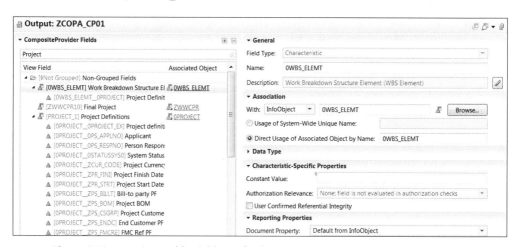

Figure 8.38 Associate Table Field to InfoObejct

Through an association with an InfoObject, the attributes and text data of the InfoObject will be available in the Open ODS view or CompositeProvider. In this way, we can avoid data redundancy in SAP HANA and avoid loading duplicate data into the SAP BW/4HANA system.

Turn on Navigation Attributes

After associating a field with an InfoObject, all attributes of the associated InfoObject are available, and you can turn on one or more attributes as navigation attributes, as shown in Figure 8.39.

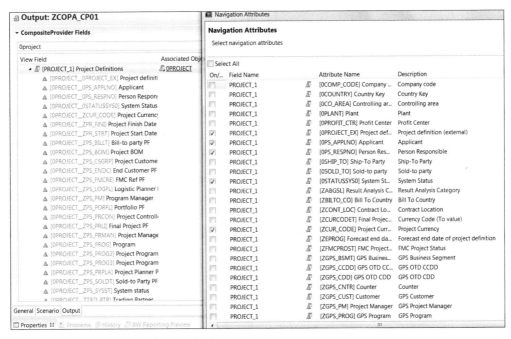

Figure 8.39 Turn on Navigation Attributes

Compound InfoObjects

Figure 8.40 shows the InfoObject OCOSTELMNT (Cost Element) compounding to OCO_AREA (Controlling Area); we also can specify the compounding in an Open ODS view or CompositeProvider in SAP HANA Studio, as shown in Figure 8.41.

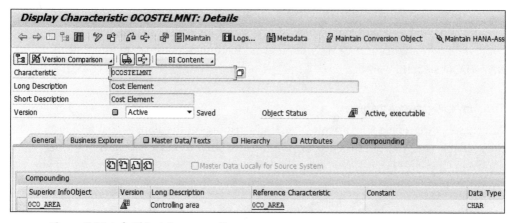

Figure 8.40 InfoObject Compounding

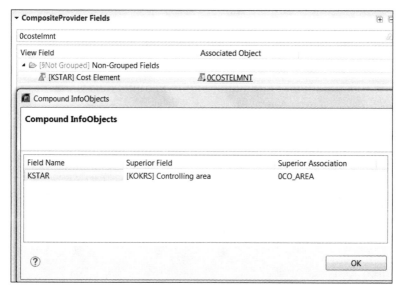

Figure 8.41 Compounding InfoObejct in Open ODS View or CompositeProvider

SAP BEx queries can be created on top of the Open ODS view or CompositeProvider. The navigation attributes and text can be used as usual in SAP BW/4HANA models. Note that even with Open ODS views and CompositeProviders created in Eclipse, you still need to use transport requests to transport them across the SAP BW/4HANA landscape.

8.4   Summary

In this chapter, SAP BW/4HANA was considered as the central layer to integrate data from external databases and data from the SAP BW/4HANA system, via the following methods:

- Access external data remotely with SDA or SDI
- Integrate with the SAP BW/4HANA system

With SDA and SDI in SAP BW/4HANA, you will be able to do the following:

- Combine or merge data from different sources with or without duplicating data to SAP BW/4HANA
- Get information in real time to make quick decisions
- Lower the cost of IT and technology

The next chapter will discuss the tools provided by SAP for data lifecycle management.

Chapter 9
Data Lifecycle Management

Effectively managing data growth in your data warehouse can be an intensive and massive task. In this chapter, we'll discuss planning for growth and performance up front during design, which can simplify and facilitate your data management efforts.

As data is loaded into a data warehouse, it's propagated through the data flow and replicated throughout the LSA++ architecture. For example, data extracted from a table in SAP ERP could be loaded into the operational delta queue (ODQ), one or more DSO layers, change logs, and corporate memory. The result of this data propagation is data replication and an increased storage requirement beyond that of the original source system. In some cases, data may be denormalized to improve data load performance and/or reporting performance (i.e., including sales order header information in the sales order item data flow). *Denormalization* is the intentional duplication of columns in multiple tables, and it increases data redundancy.

Failure to proactively manage data loaded into SAP BW/4HANA can seriously jeopardize system performance and directly affect the total cost of ownership. Housekeeping activities must be an integral part of the operational concept of a complex enterprise data warehouse. Planning and executing housekeeping activities regularly in the system will ensure optimum utilization of system resources and thereby optimize the overall system performance.

An integral part of any data monitoring and housekeeping effort is a data retention strategy, as we'll discuss in Section 9.1; such a strategy may include a hybrid approach that uses all tools at your disposal, such as aggregation, near-line storage, archival processes, and data deletion. In Section 9.2, we'll introduce the data temperature concept for managing data with different retention requirements and access frequencies. For cold data, in Section 9.3 we'll discuss in detail how to configure the data archiving process using SAP's near-line storage (NLS) on SAP IQ or Hadoop.

9.1   Data Retention Strategy

In an operational data warehouse, it's natural for the volume of data to perpetually increase, which is known as *organic growth*. Constant changes to business and legal requirements mean that this data must be available for longer than ever before. The impact of keeping a large volume of data in the system is generally a decrease in performance and an increase in administration effort. To combat and manage these impacts, you should implement a data aging strategy early in the lifecycle of the data warehouse; such a strategy can have a profound influence on design and architecture.

Efficient storage of historical data for comprehensive enterprise data warehousing is essential to maintaining a healthy and high-performing system. The following are some advantages of a carefully planned data retention strategy:

- Reduced infrastructure costs for the following categories:
  - Storage capacity costs
  - Processing capacity costs
- Improved performance of the SAP BW/4HANA system in the following areas:
  - Query performance
  - Data loading performance
  - System administration performance
- Reduced administration and maintenance effort in the following areas:
  - Reloading and repartitioning effort
  - Data management effort

When considering a data retention strategy, there are always trade-offs: benefits and costs, advantages and risks. Making a decision about what data should remain available and accessible to end users is fraught with consequences.

However, the good news is that solid advice is available, because this dilemma has been wrestled with many times before. To start, it may be helpful to consider some of the following questions:

- At what point does lack of processing capability incurred by the data volume become unacceptable? In other words, what is the data volume threshold above which response times are intolerable?
- Are there any catastrophic consequences associated with loss of processing for this system?

- What other systems or processes does the data retention strategy affect or feed? How many downstream systems rely on data availability in this data warehouse?
- What is the cost and elapsed time of restoring or recreating the data that's no longer retained?
- Are there legal requirements (such as a litigation hold, court order, or law) to retain the data or keep the system operational?
- What's the risk or exposure related to keeping old data available for reporting? What liabilities are inherent in lieu of adopting a strictly enforced data retention strategy?

The greatest complexity related to defining a data retention strategy is that answering these questions requires candid discussion and agreement among infrastructure, technical support, and business representatives. Recognizing that the data retention requirements for each subject area or line of business may be completely different adds a bit more complexity. The good news is that a data retention strategy need not be one size fits all. In fact, multiple options are available, and the success of the whole strategy may depend on defining unique data aging tactics for each area based on specific data content and the business value of accessing that data.

The specific options or tactics available range from doing nothing (i.e., keeping all data available online for all time) to deleting data directly from the database with no option for recovery. Thankfully, there are also several options in between! Again, because these options may influence design and architecture, defining the data aging or retention strategy should not be deferred; if it is, a significant effort to redesign or rearchitecture may be needed.

The key point is that as data ages, details lose relevance. Keeping irrelevant data online not only adversely impacts performance (in read and write operations) but also increases administration and maintenance efforts and costs. The following list ranks different data retention tactics in order of data availability online and, indirectly, data relevance:

1. Detail InfoProviders
2. History InfoProviders
3. Summary InfoProviders
4. NLS
5. Traditional archiving
6. Data deletion

> **Note**
>
> Traditional archiving isn't available for customer data loaded to SAP BW/4HANA InfoProviders; however, it is available for system administration data, such as IDocs and application logs.

From a purely technical perspective, the first step to defining which tactic is suitable for each data set is to determine the usage of the relevant data sets. The technical content statistics are a great place to start: Check the number of navigations and number of users executing queries on each InfoProvider for that data set (i.e., subject area). Ranking each InfoProvider by usage and performance is a good way to initiate discussions with the business about the need for a data retention strategy. The flaw in this approach is the inability to decipher the age of the data being queried from the statistical information available, so engaging the business on end user behavior is critical to fully understanding how the data is being consumed. A general guideline to follow is illustrated by Table 9.1. Data used more frequently should be kept online, and you should consider keeping data used less frequently offline.

	Detail InfoProviders	Summary InfoProviders	Historical InfoProviders	NLS	Traditional Archiving	Deletion
Frequently queried data	Yes	Yes	Yes	No	No	No
Rarely used data	Yes	Yes	Yes	Yes	No	No
Very rarely used data	No	Yes	Yes	Yes	No	No
Legal hold or audit data	No	No	Yes	Yes	Yes	No
Expired or obsolete data	No	No	No	No	Yes	Yes

Table 9.1 Data Retention Tactics versus Data Access Frequency Matrix

Although no single tactic should be employed for all data sets, Table 9.1 illustrates some general guidelines that can be employed fairly consistently. Before proceeding, we should review these tactics in a little more detail and evaluate the advantages and disadvantages of each approach.

The first three tactics (using detail, historical, and summary InfoProviders) will influence the design of the data models in the warehouse. The fourth one (using NLS) will influence the system architecture. The final two (using data archiving and data deletion) will only influence the warehouse administration.

First and foremost, all data that is frequently accessed should remain available in full detail. In fact, all available details of each transaction should be available to minimize the need to enhance the data structure by adding data fields later. This is the default tactic and is represented by the first detail InfoProviders column in Table 9.1. The other columns represent alternative tactics.

The use of historical InfoProviders involves the creation of a new InfoProvider in which old data is loaded at the original *granularity* (level of detail). Current data will remain in the original InfoProvider. After data is moved to the history cube, it must be deleted from the original InfoProvider so that queries won't return duplicate data.

The historical InfoProvider tactic provides the following benefits:

- Storing historical data in a semantic partition improves performance of read/write access to the original InfoProvider, because most loading and querying is performed against current data in the original cube, which has less data.

- All data, current and historical, remains available online and can be accessed in the same query when both the historical and current InfoProviders are part of the same MultiProvider.

- There is no custom programming required to implement historical InfoProviders, so development is simple. Mapping transformation rules from the original Info-Provider to the historical InfoProvider are 1:1.

However, the historical InfoProvider is associated with a few disadvantages:

- The cost/benefit value associated with maintaining historical data is low. As older data loses relevance and is accessed less frequently but remains online, the cost per storage unit equals the cost of more relevant data.

- Unless an automated mechanism is developed, data moved from the original Info-Provider to the historical InfoProvider must be selectively deleted from the original InfoProvider, which requires planning and execution effort, as well as data loading downtime.

- There is neither reduction in infrastructure costs (storage capacity) nor in administration effort. In fact, the existence of historical data may result in increased administration effort, because changes made to the original InfoProvider may need to be applied to the historical InfoProvider to keep results consistent.

Rather than keeping historical data at the same granularity as relevant or current data, another option is to simplify the data model and summarize the data. As the details lose relevance, this approach can be very practical to keep the relevant information available. The following are advantages of a summary InfoProvider:

- Storing summarized data in a specific InfoProvider improves performance of read/write access to the original InfoProvider, because most loading and querying is performed against current data in the original cube, which has less data.

- Summarized data, current and historical, remains available online and can be accessed in the same query when both the summarized and current InfoProviders are part of the same MultiProvider.

- There is minimal custom programming required to implement summary InfoProviders, so development is simple. Mapping transformation rules from the original InfoProvider to the summary InfoProvider are usually 1:1.

- Data in the summary InfoProvider can be aggregated by more than one characteristic, thus compounding the value of the summary InfoProvider.

- Query response times against the summary InfoProvider will be faster.

- The reduction in storage capacity will be directly correlated to the reduction in granularity so long as the data in the original InfoProvider is deleted.

- There will be a reduction in infrastructure, maintenance, and administration costs, including backups, because the database holds less data.

The summary InfoProvider tactic is prone to the following disadvantages:

- An analysis effort needs to be conducted to determine whether each InfoProvider is a candidate for summarization based on the business use cases for queries on the data contained within the InfoProviders.

- If data isn't deleted from the original InfoProvider, there's neither a reduction of cost and effort nor an improvement of performance over the original InfoProvider.

- In many cases, queries may need to be adapted if historical data is summarized, or new queries may need be to be created.

Beyond summarized data, there's no other online data storage option. The next alternative is to move data out of the database and onto a *near-line storage* (NLS) database. Near-line storage is an intermediate type of data storage representing a compromise between online storage and archiving. When data is near-lined from the SAP HANA database, it is moved to the NLS system, but is still accessible by SAP BW/4HANA for reporting. The next section will dive deeper into the NLS options, but for now, the advantages of implementing NLS include the following:

- Data stored in NLS can reach compression ratios of up to 95 percent, significantly reducing storage capacity requirements and costs in the original database.
- Less expensive media can be used for the NLS solution, thus further reducing the cost of the reduced storage capacity.
- Data in NLS can be accessed by the original queries with little or no maintenance and only a nominal performance impact.
- Data that is near-lined can be restored to the original database if necessary.

The disadvantages of NLS as a data retention tactic include the following:

- Data stored in the NLS solution doesn't meet the same performance benchmarks as data that remains online; there's a performance impact, which is usually acceptable for older data.
- Only static data can be near-lined. Once near-lined, no deltas can be loaded unless the near-lined data is restored to the original database. It will then need to be moved again to the NLS database.
- When data is moved from the original database to the NLS database, no new data can be loaded to the original InfoProvider until the NLS process is completed.
- Each NLS solution has a license and maintenance cost, which, in some cases, depends on the volume of data stored in the NLS solution.
- To look up data from NLS in transformation rules, special code needs to be added to ensure the NLS data is queried.

When data is truly no longer relevant for any end-use scenario, or liability policies dictate data should be purged from all production systems, then selective deletion of data from SAP BW/4HANA InfoProviders is the best and sometimes only option. The following are advantages of deleting data:

- It's the cheapest cost option from an infrastructure perspective; once the data is deleted, there are pure cost savings.
- Minimal maintenance is required—especially if a custom programming solution is developed to selectively delete irrelevant data from InfoProviders.
- It leads to better performance reading and writing to the InfoProviders, which have less data volume.
- Less storage capacity is needed for all InfoProviders being cleansed in this way.
- It creates a healthier system as redundant and irrelevant data is deleted.

The disadvantages of data deletion, on the other hand, are quite stark:

- It's very risky if no archiving was performed previously and important or legally needed data is no longer available.
- Recovery of deleted data can only come from the source system; if the data is archived from the source, recovery can be extremely costly and difficult. If data has been deleted from the source system, no recovery is possible.
- Additional administration is required to detect candidate data for deletion and confirm whether it can be deleted.

It's important to note that these tactics are not mutually exclusive and every tactic could be employed in a single scenario. The keys to defining a successful data aging strategy include the following:

- Forecasting the impact of future data growth on capacity and performance
- Developing a cost model for data storage and maintenance
- Profiling data activity and access for all data sets
- Defining data retention tactics for all data sets
- Choosing and implementing technology to minimize impact to the business

In the next section, we'll discuss the NLS solutions for SAP BW/4HANA in more detail and learn how to create the connections necessary to use them.

9.2   Data Temperature

The overall recommended SAP data management strategy is to use the SAP HANA database with SAP's NLS to deliver a multitemperate, color-coded persistence management concept. There are three temperatures—hot data, warm data, and cold data—as illustrated in Figure 9.1:

- *Hot data* is defined as active data that needs to be accessed frequently by read and write processes. This data is stored online in the main memory of the SAP HANA database.
- *Warm data* is defined as less frequently accessed data, which is stored in the SAP HANA database file system. This data is loaded into the main memory for processing but is then displaced with higher priority hot data once processing is finished.

- *Cold data* is defined as rarely used data, which is stored in the SAP IQ database or Hadoop cluster (NLS). This data can be accessed from SAP BW/4HANA for read-only operations.

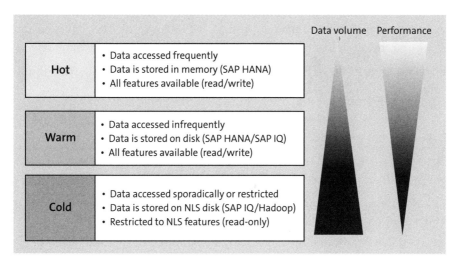

Figure 9.1 Multitemperature Data Management Strategy

Hot data includes all detailed and summary InfoProviders and perhaps even the most recent partitions of the history InfoProviders (see Table 9.1), which are frequently queried, as well as system tables required for SAP BW/4HANA system operation and administration. Because hot data is stored in the main memory of the SAP HANA database, we don't need to spend much time discussing it here. This chapter is more concerned with warm and cold data.

Warm data is accessed less frequently and therefore doesn't need to be loaded into main memory until it's queried. In other words, warm data isn't actively used. The *nonactive data* concept was originally defined to optimize the displacement strategy for SAP BW tables in SAP HANA, in which tables with warm data are flagged and prioritized for displacement from the main memory after they're used. If the warm data tables are partitioned, only the partitions needed by the transaction or query are loaded into main memory. The nonactive concept facilitates a more efficient use of main memory and allows for a relaxed memory to data ratio.

With SAP HANA SPS 09, SAP built on the nonactive data concept and introduced *dynamic tiering*, which is a native big data solution for SAP HANA. Dynamic tiering enhances SAP HANA with a large volume, warm data management capability by adding smart, disk-based extended storage to the SAP HANA database.

Initially, dynamic tiering was developed for use with SAP BW, but it required separate dedicated hosts in the production environment, making the hardware architecture overly complex and burdensome for SAP BW implementations. SAP has now restricted dynamic tiering for use with native SAP HANA solutions and has simplified the warm data management capability with SAP BW/4HANA by offering extension nodes, which provide similar benefits as dynamic tiering but with less complexity.

In the following sections, we'll discuss extension nodes for warm data storage and NLS solutions for cold data storage in more detail.

9.2.1   Warm Data in Extension Nodes

Let's start with a quick recap of the previous section. SAP HANA initially offered two options to manage the warm data in your SAP BW system:

1. *The nonactive data concept*: Tables with warm data are flagged and prioritized for displacement from the main memory after they're used.

2. *SAP HANA dynamic tiering*: Dedicated hosts in your landscape (ExtendedStorage servers with disk only and no in-memory component) are used to store warm data objects, which can be read into the memory of other hosts on request.

SAP has reevaluated these options for use with SAP BW/4HANA and has determined that advancements in both hardware technology and in SAP HANA provide an even simpler option. Rather than introducing a new ExtendedStorage server into your SAP HANA cluster to store the warm data on disk, it's simpler to use standard SAP HANA nodes with a relaxed sizing formula and RAM/CPU ratio.

The additional SAP HANA nodes form an asymmetric SAP HANA scale-out landscape: a standard group of nodes for hot data with standard sizing and an extension group for warm data with relaxed sizing (see Figure 9.2). The extension group nodes are then used to store more warm data than they have available memory. Leveraging an extension group allows you to run an SAP HANA scale-out landscape with fewer nodes and less overall memory but a larger data footprint.

Architecting an extension group in your landscape is easier to set up and administrate than using ExtendedStorage servers, and it offers all the operational, administration, and data management features of SAP HANA right out of the box. The allocation of data as hot or warm can be handled easily via the SAP BW/4HANA application, and existing data can be moved using standard SAP HANA techniques to relocate data between nodes.

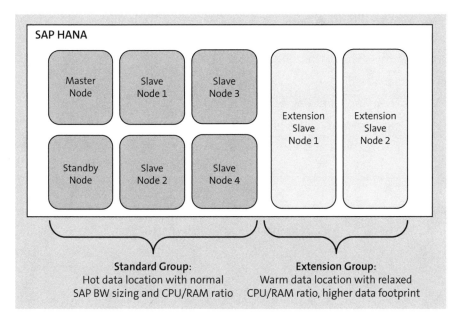

Figure 9.2 SAP HANA Warm Storage in Extension Groups

Note

This set up relies heavily on SAP BW/4HANA partitioning, pruning, and control functionality. For native SAP HANA applications looking for a more generic warm data management concept, the SAP HANA dynamic tiering feature is still a valid option.

In the following subsections, we'll review the extension node deployment options in more detail, then we'll cover how the extension nodes work, followed by a review of which SAP BW/4HANA objects you can classify as warm data.

Extension Node Deployment Options

There are three different deployment options for extension nodes in an SAP BW/4HANA system. You should choose an option based on the volume of warm data in your system, but also take into consideration the SAP BW/4HANA version, the SAP HANA database revision, and the hardware vendor. The options are as follows:

- Option 1: Simple
  - Assign one or more existing nodes as extension nodes

- – Reconfigure extension node(s) to use 100 percent of available memory for data
- – Distribute warm data to extension node(s)
- **Option 2: Advanced**
  - – Assign one or more existing nodes as extension nodes
  - – Reconfigure storage and I/O (hardware vendor dependent)
  - – Reconfigure extension node(s) to use 200 percent of available memory for data
  - – Distribute warm data to extension node(s)
- **Option 3: Special**
  - – Add one or more special extension nodes with specific memory, storage, and I/O as offered by hardware vendor
  - – Add one standby node for extension nodes
  - – Configure extension node(s) to use as much data as vendor specifies
  - – Distribute warm data to extension node(s)

An SAP HANA system with one or more extension nodes behaves just like a standard SAP HANA scale-out system. All operations and features work as expected, such as system replication, backups, statistics capturing, and logs and tracing.

However, there are a few differences that should be noted:

- The SAP HANA system can now store more data, which will increase backup and recovery times. Specifically, the higher data volumes on the extension nodes may now dominate the backup and recovery times—depending on the extension node hardware, of course.
- Forced unloads will likely occur frequently on the extension nodes, but if unloads also occur on standard nodes, this indicates insufficient sizing.
- In option 3, and possibly even option 2 (depending on hardware), the setup of high availability using host auto-failover may need to be adjusted if there is no dedicated standby for the extension node. For example, it may be necessary to explicitly return to the original configuration as soon as the failing node is brought online again.
- For non-SAP BW/4HANA data, the warm classification with the relocation to an extension node isn't supported. If non-SAP BW/4HANA data is stored in the same SAP HANA database, this data has to be located on standard nodes.

Note

Options 1 and 2 have been generally released since the Datacenter Service Point (DSP) of SAP HANA SPS 12. Offerings for option 3 are still under discussion.

How Extension Nodes Work

The standard SAP HANA sizing guidelines limit the data footprint to approximately 50 percent of available memory. The sizing guidelines ensure all data can be retained in-memory while providing sufficient space for temporary calculations and intermediate result sets. These guidelines can be significantly relaxed on extension nodes, because warm data is accessed less frequently than hot data and usually is accessed with reduced performance SLAs and less CPU-intensive processes.

The SAP BW/4HANA application controls and prioritizes the access patterns to SAP BW/4HANA tables and determines the appropriate partitioning and table distribution requirements for warm tables. SAP BW/4HANA leverages efficient partition pruning to prevent warm data tables from loading completely into memory. The partial load into memory of much smaller table partitions doesn't result in critical out-of-memory scenarios.

Based on the SAP BW/4HANA object type, SAP BW/4HANA defines default restrictions on objects containing warm data:

- No more than 50 percent of all data in the SAP BW/4HANA system should be classified as warm or nonactive.
- Access to warm tables should be partition-based in greater than 95 percent of all cases for writes, merges, and reads.
- Ideally, data should only be read from warm tables during batch processing when load-to-memory performance isn't critical.
- Query access to warm data will be significantly slower than access to hot data; this must be accepted by the user community.

SAP BW/4HANA Object Classification

SAP BW/4HANA objects can be classified as warm during object creation or later during remodeling. The default setting for all objects is hot. The default setting can be overwritten and objects can be classified as *warm*, however, the system behavior will be different for these objects, as follows:

- Newly created objects classified as warm will have all database tables created on an extension node during activation.
- Existing objects containing data reclassified as warm will not be relocated automatically to an extension node during object activation. Instead, only the metadata of the object will be updated during activation. The tables will need to be moved manually using one of the following two alternatives:
  - Execute a table redistribution using the SAP HANA data warehousing foundation Data Distribution Optimizer (DDO).
  - Use Transaction RSHDBMON to manually move single tables or partitions.

Table 9.2 provides information about which SAP BW/4HANA objects can be classified as warm. Depending on the type of object, the data loading operations and reporting requirements may determine whether the object should be classified as warm. In any case, recommendations are provided for you to make case-by-case evaluations.

BW Object	Classification Comment	Recommendation
Advanced DSOs without activation	Can be classified as warm. Advanced DSO tables are partitioned by load request. Load operations only change the latest partition, which limits the merge process to a small amount of data. Extract operations only use the latest partition in most cases (i.e., delta loads).	Only Advanced DSOs with usage type **Corporate Memory** should be classified as warm, because they don't support reporting access ,nor are they used heavily as data lookup targets.
Advanced DSOs with activation	Load and extract patterns are request/partition-based.	DSO activation needs to load and process the complete table in-memory, so only Advanced DSOs with very infrequent load activity should be classified as warm; use range partitioning of the Advanced DSO where possible to allow pruning.

Table 9.2 SAP BW/4HANA Objects: Warm Classification Specifications

BW Object	Classification Comment	Recommendation
Advanced DSOs with reporting access	Load patterns are request/partition-based.	Query read access can load the complete table (all requested attributes/fields) to memory, and query processing may be very CPU-intensive. Only classify objects with the following: ■ Very infrequent reporting access ■ Highly selective access (few fields, selective filters hitting range partition criteria, if available) ■ Reduced performance expectations due to load-to-memory time and less CPU available
Range partitions of Advanced DSOs	Selected range partitions of Advanced DSOs can be classified as warm. Load and read patterns are request/partition-based.	DSO activation uses partition pruning; activation loads and processes the complete partition to memory. Only classify Advanced DSO partitions with very infrequent load activity as warm.

Table 9.2 SAP BW/4HANA Objects: Warm Classification Specifications (Cont.)

Note

Data can only be classified as warm if it fulfills the SAP BW/4HANA restrictions listed in Table 9.2. It isn't realistic to distribute more than 30–50 percent of your data into warm extension nodes. See SAP Note 2343647 for more information.

9.2.2   Cold Data in Near-Line Storage

The SAP's NLS interface was introduced in SAP BW 7.0 but could only be used with software developed by SAP development partners. The most promising solution was developed in Germany by software company PBS, a longtime SAP development partner with a primary focus on archiving. In its SAP BW NLS implementation, PBS opted for the analytic database platform Sybase IQ as the storage location for its NLS data and leveraged the column-based architecture of the database to achieve compression rates of 85–95 percent. SAP subsequently acquired Sybase and developed its own NLS solution for Sybase IQ, now referred to as SAP IQ, which was delivered with SAP BW release 7.3 SP 09 and can be used with all supported database versions. Even more recently, SAP has introduced NLS connectivity with Hadoop clusters.

SAP's NLS integration with SAP BW enables the archiving of rarely accessed data from the online database to a near-line database, where it's dramatically compressed. The near-line data can still be accessed by SAP BW/4HANA processes such as queries and data loads while reducing the storage capacity requirements of the online database. SAP's NLS thus provides a balance between cost and performance. Additional benefits can include data loading performance improvements and a reduction in the SAP BW/4HANA footprint.

The objective is to achieve a steady state for storage capacity by near-lining historical data and keeping current data online. Figure 9.3 shows a real-world projection for a 5 TB database. In this example, all but three months of data would remain online; anything older would be near-lined. Over time, the online database size would grow much more slowly than the compressed near-line data, thus reducing the future costs of additional in-memory storage capacity.

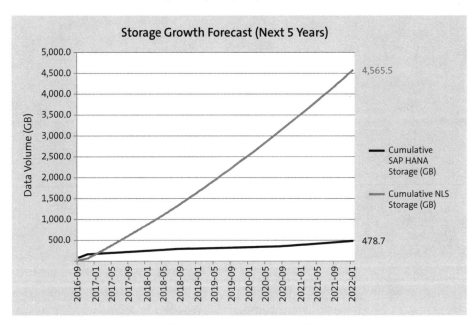

Figure 9.3 Example of Organic Storage Growth Forecast with NLS

The near-line process removes data in time slices to the SAP IQ database. All near-lined time intervals of an InfoProvider are then locked for load processes in SAP BW/4HANA, so only static data is a candidate for NLS. Any data that could change—either by full load or delta—should remain online or, if already near-lined, will need to be restored from NLS before it can be loaded successfully. The archival process is highly complex but can be easily managed in both directions using SAP BW/4HANA data archiving processes (DAPs), which can also be scheduled in process chains.

Apart from this restriction, the near-lined data remains available at any time for all other processes in SAP BW/4HANA, such as query read accesses and ETL process lookups. Queries that analyze data over longer periods of time are split and procure data from the online database and from SAP IQ.

Tip

Consult SAP Notes 1737415 and 1796393 to install and configure NLS using SAP IQ.

9.3 Data Archiving

As described in Section 9.2.2, the DAP is used to move data from SAP BW/4HANA to NLS (SAP IQ or Hadoop) before it's deleted from SAP BW/4HANA. The data can then be accessed directly from NLS or loaded back into SAP BW/4HANA as required, depending on how the data was archived.

For Advanced DSOs, you can store the data in NLS using a data archiving process. Storing historical data in NLS reduces the data volume of InfoProviders, but the data is still available for queries. You don't have to load the data back into the SAP BW/4HANA system. The database partitions and the NLS partitions for an InfoProvider consistently reflect the total dataset.

The data archiving process consists of three main steps:

1. Creating the archive data/near-line objects
2. Storing the archive file in NLS
3. Deleting the archived data from the database

A data archiving process can only be assigned to one specific InfoProvider. It always shares the same name as the InfoProvider but can be created at any time after the InfoProvider—even if the InfoProvider is already filled with data.

The data archiving process will generate a near-line object for every InfoProvider directly in the NLS solution for you, meaning you don't need access to the NLS solution yourself. Near-line objects consist of different near-line segments that reflect different views and different versions of the InfoProvider.

The data archiving processes can also be transported like all TLOGO objects, but the NLS connection name must be the same in all the systems in the landscape; there is no NLS connection mapping table like there is for source systems.

In the following subsections, we'll cover how to create NLS connections in SAP BW/4HANA and how to create remote sources in SAP HANA directly. We'll review specifics for using SAP IQ and Hadoop as near-line solutions and then dive into creating data archiving processes to move data from hot storage (SAP HANA) to cold storage (NLS). We'll wrap up the chapter by discussing how to administrate data archiving processes and how to read data from NLS in transformations.

9.3.1 Creating Near-Line Storage Connections

Before you can create a data archiving process with NLS, you first must create a connection to your NLS solution as follows:

1. Call the transaction for processing near-line storage, either in Customizing under **SAP BW/4HANA Customizing Implementation Guide • SAP BW/4HANA • Information Lifecycle Management • Edit Near-Line Storage Connection** or in the Data Warehousing Workbench under **Administration • Current Settings • Near-Line Storage Connections**.

2. Choose **New Entries**.

3. Enter a name for the NLS connection (see Figure 9.4). This name is then offered for selection when you create a data archiving process.

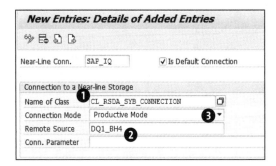

Figure 9.4 Creating New NLS Connection

4. Specify if you want the connection to be the default connection. When you create a new data archiving process, the default connection is used automatically.

5. Enter the name of the class that implements the NLS connection. There are two options in the dropdown list: CL_RSDA_SYB_CONNECTION for SAP IQ and CL_RSDA_HDP_CONNECTION for Hadoop. Choose the class for the NLS solution you're implementing.

6. Specify the near-line connection mode. This defines the operation mode of the NLS connection. The following modes are supported:

   – **Productive Mode**
   This mode is recommended for productive use. Every operation on the near-line connection is passed to the near-line provider. If the NLS isn't available while in productive mode, queries against near-line providers will be terminated with an error message unless a pruning mechanism has been designed into the data model to exclude near-line access when querying online data.

   – **Query Emergency Mode**
   Use this mode if NLS is temporarily unavailable. While in this mode, queries return empty result sets from every near-line provider assigned to this near-line connection, and a warning message is sent to the frontend as well. All other operations—such as moving data into or out of NLS (like archiving and restoring), data extraction from NLS (for ETL processes in SAP BW/4HANA), or creating new near-line tables/editing existing ones—terminate with an error message, without the corresponding near-line interface method being called. Use this mode during NLS maintenance or service interruptions.

   – **Read-Only Mode**
   This mode is like the productive mode, except no operations can be transferred to NLS. In other words, no DDL commands (create, edit and store near-line tables) or DML commands (create, edit near-line requests, open writer handles) are allowed at the near-line interface level. Any SAP BW/4HANA process that triggers a command of this type will prompt an error message indicating that the command isn't possible in this mode.

   This mode can be used during system migrations to SAP HANA if both the original system and the copied system will use the same NLS.

   – **Off**
   This mode should only be used if the NLS has been permanently disconnected from the system, but there are still active DAPs in the system. In this mode, all DDL and DML commands return an error message. Errors of type DROP_TABLE are

ignored to allow deletion of DAPs without having to connect the NLS system again. Every read access on near-line data returns an empty result set, because the system expects all near-line requests and the corresponding data to be deleted.

7. In the **DB Connection** field, enter the destination name of the host on which the SAP IQ or Hadoop WebHCat service is running.

8. In the **Remote Source** field, enter the SAP HANA smart data access (SDA) remote source, which should have already been created in SAP HANA Studio. See Section 9.3.2 for information on creating remote sources.

Note

With SAP BW/4HANA SPS 01 and higher, it's mandatory to access the data in SAP IQ via SDA. If you've upgraded from a previous version of SAP BW to SAP BW/4HANA and you have an existing NLS connection that was previously defined without a remote source, you'll need to assign a remote source to the connection. New NLS connections can only be created if a remote source has been specified.

If a remote source has been assigned to an existing near-line connection, then SDA is used for a query on the near-line provider, SAP HANA. To ensure that existing data archiving processes can use SDA, they need to be reactivated.

When you create new DAPs or reactivate an existing DAP, a virtual table is created in SAP HANA when the DAPs are activated. The creation of the virtual table is written to the activation log.

---

9. Enter a connection string in the **Connection Parameters** field. The connection string generally comprises a list of name/value pairs separated by semicolon and specific to your NLS solution. Each name/value pair must be entered as follows: `<Name of the parameter>=<Value of the parameter>`. For more information on individual parameters, see the `F1` help. For Hadoop, enter the following string: `HDFS_DEST=<Name of host destination on which the WebHDFS service is running>;REMOTE_SOURCE=<Name of remote source>`.

10. Save your entries. When you save, the connection to the NLS solution is opened and then closed again. The NLS solution then returns a status that indicates whether the connection is working and providing system information. In the top area of the screen, the system displays the connection, the connection status, and system information. The log is displayed in the bottom area of the screen.

9.3.2   Creating a Remote Source in SAP HANA Studio

To access the data in NLS via SDA, you need a remote source. The remote source in SAP HANA should point to the same SAP IQ database used as NLS for the SAP BW/4HANA system. The remote source should also be bound to the same user as the NLS connection. You create the remote source under the **Provisioning** folder in SAP HANA Studio, as shown in Figure 9.5. Right-click the **Remote Sources** subfolder ❶ and choose **New Remote Source**.

Figure 9.5 Provisioning Folder in SAP HANA Studio

- Object privilege: CREATE VIRTUAL TABLE on VIRTUAL_TABLES (SYS)
- Object privilege: DROP on VIRTUAL_TABLES (SYS)

A screen will open in which you can define the type of remote source you want to create, as shown in Figure 9.6. To create a remote source for SAP IQ, select **IQ (ODBC)** from the dropdown list for **Adapter Name ➋** and enter the following information:

- **Source Name**
  Enter a name for the remote source ➊.
- **Source Location**
  Enter "indexserver".
- **Connection Properties**
  - **Connection Mode**
    Choose **Adapter Properties** to inherit the properties of the installed adapter.
  - **DML Mode**
    Choose **readonly** to improve performance.
  - **Extra Adapter Properties**
    Specify the IQ connection details ➌.
- **Credentials**
  - **Credentials Mode**
    Choose **Technical User**.
  - **User Name**
    Enter a user with database rights on the SAP IQ server ➍.
  - **Password**
    Enter the user's configured password.

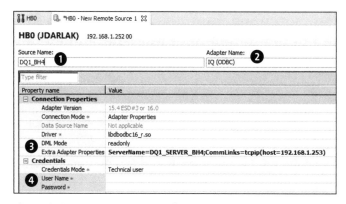

Figure 9.6 New Remote Source for ODBC Connection to SAP IQ

To create a remote source for Hadoop, you must have already installed and configured the SAP HANA Spark Controller, as described in the documentation delivered
with SAP Note 2344239. In the new remote source screen, shown in Figure 9.7, choose
SPARK SQL (DESTINATION) from the **Adapter Name** dropdown list ❷ and enter the following information:

- **Source Name**
  Enter a name for the remote source ❶.

- **Source Location**
  Enter "indexserver".

- **Connection Properties**
  - **Server**
    Enter the fully qualified domain name for the Hadoop node on which the Spark
    Controller is running ❸.
  - **Port**
    Set to **7860** by default, but enter the configured port for the Spark Controller if
    different.
  - **SSL Mode**
    Choose either **Enabled** or **Disabled** depending on your security strategy.

- **Credentials**
  - **Credentials Mode**
    Choose **Technical User**.
  - **User Name**
    Enter the user name that you created in the first step of the Hadoop configura-
    tion ❹.
  - **Password**
    Enter the user's configured password.

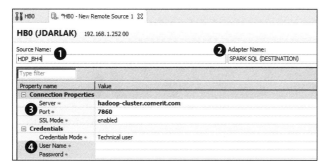

Figure 9.7 New Remote Source for Connection to Hadoop Spark Controller

After the remote source is saved, you can test the connection to confirm a connection to the source can be successfully established. Once connected, the remote source and all its tables are now displayed in the **Remote Source** folder.

9.3.3   Using SAP IQ for Near-Line Storage

The adapter for SAP IQ as a near-line solution is delivered with SAP BW/4HANA. The integration of SAP IQ into your landscape enables the separation of data accessed frequently from data that is rarely accessed, thus reducing the demand on system resources in your SAP BW/4HANA system. The near-line data is stored in compressed form and needs to be backed up less frequently. SAP IQ is simply a lower-cost storage solution for data accessed less frequently.

To ensure consistency between online data and near-line data, the archived time partitions are locked and are read-only. The online data also becomes read-only by means of a logical lock on the time slice. The data in NLS can be read directly using queries against the SAP BW/4HANA InfoProvider.

The data in the SAP IQ NLS is accessed via SDA. As covered in Chapter 8, SDA reads the remote data without replicating the data into the SAP HANA database. Only the requested data at the desired granularity is read back into SAP HANA across SDA, because the SELECT statement with a GROUP BY clause is pushed to SAP IQ.

More Information

Consult SAP Notes 2165650 and 2100962 for more information and FAQs on SDA.

Prerequisites

Before you can define an SAP IQ connection, you must have installed the SAP IQ Server and SQL Anywhere ODBC driver. For more information, see SAP Notes 1737415 and 1796393.

Backup for the Near-Line Connection

You can set up an automatic data backup for the near-line connection between SAP IQ and SAP BW/4HANA. If errors occur, it will then be possible to restore consistency between SAP BW/4HANA and SAP IQ.

As a prerequisite, the database user used for the near-line connection between SAP IQ and SAP BW/4HANA needs sufficient authorizations to trigger an event via the following process:

1. Define a suitable event in Sybase IQ.
2. Specify the name of the event in the connection parameters for the near-line connection in the SAP BW/4HANA system. For more information about defining the event and about the process in general, see SAP Note 1900379.

Moving data from SAP BW/4HANA into SAP IQ creates a partitioned table for every InfoProvider in the SAP IQ database. The system creates a new partition for every new archiving request. It does this either by splitting the MAX partition, which should always be empty, or by splitting the partition that belongs to the previous archiving request.

SAP IQ version 16 can manage up to 1,024 partitions per table. If you move data to SAP IQ very frequently, you might reach the upper limit for partitions, in which case you can manage the partitions.

You can monitor and reduce the number of partitions using report RSDA_SYB_PAR-TITION_MONITOR. The report attempts to reduce the partitions by deleting or merging them. To start, all partitions are deleted that are flagged for deletion or as invalid. The system deletes the partitions in order of age, starting with the oldest. If this deletion step doesn't bring the number of partitions back below the limit, the system merges the partitions.

Prerequisites

To run the report to display which activities are being executed or to run it in simulation mode, you need authorization STOR for field S_ADMI_FCD in authorization object S_ADMI_FCD and authorization 03 (Display) for field ACTVT in authorization object S_RZL_ADM.

To merge or delete partitions manually, you also need authorization 01 (Add or Create) for field ACTVT in authorization object S_RZL_ADM.

You can run the SAP IQ Partition Monitor manually by running report RSDA_SYB_PARTITION_MONITOR in the dialog, or you can schedule it to run periodically in the background. You can choose to run it for the NLS connection and it will check all the tables, or you can specify a specific database table or tables in SAP IQ.

The report also allows you to specify a lower and upper threshold value for the number of partitions per table. The default setting is 20 percent for the lower threshold and 80 percent for the upper threshold. The system will first check for tables exceeding the upper threshold (i.e., with over 80 percent of the maximum number of partitions) and then reduce the partitions for this table until the lower threshold is reached.

If you run the report in the background, the partitions are processed automatically in accordance with the system proposal, but if you run the report in the dialog, the system first displays a list of all selected tables. All tables in which the number of partitions exceeds the upper threshold value are marked in red in the **Partitions** column. By double-clicking a row, you can access the detail view for the partitions in the table. Here, you'll see one partition per row. In the **Action** column, you can see the options available for reducing the number of partitions. If you choose execution mode **Drop and Merge Partitions**, you have the following options:

- No icon: This partition can't be deleted or merged with another partition.
- 🗑: This partition can be deleted.
- 🗗: This partition can be merged with the following partition.

In **Drop Partitions (no Merge)** execution mode, you'll only see partitions that can be deleted. In **Merge Partitions (no Drop)** execution mode, you'll only see partitions that can be merged.

You can select one or more rows and choose 🔄 **Drop & Merge** to initiate the actions proposed for the selected rows. Initially, all rows are selected that need to be processed to reach the lower threshold value. In the **Seq.No** column, you can see the sequence in which the merge will be performed.

The report starts by attempting to delete all partitions that only contain requests with request status **Invalid (8)**. It will process the oldest requests first. As soon as the lower threshold is reached, the report stops deleting. If the deletion completes and the lower threshold hasn't been reached, the report attempts to merge neighboring partitions. Neighboring partitions are always merged if they only contain requests that have the request status **Active (7)**. The system starts by merging neighboring partitions that produce the smallest result partitions. As soon as the lower threshold is reached, the report stops merging.

The Partition Monitor can also be scheduled via a process chain by using the application process type **SAP IQ Partition Monitor**, which can be found in process category **Others** in the **Process Chains** of the Data Warehousing Workbench.

The process step is completed successfully once the upper threshold value is no longer exceeded for any of the selected tables. If the upper threshold value remains exceeded for one or more of the selected tables, the process step ends with an error. You now can use the alerting function in the process chains to send an email to the system administrator.

9.3.4 Using Hadoop for Near-Line Storage

You can use Hadoop as NLS for SAP BW/4HANA and store archived data in Hadoop for all objects supported by NLS. The adapter for Hadoop as a near-line solution is delivered with SAP BW/4HANA.

The *Hadoop Distributed File System (HDFS)* provides inexpensive, distributed storage that's been created for mass data. The integration of Hadoop enables you to separate data for which there is limited access or no access at all from data accessed frequently. This reduces the strain on the system and thereby reduces the costs of data with limited access.

To ensure consistency between online data and near-line data, the archived time partitions are locked and are read-only. On the online side, the data is made read-only by means of a logical lock on the time slice. The data in NLS can be read directly using analytic queries without having to be reloaded. SDA is used for query access related to data stored in NLS. The data is accessed from Hadoop via the Spark SQL adapter.

Caution

SAP recommends that you only use Hadoop as NLS if a Hadoop cluster has already been configured in your IT landscape. To use a Hadoop cluster as NLS, you need sufficient knowledge of cluster management.

SAP recommends Hadoop as NLS specifically for the entry layer of the data warehouse (data collection and corporate memory only; no reporting).

Note that the data archived to Hadoop still belongs to SAP BW/4HANA and therefore no direct data manipulation with HDFS-based tools is possible.

More Information

For more information on prerequisites, recommendations, and restrictions, see SAP Note 2363218.

See Figure 9.8 for an overview of the architecture of the Hadoop NLS solution. The NLS table definitions in Hadoop are created via Hive. Data is archived via a RESTful API from SAP BW/4HANA to Hadoop Hive. Query access and reloading are supported by the Spark SQL adapter via SDA.

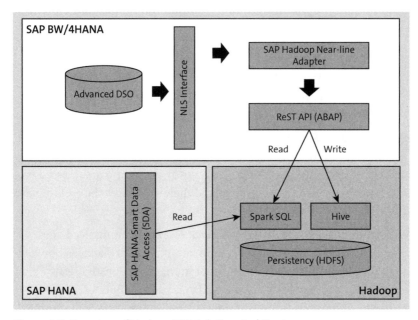

Figure 9.8 Overview of Hadoop NLS Solution Architecture

In the following subsections, we'll cover in detail how to configure Hadoop as an NLS solution in both SAP BW/4HANA and SAP HANA. We'll also provide recommendations for archiving with Hadoop.

Configuring Hadoop as a Near-Line Storage Solution

Before you can use Hadoop as an NLS solution, you need a Hadoop cluster and the required components with the minimum recommended versions or higher. To ensure you have all the components, check the list of required components and versions in Table 9.3.

More Information

For more information on prerequisites, recommendations, and restrictions, see SAP Note 2363218.

Component	More Information
HDFS 2.7.1 Apache Hadoop Distributed File System	*https://hadoop.apache.org/docs/stable/*
MapReduce2 2.7.1 Apache Hadoop NextGen MapReduce (yet another resource negotiator [YARN])	*https://hadoop.apache.org/docs/stable/*
YARN 2.7.1 Apache Hadoop NextGen MapReduce (YARN)	*https://hadoop.apache.org/docs/stable/*
Tez 0.7.0 (Tez is the next generation Hadoop Query Processing framework written on top of YARN)	*https://tez.apache.org/*
Hive 1.2.1 Data warehouse system for ad hoc queries and analysis of large datasets and table and storage management service	*https://hive.apache.org/*
Pig 0.15.0 Scripting platform for analyzing large datasets	*https://pig.apache.org/*
ZooKeeper 3.4.6 Centralized service that provides highly reliable distributed coordination	*http://zookeeper.apache.org/*
For SDA with SAP HANA's Spark controller, Spark 1.5.2 (Apache Spark is a fast and general engine for large-scale data processing.)	*https://spark.apache.org/*
SparkController 1.6.0 PL1 SAP HANA Spark Controller	SAP Note 2344239
Optional for authentication: Knox	*https://knox.apache.org/*

Table 9.3 Components (Specified Versions or Higher) Required for Hadoop Cluster

When you've confirmed your Hadoop cluster has all the prerequisite components and versions, then you can complete the necessary configuration tasks:

1. Perform the configuration steps for Hadoop.

2. Perform the configuration steps for SAP HANA.

3. Perform the configuration steps in SAP BW/4HANA.

The following steps describe the procedure for simple authentication on Hadoop (you can find information on other authentication methods in the Hadoop documentation under *https://hadoop.apache.org/docs/stable/hadoop-auth/* or in the relevant documentation):

1. Create a user for the SAP BW/4HANA system on Hadoop. This user is used to establish a connection to Hadoop and controls the authorizations for data access on Hadoop. Create the user at the operating system level on all Hadoop nodes. The recommended naming convention for the user is as follows:

   ```
   sap<SAP BW/4HANA system ID in lowercase letters> (sap<sid>).
   sudo useradd sap<sid>
   ```

2. Create a group for the SAP BW/4HANA system. Use the same name for the group as you did for the user just created, as follows:

   ```
   sudo groupadd sap<sid>
   ```

3. Add the user you created in step 1 and the dfs, hive, spark, and hanaes users to the new group, as follows:

   ```
   sudo usermod <user name> -a -G sap<sid>
   ```

   User names:

   - hdfs

   - hive

   - spark

   - hanaes

4. Using a user authorized to create folders in the root directory of HDFS, create a directory for the SAP BW/4HANA system. In a local operating system, this is usually the hdfs user. The recommended naming convention for this directory is as follows:

   - */sap/bw/<SAP BW/4HANA system ID in lowercase letters> (/sap/bw/<sid>).*

   ```
   hdfs dfs -mkdir -p /sap/bw/<sid>
   ```

   Confirm the */sap/bw/<sid>* directory exists.

5. Change the owner rights for the directory */sap/bw/<sid>* so that the directory belongs to the user and group which you created in the first two steps (sap<sid>):

```
hdfs dfs -chown <user name>:<group name> /sap/bw/<sid>
hdfs dfs -chown sap<sid>:sap<sid> /sap/bw/<sid>
```

6. Change the access rights for the folder so that the sap<sid> user who owns the directory has all permissions (read, write, execute) and the sap<sid> group has at least read and execute permissions, as follows:

```
hdfs dfs -chmod 750 /sap/bw/<sid>
```

7. Optional: Using the sap<sid> user, create additional directories under the /<sid> directory, as follows (see Table 9.4 for directory specifications):

```
hdfs dfs -mkdir -p /sap/bw/<sid>/<NLS directory>
```

NLS Directory	Purpose
nldata	Data directory that contains files for external Hive tables
nlmeta	Metadata directory that contains the DDL statements for the Hive tables created
nljobs	Control data and log data for Hive jobs

Table 9.4 NLS File Directories for Hadoop

> **Note**
>
> The NLS directories step is optional because the directories are created automatically by the SAP BW/4HANA system when accessed for the first time. However, this step can be useful—for example, if you need to assign specific access rights for the directories.

8. Create a database named sap<sid> in Hive. A database in Hive corresponds to a schema. You can use the hive user to run the following command in a node where the hive client is installed:

```
hive -e 'create database sap<sid>;'
```

Check if the sap<sid> database already exists.

9. Create a dedicated YARN queue for templeton controller jobs.

10. Assign the name of the YARN queue in the Hive configuration file hive-site.xml to the property with the key templeton.hadoop.queue.name.

11. Ensure that the WebHDFS and WebHCat services are correctly configured.

12. *Optional*: Install and configure the Apache Knox Gateway to establish secure WebHDFS and WebHCat connectivity to the SAP BW/4HANA system.

13. Install and configure the SAP HANA Spark Controller as described in the documentation delivered with SAP Note 2344239.

Configurations in SAP HANA and SAP BW/4HANA

In SAP HANA, you need to create a remote source, as described previously in Section 9.3.2. In SAP BW/4HANA, you need destinations for communication with Hadoop and you need to create a connection to Hadoop NLS, as described previously in Section 9.3.1.

Communication between SAP BW/4HANA and Hadoop occurs via the WebHDFS and WebHCat (Templeton) RESTful APIs. In the configuration screen for each RFC connection, create an HTTP connection for the server on which the WebHDFS or WebHCat service is running, as follows:

1. Go to the **Configuration** screen of Transaction SM59 (RFC Connections).

2. Choose **Edit/Create** from the menu.

3. Enter a name for the RFC connection and assign a description.

4. Choose the **G-HTTP** connection to an external server as the connection type.

5. Make the following settings on the **Technical Settings** tab:
   - For WebHCat:
     - **Target Machine**
       Enter the hostname where the WebHCat service is running.
     - **Service Number**
       50111 is the default value, but use the port selected in the Hadoop configuration if it's different.
     - **Path Prefix**
       Enter "/templeton".
   - For WebHDFS:
     - **Target Machine**
       Enter the hostname where the WebHDFS service is running.
     - **Service Number**
       50070 is the default value, but use the port selected in the Hadoop configuration if it's different.
     - **Path Prefix**
       Enter "/webhdfs".

6. If you use plain HTTP communication and you haven't implemented any security mechanisms on Hadoop, then keep the default settings for the destination.

7. To run a connection check, press ⌈Enter⌋. The system will open the connection to the NLS and then close it again. The NLS solution returns a status indicating whether the connection is working and providing system information. In the upper area of the screen, the system displays the connection with its status and system information. The log is displayed in the lower part of the screen. A successful check is indicated by an appropriate successful status message.

8. Save your settings.

Recommendations for Archiving with Hadoop

To achieve the optimal archiving throughput, SAP recommends using the available parallelization options for DAPs for NLS and Hadoop (e.g., separate variants in process chains and settings for parallelization). Make sure that the configured parallelization is compatible with the existing resources on the Hadoop cluster. For the archiving process, it's necessary to convert the CSV files created during the copy phase to ORC (Parquet) format. This requires sufficient resources. If there aren't enough resources available, this results in a suboptimal serialization of the processes, which can lead to long-running background processes or timeouts in SAP BW/4HANA.

To establish a secure connection, you can use the Apache Knox Gateway as a reverse proxy on Hadoop, configure a suitable authentication method (e.g., Kerberos), and import the relevant certificates in the SAP BW/4HANA system using Transaction TRUST (Trust Manager). Then, you can call Transaction SM59 (HTTP Destination for WebHCat and WebHDFS), go to the **Logon and Security** tab, choose **Basic Authentication** as the logon procedure, and activate SSL in the security options.

9.3.5   Creating Data Archiving Processes

In the following subsections, we'll cover in detail how to activate and configure a DAP. Then, we'll review a few points to consider for Advanced DSOs with inbound tables before describing how to change existing DAPs.

Activating and Configuring Archiving

For Advanced DSOs with the properties **Activate Data** and **Write Change Log** or **Activate Data** and **All Characteristics are Key, Reporting on Union of Inbound and Active Table**, the data must be activated before it can be archived.

> **Note**
>
> Advanced DSOs must adhere to the following prerequisites to be eligible for archiving:
>
> - They must not contain any noncumulative key figures.
> - One of the modeling properties must have been selected.
> - The maximum length for any field is 18 characters.

To configure archiving for an Advanced DSO, follow this procedure:

1. In the SAP BW/4HANA modeling tools, go to the editing screen of the Advanced DSO to be archived. Choose **Manage the Data Archiving Process**.
2. The DAP contains the same technical name as the InfoProvider. Enter a description.
3. Select a near-line connection in the **General Settings** tab. The default near-line connection is predefined for a new data archiving process.
4. Specify which data should be archived from the InfoProvider in the **Selection Profile** tab.

   As far as the selected time characteristic is concerned, time slice archiving always creates time intervals that directly follow one another chronologically. These intervals can be linked to additional, time-independent partitioning characteristics. You can use these characteristics to further refine the selection of data to be archived.

> **Note**
>
> To create the best possible conditions for using queries against data in NLS, the selected time characteristic should be included in the filter conditions of each query execution.
>
> For a DSO, you can only select a key characteristic as the partitioning characteristic in time slice archiving. This is necessary to ensure that the archived records are consistent, which isn't the case with non-key fields. The characteristic for the time slice generation can also be a non-key characteristic. However, you then must select a separate partitioning characteristic from the key with no relationship to the time characteristic so that the time conditions can be applied to it (such as **Clearing Date** in the data part and **Document Number** in the key). At runtime, the system attempts to apply the time restriction to a partitioning characteristic restriction. For more information, see SAP Note 1000784.
>
> You can't select constant values as characteristics for time slice archiving.

> You can also specify that uncompressed data can be archived. If you don't compress data, you can save time and memory space during compression. You can change this setting while the system is running. However, you should only do this once all archiving runs have finished. Note that requests can no longer be deleted once compressed.

5. Specify a maximum size for the data package in the **Near-Line Storage** tab. You should take the memory capacity of your storage medium into account, which can be restricted by the number of data objects. During an archiving run, a new data package is created when the maximum size is reached.

6. Activate the DAP. Once it's active, you can no longer change many of the settings.

The activated DAP can be executed manually or scheduled via process chains.

Advanced DSOs with Inbound Tables: Points to Consider

To archive data from Advanced DSOs with inbound tables, all requests must be updated first. There are also several additional points to consider when creating a data archiving process. On the **General Settings** tab, request-based archiving is the default setting and can't be changed, because the contents of these DSOs are managed by requests and because the request transaction number (TSN) is the primary technical key characteristic of this type of DSO.

Request-based archiving is a special form of time slice archiving, and only complete requests can be archived. The time slice condition is converted into a request condition. If it isn't possible to select an entire complete request with the selected time slice condition, then no data is archived.

A technical attribute of the load request (e.g., **Request Creation Date** or **Request Load Date**) can also be selected as a time slice characteristic. Subsequent processing is the same as for standard DSOs.

On the **Selection Profile** tab, you can also select the **Request Load Date** or **Request Creation Date** technical characteristic as the characteristic for time slices. This type of DSO doesn't have a semantic key; therefore, it's only possible to select a characteristic for time slices, rather than a partitioning characteristic.

> **Caution**
> This means that when data is being archived or loaded, no check is performed to determine if the data has already been archived or loaded.

Individual requests can't be reloaded, because no gaps are allowed in this kind of Advanced DSO. The subsequent requests must therefore always be reloaded as well.

Changes to the Data Archiving Process

If you've created a data archiving process for an InfoProvider, you can only make limited changes to the InfoProvider. This ensures that you can still archive data and access archived data.

The following changes aren't permitted:

- If you delete a DAP, you lose the connection to the data that has already been archived.
- Only the type changes or structure changes listed ahead are permitted if data has already been stored in NLS.

You can only make incompatible structure changes if no data has been archived or if the archived data has been completely reloaded. The following type changes and structure changes are permitted when using NLS:

- You can add new characteristics and key figures.
- You can increase the length of characteristics of data type CHAR.
- You can change characteristics of data type DATS, NUMC, and TIMS into data type CHAR, so long as you don't shorten the character length.
- You can change characteristics of data type DATS and TIMS into data type NUMC, so long as you don't change the character length.
- You can change key figures of data type INT4 into data type DEC, CURR, or QUAN, so long as you don't reduce the value range (number of whole number places).
- With key figures of data type CURR, DEC, and QUAN, you can expand the value range (number of whole number places) or the accuracy (number of decimal places).
- You can change key figures of data type CURR, DEC, and QUAN into data type INT4, so long as you expand the value range.

9.3.6   Administration of Data Archiving Processes

In the administration of an InfoProvider, you can create an archiving request for active DAPs. With data archiving processes that store the data in NLS, you can create a request, lock the selection area, write the data to NLS, verify the storage, and delete the data from the InfoProvider. At any point before the verification, you can mark the request as invalid. Once the request has completed, all the steps involved and the overall status are green. You can now reload the data back into the InfoProvider.

In the following subsections, we'll review step by step how to create and execute archiving requests, check the status of an archiving request, and invalidate an archiving request.

Creating and Executing Archiving Requests

When you've created and activated a DAP for an InfoProvider, you can create an archiving request manually without using a process chain.

1. In the SAP BW/4HANA modeling tools, go to the editing screen for your Advanced DSO. Choose ▥ **Manage DataStore Object (advanced)**.
2. Under ▣ **Manage Archiving**, you can create an archiving request.
3. Choose ▯ **Create Archiving Request**.
4. Make the required settings:
   - Under **Primary Time Restrictions**, specify the exact partition range you want to archive.
   - Under **Further Restrictions**, you can set further restrictions using the characteristics you defined as additional partitioning characteristics.
   - Under **Process Flow Control**, specify whether you want to resume unfinished archiving processes or whether archiving processes should only run until a specific status is reached.
   - Choose between **Test Mode** and **Productive Mode**. In test mode, only tests are run; no data is archived.
5. Before starting the archiving session in productive mode, you can execute it in test mode:
   - To perform the run in test mode, choose ▦ **In the Background** or ▦ **In Dialog**.
   - To perform the run in productive mode, choose ⊕ **In the Background** or ⊕ **In Dialog**.
6. Choose **Back**. The generated archiving request is displayed.
7. You can start other processing steps using the status columns, discussed in the next subsection. The status of the request depends on what was specified under **Process Flow Control**. You can execute the rest of the steps by choosing the pushbutton for the last status entry.
8. In the **Archiving Request Monitor**, you can view a list of archiving requests. By double-clicking a request, you can view the archived data.

By choosing **Goto • Sybase IQ** (may be **SAP IQ**, depending on version), you can view the table contents for a selected near-line connection and a schema. If you switch to ▣ **Expert Mode**, you can create your own SELECT statement to display certain data. Via **SQL statements**, you can view a list of the current statements. Via **SQL statistics**, you can view the SAP IQ statistics.

If the archiving request has run in productive mode and the status is green, the data has been archived.

> **Note**
>
> The DSO being archived isn't locked against data loading during the entire process. It only needs to be locked for a short period before the data is copied. After this, only the previously archived data areas and the area that is currently being archived are locked.

Status of Archiving Request

In the administration of an archiving request, you can view and execute additional processing steps using the last status. The **Copy Status**, **Verification Status**, **Deletion Status**, and **Overall Status** columns show the status of the various phases of the archival process using icons and traffic lights. An icon in one of the four status columns becomes a pushbutton via which you can execute further processing steps if there's no longer an active process for the request, and the request can be continued or repeated (after an error) in the corresponding phase. When you press the button, a dialog appears in which the request can be continued.

The following list explains what's executed during the phase when each status is set:

- **Lock Status**
  You can lock the selected data area of the archiving request to prevent any changes. This is necessary before data archiving begins. This step can be executed in dialog mode.

- **Copy Status**
  The data to be archived is copied into NLS or the archive. This step is executed in the background. When the write phrase is complete, the archiving request can be marked as invalid if your requirements have changed in the meantime. The data to be archived is still available in the InfoProvider.

- **Verification Status**
  In the verification phase, the system checks that the write phase was successful

and the data can be deleted from the InfoProvider. The archive file assigned to the process is opened in test mode and read completely. This ensures the archive file is complete and can be accessed. If the check is successful, this is noted in a separate status table for the archive file.

- **Deletion Status**
When the archived data is deleted from the InfoProvider, the archiving process is complete. The archived data is deleted from the InfoProvider with the same selection conditions used to copy the data from the InfoProvider. Once the data has been successfully deleted from the InfoProvider, all the archive files from the archiving run are confirmed using NLS.

- **Overall Status**
Once all steps of the archiving request have been completed, you can't change the status of the request any longer, but you can reload the data by creating another request for the reload.

Setting Archiving Requests to Invalid

An archiving request can have a yellow status during the write and verification phases for a variety of reasons. You can set such a request to invalid either automatically or manually to create a new archiving request and restart archiving. The archiving request is then automatically flagged for deletion if it has already been created as a near-line request.

With automatic request invalidation, an archiving request with a yellow status during the write or verification phase is automatically set to invalid. This prevents an InfoProvider from being locked against further actions. This is beneficial when a DSO has a time slice characteristic used as a primary partitioning characteristic in the archive. Without automatic invalidation, the DSO remains locked, which can impact data loads and report activation.

You can set an archiving request to invalid manually in the archiving administration transaction. This allows you to automatically set to invalid both archiving runs that have a yellow status during the write or verification phase and terminated reload requests.

9.3.7 Reading Near-Line Storage Data in Transformation Rules

The CL_RSDA_INFOPROV_QUERY lookup API allows you to use a transformation rule routine to read data from the active table of a DSO containing data that's been partially stored in NLS.

The static method SELECT has the following parameters:

- Importing parameters
  - I_INFOPROV: InfoProvider
  - I_T_ENTRIES (optional): table FOR ALL ENTRIES
  - I_T_ENTRY_FIELDS (optional): Fields of table FOR ALL ENTRIES
  - I_T_FIELD_SELECTIONS (optional): Selection clause
  - I_R_SELECTION_SET (optional): Selection condition as a multidimensional set object
  - I_WHERE_CONDITION (optional): Selection condition as an OpenSQL expression on the active table
  - I_APPEND (optional): Indicator: Adding selected records to C_T_DATA
- Changing parameters
  - C_T_DATA: Return table for selected data records of the active table
- Exception conditions (exceptions)
  - CX_RSDA_INPUT_INVALID: Incorrect input parameterization
  - CX_RSDA_ACCESS_ERROR: Error while accessing data

Note

The lookup API works with the field names derived from the characteristic names (e.g., field name EMPL_ID for characteristic **OEMPL_ID** or field name /BIC/EMPL_ID for the characteristic **EMPL_ID** in the customer namespace) and not with the characteristic names themselves.

For more information, see SAP Notes 985609 and 1028450.

In the following subsections, we'll briefly cover what near-line data can be reloaded back into SAP BW/4HANA and how to reload such data with DTPs. We'll also specify how to read NLS data in queries from CompositeProviders.

Reloading Near-Line Storage Data Using the Data Archiving Process

You can reload data that has already been archived back into the same InfoProvider with a data archiving process. This restores the content of the InfoProvider to its original, unarchived composition. When near-line requests are reloaded, the archiving request is automatically flagged for deletion.

The reload request is directly related to the archiving request for which it's created. If it terminates in error, you can flag the reload request as invalid and create a new one.

> **Note**
>
> You can only reload the data to the original InfoProvider using the reload function. You can't use a DTP. Follow this procedure:
>
> 1. Go to the InfoProvider administration screen.
> 2. Create a reload request by click the button in the completed request's **Overall Status** column.

Loading Near-Line Storage Data Using a Data Transfer Process

InfoProvider data that has been archived using a DAP can be loaded into other Info-Providers with a DTP. Create a transformation and a DTP using the archived InfoProvider as a source to load data to a target InfoProvider directly from the archive.

In the DTP, you can decide whether you want to extract from the archive by choosing the appropriate option in the **Extraction** tab under **Extraction From**. You don't need to select the pertinent archiving sessions.

The filter conditions of the DTP are mapped to the selection conditions of the current archiving sessions before the archive is accessed, meaning that an intersection is calculated. If they overlap, the relevant archiving request is opened automatically for extraction.

Reading Near-Line Storage Data in a Query

You can read the data archived to NLS when executing a query by configuring access to the near-line data either in the properties of the CompositeProvider or in the properties of the query created on the InfoProvider. In the default setting, access to data in NLS is deactivated, even if a DAP with NLS exists for an InfoProvider.

> **Tip**
>
> Create a variable on characteristic ONEARLINE to enable the flexibility to choose whether to read from NLS when executing queries.

To enable access to NLS in a CompositeProvider, perform the following steps:

1. In the BW modeling tools in SAP HANA Studio, go to the **General** tab in the editing screen of the CompositeProvider.

2. Under **Common Runtime Properties**, change the **Near-Line Storage Read Mode** to **Read Near-Line Storage**.

3. Save the CompositeProvider.

To enable access to NLS in a query:

1. In the BW modeling tools in SAP HANA Studio, go to the **General** tab in the editing screen of the query.

2. Under **Extended**, change the read mode under **Near-Line Storage** to one of the following options:

   - **Do Not Read Near-Line Storage**
     - The query doesn't read any data stored in NLS. This setting overrides a CompositeProvider level setting to allow access.
     - If you've disabled access in the CompositeProvider, you can't enable it again in the query properties.
   - **Read Near-Line Storage**
     - The query can read data stored in NLS assuming the InfoProvider is connected to NLS and the user selects data that's been archived.
   - **Use Near-Line Storage According to InfoProvider**
     - The CompositeProvider-level configuration is passed to the query.

3. Save the query.

9.4   Summary

In this chapter, we started with a discussion of the importance of a data retention strategy that includes all available tools. Then, we presented the data temperature concept for managing data with different access requirements and access frequencies. Finally, we reviewed in depth how to configure the data archiving process using SAP's NLS on SAP IQ or Hadoop for cold data storage. In the next chapter, we'll cover administration and monitoring of routine tasks within your SAP BW/4HANA system to keep it performing at an optimal level.

Chapter 10
Administration

Proactive administration and monitoring allows support organiza-
tions to identify and anticipate technical issues affecting end users
before they escalate. In this chapter, we'll discuss monitoring and
resolution of these issues, which can give support organizations
credibility in the eyes of their stakeholders.

In many companies, IT support for SAP BW/4HANA is divided between the project delivery team and the support organization. The support organization's main role is to ensure the system operates within defined *service-level agreement* (SLA) parameters. The SLA parameters usually specify how much time the support organization has to address incidents by severity. For example, it might have four hours for a very high severity incident, twenty-four hours for a high incident, one week for a medium incident, and four weeks for a low incident. Support organizations that proactively monitor and resolve issues are much more successful at meeting SLA parameters than those that don't.

This chapter will focus on routine or daily administration (Section 10.1) and data load monitoring (Section 10.2) tasks, which should be performed by SAP Basis, SAP BW/4HANA technical, and/or data load monitoring subteams within the support organization. In Section 10.3, you'll find a list of weekly, monthly, quarterly, and annual tasks. Some of these tasks only need to be performed when there are specific concerns regarding performance or operational stability, but others may need constant supervision. You should consider any opportunity to automate daily tasks, such as leveraging SAP Solution Manager to configure thresholds and send alerts by email.

10.1 Daily Administration Tasks

The first technical resource to arrive in the office every morning should conduct routine daily administration checks manually as a quick health check of the system.

If the system is monitored globally, 24-7, then the technical resource receiving handover should conduct the check at the beginning of every shift. Over time, thresholds for normal behavior will become apparent; technical resources should document these thresholds and investigate any abnormal behavior or deviations above or below thresholds.

In addition, when performance or systematic issues are reported, these checks should be executed first so the technical team is knowledgeable and aware of the system's operational health.

This section will highlight a few important administrative checks to execute on a daily or routine basis:

- Check database storage
- Check workload
- Perform system checks
- Automate daily tasks

10.1.1   Check Database Storage

Every database grows consistently when in operational use. In SAP BW/4HANA systems, there are usually four main reasons for growth:

1. Organic growth
2. New development/content-related growth
3. System administration table growth
4. Lack of management by project and/or support teams

The final contributor to growth—lack of management by project or support teams—is completely preventable. This type of growth is usually the result of negligent housekeeping, such as failing to delete uploaded requests or change log tables after they're no longer valuable. Following the data management principles covered in Chapter 9 and the guidelines in this section should not only help you eliminate this type of growth from your system but also help you manage the other three types of growth.

When database usage grows quicker than available capacity, you can expect significant performance problems or operational problems. It's therefore extremely important to monitor free space (or lack thereof) in the database. With SAP HANA, free space monitoring can be automated and table unloads can be prioritized. However, if there's too high a demand on database memory and not enough capacity can be freed by unloading to disk, the host or even the database may failover or crash completely. In the next two subsections, we'll review how to monitor SAP HANA memory usage and the delta merge process.

SAP HANA Memory Usage

The allocation limit and available capacity of the database can be found on the overview screen of Transaction DB02 (Database Monitor). Figure 10.1shows the database monitor overview for a small SAP BW/4HANA system with a memory allocation limit of 110 GB and used memory of 61 GB ❷. Although this data footprint is small, it exceeds 50 percent of the allocation limit, so there's no room to grow.

> **Note**
>
> The information contained in the database monitor is the same information available in the administration console of SAP HANA Studio.

There are a few key things to check in SAP HANA databases, which are labeled in Figure 10.1, although not necessarily with any specific priority. The first item to confirm is the operational state ❶ in the top-left quadrant. Second, check the number of alerts in the top-right quadrant ❷. In the bottom-left quadrant, you can check the overall memory consumption and CPU usage for all hosts ❸ against the global allocation limit. In the bottom-right quadrant, check the disk, log, and trace file sizes for all volumes ❹.

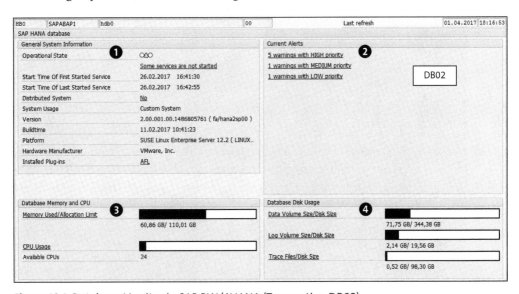

Figure 10.1 Database Monitor in SAP BW/4HANA (Transaction DB02)

Each of these quadrants has a detailed view. In a scale-out or distributed system, it's more important to monitor memory usage by host than usage overall. It's possible that memory on a single host could be overloaded while others are underutilized. In such a case, reorganization or redistribution may be necessary.

To see memory consumption by host, go to the menu item **Configuration • Services**, as shown in Figure 10.2. In this view, the memory usage of each service ❶ on each host is specified. Pay attention to any index server ❷ consuming more than 50 percent of available memory ❸ on any single host.

Active Host		Port	Service Name	Process ID	Detail	SQL Port	Start Time	P	T	ΣProcess Memory (GB)	Total Memory (GB)	Available Memory
◉	hdb0	0	xsexecagent	0		0		0	0	0,00	0,00	0,00
△		30.000	daemon	29.631		0	26.02.2017 16:41:30	1	1	0,00	0,00	0,00
☐		30.001	nameserver	29.682	master	0	26.02.2017 16:41:32	0	0	6,47	76,60	138,04
☐		30.002	preprocessor	29.769		0	26.02.2017 16:41:41	0	0	5,32	76,60	138,04
☐		30.003	indexserver ❶	29.801	master	30.015	26.02.2017 16:41:45	0	0	❷ 75,37	76,60	❸ 138,04
☐		30.006	webdispatcher	30.499		0	26.02.2017 16:42:27	0	0	5,12	76,60	138,04
☐		30.007	xsengine	29.803		0	26.02.2017 16:41:45	0	0	7,15	76,60	138,04
☐		30.010	compileserver	29.767		0	26.02.2017 16:41:39	0	0	4,96	76,60	138,04
☐		30.025	diserver	30.497		0	26.02.2017 16:42:28	0	0	4,86	76,60	138,04
◉		30.029	xscontroller	0		0		0	0	0,00	0,00	0,00
☐		30.031	xsuaaserver	30.507		0	26.02.2017 16:42:55	1	1	0,00	0,00	0,00
										109,25		

Figure 10.2 Memory Usage by Host (Transaction DB02)

The memory consumption for each service includes memory used by the following components:

- Database administration
- Code and stacks
- Column-store tables
- Row-store tables

A more detailed memory consumption report can be executed to identify how much memory each component is using. This report is available in SAP HANA Studio on the **System Information** tab and is called **Component Memory Usage**. Using this report can help identify memory leaks if components that are normally small are suddenly large.

> **Note**
>
> The row-store tables may need to be compacted if they've been cleansed since migration to SAP HANA. Check SAP Note 1813245 for instructions on how to check whether row-store compaction is recommended.

SAP HANA Delta Merge

In the SAP HANA database, inserts or updates to data tables are initially written to delta storage optimized for write access. The data modifications then must be transferred to main storage by means of a delta merge.

Most main storage data is saved in a highly compressed format optimized for reduced memory space and improved read performance. A delta merge is used to transfer data modifications from the delta storage to the main storage. First, an asynchronous check determines whether a delta merge is necessary. If the delta storage threshold value is exceeded, the merge is executed. At any time when data is accessed from the table, the data is read from both the main storage and the delta storage and the results are merged.

> **Note**
>
> Merge functionality doesn't apply to extended tables, because they don't contain main storage and delta storage.

The check and the delta merge either are performed automatically by the system or must be triggered manually. Automatic checks and delta merges can be controlled for the following object types:

- Advanced DSOs are automatically checked and merged after activation when the **Trigger Database Merge** checkbox is selected, which is the default setting.
- The DTPs are automatically checked and merged after the DTP request has been successfully processed when the **Trigger Database Merge** checkbox on the **Update** tab is selected, which is the default setting.
- For write-optimized classic DSOs, standard InfoCubes, and SAP HANA–optimized InfoCubes, the check and the delta merge (if possible) aren't performed automatically. This also applies to objects that belong to a semantically partitioned object.

> **Note**
>
> Due to load distribution issues, there are some exceptional cases in which it's not recommended to perform a delta merge after processing a DTP request.

When data is loaded from multiple sources into a single target in parallel, SAP recommends deselecting the checkbox in the DTP and using the **Trigger Delta Merge** process type to trigger the delta merge. Then, the delta merge check can be controlled so it's only performed at the end of the entire loading process.

> **Note**
>
> Ensure the DTP or process type always triggers a delta merge. If no delta merge takes place, a large delta storage could lead to increased memory consumption, longer recovery times, performance degradation, and increased disk size.

Merge statistics are captured in table M_DELTA_MERGE_STATISTICS in the SYS schema. This table can be queried via the SQL console in SAP HANA Studio or via **Diagnostics • SQL Editor** in Transaction DB02.

> **Note**
>
> See SAP Note 2119087 for more information on increasing the database trace level for merges.

10.1.2   Check SAP HANA Workload

It's always a good idea to monitor the workload on the database to help you understand what jobs are running in the system and who's running them. As with memory usage, the database workload can be monitored via Transaction DB02, the administration console of SAP HANA Studio, or the SAP HANA Cockpit.

> **Note**
>
> The SAP HANA Cockpit can be accessed directly through its URL or via SAP HANA Studio by right-clicking the system in the navigation pane and selecting **Configuration and Monitoring • Open SAP HANA Cockpit**. To access the cockpit, you will need the following roles:
>
> - sap.hana.admin.roles::Monitoring
> - sap.hana.admin.roles::Administration
> - sap.hana.admin.cockpit.roles::SysDBAdmin (for multitenant systems)
>
> To access via the URL, enter the following in your web browser: *http://<host_fqdn>:<port>/sap/hana/admin/cockpit*
>
> Note that the hostname is the fully qualified domain name (FQDN) of the system (or the tenant in an MDC system).

Figure 10.3 shows the overview screen of the SAP HANA Cockpit. The database workload can be monitored via **CPU Usage** ❶ and the number of active threads ❷ in the system. By selecting each tile, the user can access more detailed information.

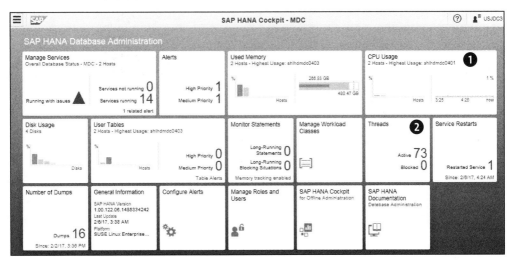

Figure 10.3 Entry Screen of SAP HANA Cockpit

In the following subsections, we'll cover how to monitor CPU usage and threads in SAP HANA. In addition, we'll cover the two most useful statistics' content from a performance troubleshooting perspective: expensive statements and the SQL plan cache.

CPU Usage

SAP HANA is optimized to consume all memory and CPU available. In other words, the SAP HANA database will execute queries in parallel to the extent possible to provide optimal performance. Therefore, if the CPU usage is near 100 percent for a query's execution, that doesn't always mean there's a performance or hardware issue. However, consistently elevated CPU consumption can lead to a considerably slower system if no more requests can be processed. From an end user perspective, the application behaves slowly, is unresponsive, or can even seem to hang.

To monitor CPU usage trends for periods of increased elevation, go to the **Performance • Load** tab in the SAP HANA Studio administration console as shown in Figure 10.4 ❶. Be sure to select the timeframe of the graph and CPU KPI from the list at the bottom of the screen ❷.

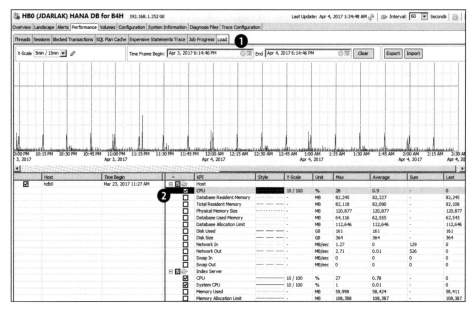

Figure 10.4 CPU Usage Monitoring in SAP HANA Studio

Threads

During periods of high CPU usage, you can monitor the active threads executing in the system via the **Performance • Threads** item in the navigation pane of Transaction DB02, as shown in Figure 10.5 ❶.

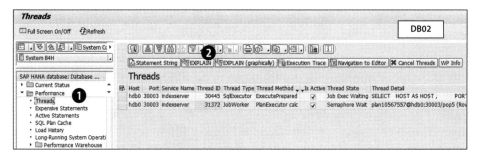

Figure 10.5 Active Threads in Database Monitor

From the **Threads** detail, it's easy to display the **EXPLAIN** plan ❷, the **Statement String**, and the **Execution Trace**. Each of these items can provide insight into the active thread and help troubleshoot performance issues where deemed appropriate.

Expensive Statements

If you encounter specific performance issues, check the expensive statements in Transaction DB02 under the **Performance • Expensive Statements** menu item, as shown in Figure 10.6 ❶. This figure shows an example from an SAP HANA database indicating specific statements executed by a user that ran for more than 10 seconds ❷.

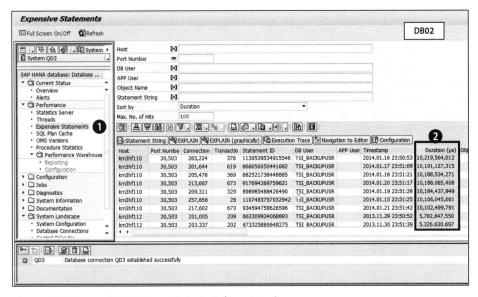

Figure 10.6 Expensive Statements in Database Monitor

Expensive statements should be traced to identify why they're taking so long. Transaction ST05 can be used to complement the analysis performed in the database monitor.

Note

To improve the value of expensive statement traces, you can enable per-statement memory and CPU time tracking by setting the following parameters in the *global.ini* configuration file:

- `[resource_tracking] enable_tracking = on`
- `[resource_tracking] memory_tracking = on`
- `[resource_tracking] cpu_time_measurement_mode = on`

SQL Plan Cache

When expensive statements are identified in the expensive statements trace, the next area to investigate is the SQL plan cache, or table SYS.M_SQL_PLAN_CACHE, which can capture statistics for the SQL code executed against the database. You can access the SQL plan cache via the menu item in Transaction DBO2 as shown in Figure 10.7 ❶. Filtering on the **statement_hash** column ❷ is the most direct way to find a specific SQL statement from the expensive statements trace.

This table holds information about the number of times a SQL statement has been executed, when it was last executed, the total and average execution time, and the memory consumed, as well as which tables and objects were accessed, which can be very useful when troubleshooting performance issues.

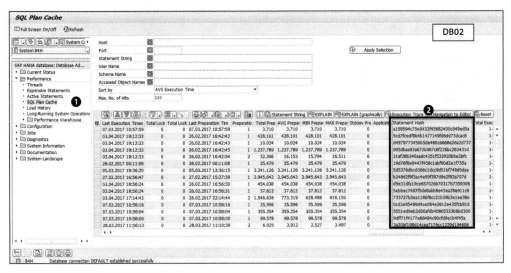

Figure 10.7 SQL Plan Cache Entries in Database Monitor

10.1.3   Check ABAP Workload

After checking the database, the next step is to check the workload on the system's application servers. It's always good to understand what jobs or transactions are running in the system and who's running them.

In the following subsections, we'll explain how to monitor the application server workload. More specifically, we'll cover transaction codes that enable you to monitor the process overview, workload statistics, memory tuning analysis, and operating systems monitor.

Process Overview

The easiest place to find information on work process usage is in the process overview transactions. Transaction SM66 provides a list of all actively used processes in the system across all application servers. This complements Transactions SM50/SM51 well; all processes (both used and available) for each individual application server can be monitored.

As shown in Figure 10.8, Transaction SM50 (Process Overview) provides an overview of all work processes for a specific application server (Transaction SM51 displays all available application servers; Transaction SM50 can be reached by selecting one application server from the list). In the process overview, pay attention to long-running activity. Any job that runs for more than five hundred seconds will show in this screen with a red status.

10

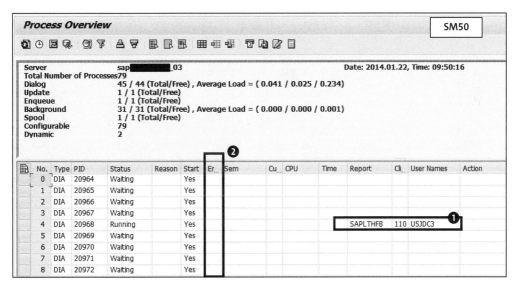

Figure 10.8 Process Overview (Transactions SM51 and SM50)

In addition, check the **Error** column ❷ for any number greater than zero, which indicates the number of times the work process has been killed at the operating system level since the last restart. If many work processes have been killed, it suggests that a systematic performance issue is affecting the system.

Workload Statistics

Armed with knowledge about what's running in the system, the next check should be to review the workload and performance statistics being captured by all workload components. Transaction STO3N (Workload Monitor) is available for this purpose, as shown in Figure 10.9.

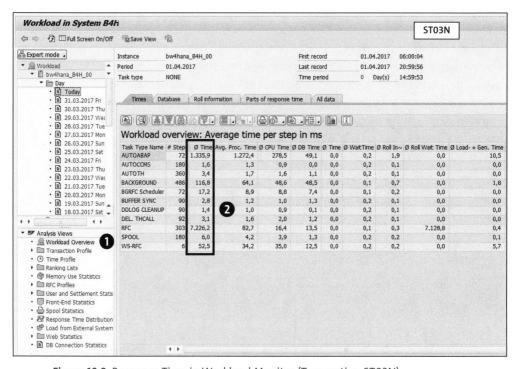

Figure 10.9 Response Time in Workload Monitor (Transaction STO3N)

The workload overview ❶ provides valuable information regarding response times of all work processes ❷. Notice that the average time for **Background** processes is 116.8 milliseconds, or 0.12 seconds; background processing should be the primary area of focus for improving response time, but in this example, **RFC** time has the worst performance, with an average response time of 7.2 seconds. This transaction also provides load history and distribution, so you can also perform a statistical analysis of different servers by different time periods.

Memory Tuning Analysis

To evaluate whether the system profile parameters related to memory usage have adequate values for the system needs, check Transaction STO2 (Tune Summary), as shown in Figure 10.10.

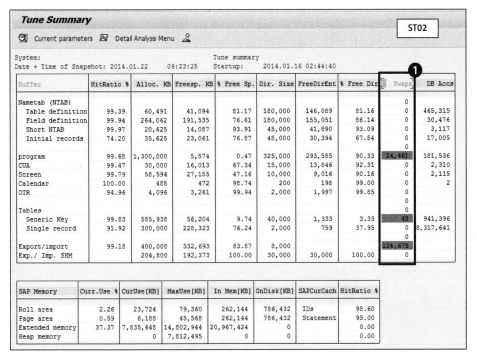

Figure 10.10 Memory Swaps Tune Summary in Transaction STO2

This transaction contains information on buffer size, swap usage, and extended heap memory. The most obvious item to check is whether swap space is being used, which would indicate that existing buffer sizes are too small and need to be increased. Figure 10.11 shows an example in which swap space is being used for the program buffer and the export/import buffer.

In these cases, the profile parameters that need to be tuned can be identified by double-clicking on the buffer line item in the tune summary to go to the **Tune Detail Analysis** screen. In the detail screen, select the **Current Parameters** button ❶ and ❸. The next screen will display the profile parameters that control the buffer size and their current values ❷ and ❹. From this last screen, it's also possible to maintain the profile parameter directly.

Some parameters can be changed and be active immediately, whereas others require a system restart. Regardless, all parameter changes should be tested for efficacy before being enacted directly in a production environment.

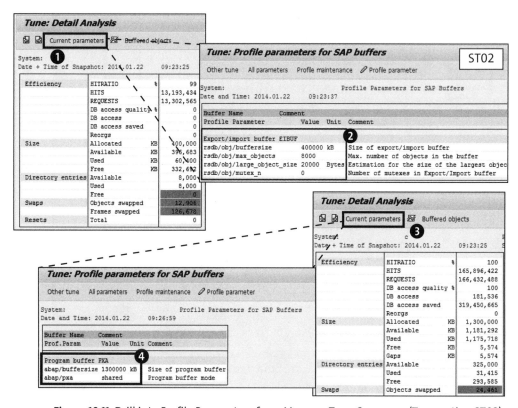

Figure 10.11 Drill into Profile Parameters from Memory Tune Summary (Transaction ST02)

Figure 10.12 offers an example of a well-tuned system. This system has quite a lot of memory allocated to each buffer but only has a few swaps. Ideally, there would be no swaps at all.

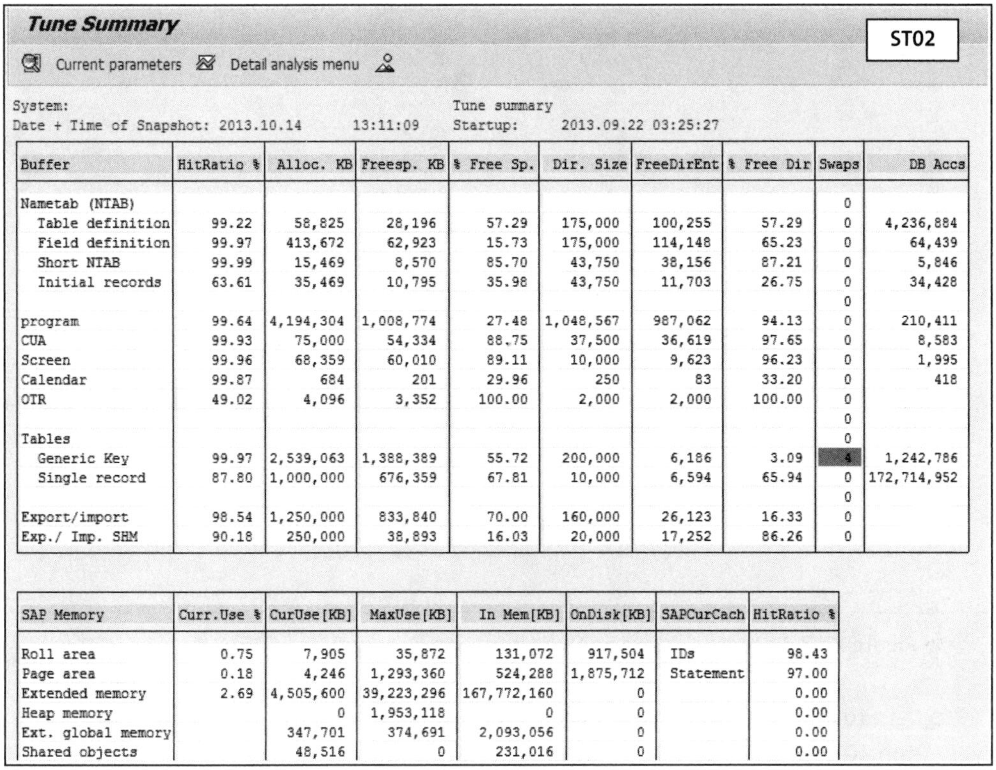

Figure 10.12 Large but Well-Tuned System (Transaction STO2)

All the memory controlled by profile parameters is SAP application–level memory. To monitor the memory usage by all servers, it's necessary to go to the operating system.

Operating Systems Monitor

The operating system can be checked in Transaction STO6 (Operating Systems Monitor). In this monitor, check the current capacity and analyze average and peak CPU utilization. If it routinely exceeds 70–80 percent, then additional capacity is likely needed before rolling out additional functionality or content. Figure 10.13 shows an example of good system CPU utilization.

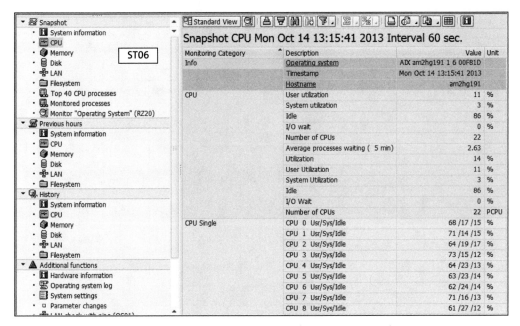

Figure 10.13 Snapshot of System CPU Utilization (Transaction ST06)

As a rule, 20 percent of the processes cause 80 percent of the load, so monitoring the top 40 processes (also in this transaction) will identify the areas needing the most focus. If an analysis in the OS monitor indicates a need for more CPU capacity, you can extend existing hardware in the following ways:

- Adding application servers
- Adding CPUs
- Replacing existing CPUs with faster CPUs

All these solutions can require long lead times, so you'd be wise to monitor CPU proactively in order to identify bottlenecks before they crash the system.

From an operating system perspective, it's also necessary to monitor memory capacity and usage of the following:

- Physical memory
- Swap size
- Free memory
- Virtual memory

The OS monitor also provides information on the current memory capacity and enables analysis of average and peak memory utilization. Figure 10.14 shows an example of current memory use in a sample system with 240 GB physical memory allocated.

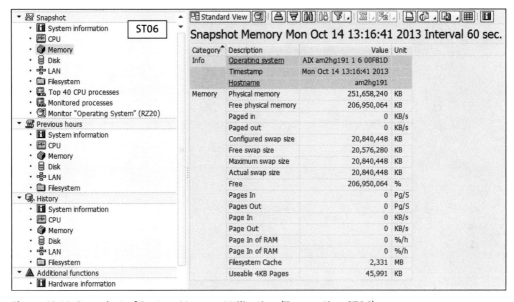

Figure 10.14 Snapshot of System Memory Utilization (Transaction ST06)

10.1.4   Perform System Checks

Not all daily administration tasks can be categorized as database storage or workload analysis tasks. The system checks covered in this section represent all other categories of health checks, which are no less important. In fact, you may prefer to execute these checks first before checking database storage and system workload.

SAP HANA Mini Checks

Over time, the configuration parameters set in the system may need to be updated to current SAP best practices or may become obsolete after patches or upgrades are applied to the system. It's a good practice to routinely check configuration parameters against SAP recommendations and act to minimize discrepancies.

SAP mini checks are a collection of SQL statements that can be executed against your SAP HANA system to compare its configuration against SAP best practice. You can download the mini checks from SAP Note 1969700 and upload them directly into SAP HANA Studio, or you can upload them directly into the SQL editor of Transaction DB02, or you can even use report Z_INSERT_INTO_SQL_EDITOR, which is also attached to the SAP Note.

Note

The mini checks are compiled into a *ZIP* file and attached to SAP Note 1969700 (SQL Statement Collection for SAP HANA).

To execute a mini check SQL statement directly via the SQL editor, as shown in Figure 10.15, call Transaction DB02 and go to **Diagnostics • SQL Editor** in the navigation pane ❶, then paste the mini check SQL statement into the **Input Query** box ❷, then click **Execution** ❸.

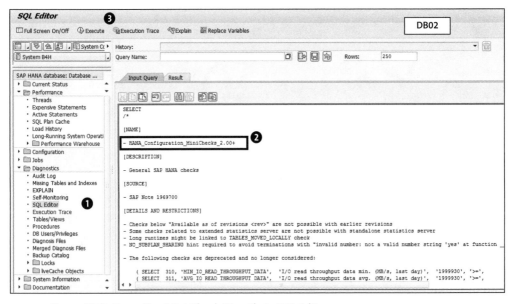

Figure 10.15 Executing Mini Check Directly in SQL Editor

The results of the mini check SQL statement will be displayed in the **Result** tab and will be delivered in a consistent format, as shown in Figure 10.16. Each configuration check will be listed in a table with the actual value ❶, the expected value ❷, and a check column ❸, in which an **X** indicates a discrepancy. In most cases, an SAP Note will be documented, so you can research the impact any discrepancies may have on system operations, stability, or performance.

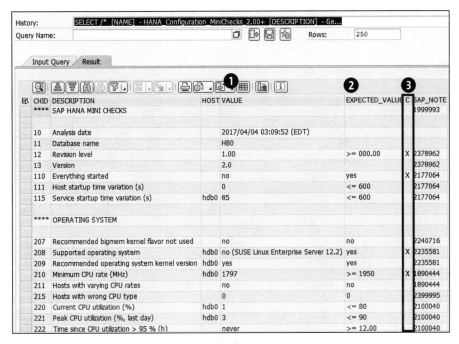

Figure 10.16 Results of SAP HANA Mini Check SQL Statement

Short Dumps

The frequency of runtime issues encountered by users and batch processes in the system are indicative of the stability of the system. Check the number of runtime errors, or short dumps, via Transaction ST22 (ABAP Runtime Error Analysis) to list the ABAP runtime errors that have occurred recently.

Figure 10.17 shows an example of short dumps in an SAP BW/4HANA system. The current day's short dumps for all users can be easily accessed by clicking the **Today** button ❶. There are two runtime errors represented ❷. The timeout error indicates a performance issue that could be related to external RFC connections. The duplicate key issues indicate a data load error, which could be resolved programmatically by checks in the ETL logic.

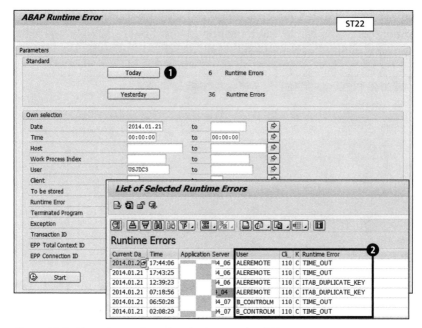

Figure 10.17 Short Dump Overview in Transaction ST22

System Log

SAP systems log all system errors, warnings, user locks (due to failed logon attempts from known users), and process messages in the system log. There are to two different types of logs created by the system log:

- **Local logs**

  Each application server has a local log for all the messages output by this server. The system log records these messages in a circular file. When this log file reaches the maximum permissible length, the system log overwrites it, starting over from the beginning.

- **Central logs**

  Central logs are optional; when configured, the central log maintains a file on a selected application server. Each application server then sends local log messages to the central log server, which collects the messages and writes them to the central log. The central log consists of two files: the active file and the old file.

  The *active file* contains the current log. When it reaches the maximum size, the system performs a *log file switch*, in which it deletes the old log file, makes the previously active file the "old" file, and creates a new active file. The switch occurs when the size of the active log file is half the value specified in the rslg/max_disk-space/central parameter.

> **Note**
>
> The location of the local log is specified in the rslg/local/file profile parameter. The location of the central log active file is specified in the rslg/central/filepro-file parameter, and the location of the old file is specified in the rslg/central/old_file parameter.

Use Transaction SM21 to access the system log output screen. With this transaction, it's possible to read all the messages contained in any of the system logs by choosing **System log • Choose • All remote system logs**, as shown in Figure 10.18 ❶. Enter the date and time ❷ to start reading the log, and click the **Reread System Log** button.

The resulting list can be restricted for **Problems Only**, **Problems and messages**, and **All messages** ❸. The information in this list, such as transaction code and user, can be used to analyze the errors indicated by a red icon in the **Priority** column. Double-clicking any line opens the detail text and provides more information.

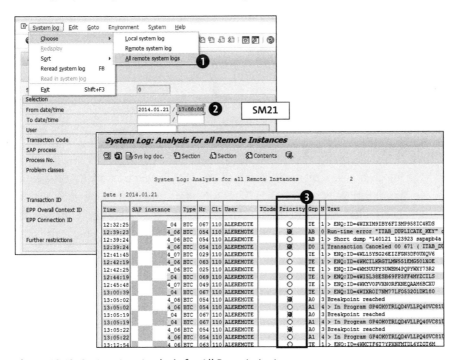

Figure 10.18 System Log Analysis for All Remote Instances

Each error message in the log should be scrutinized for root-cause analysis. Errors that aren't resolved will continue to consume system resources (CPU, memory, and storage space), which may lead to unrelated follow-up issues. Sometimes, log entries point to more information in a runtime error dump (Transaction ST22) or other location.

Job Overview

The **Job Overview** screen is a single, central area for completing a wide range of tasks related to monitoring and managing background jobs, including the following:

- Defining jobs
- Scheduling, rescheduling, and copying existing jobs
- Rescheduling and editing jobs and job steps
- Repeating jobs
- Debugging active jobs
- Reviewing information about jobs
- Canceling a job's release status
- Canceling and deleting jobs
- Comparing the specifications of several jobs
- Checking the status of jobs
- Reviewing job logs
- Releasing jobs to run

Jobs should be monitored daily for errors. When errors arise, spool output files or job logs should be evaluated for their causes.

To reach the **Job Overview** screen, call Transaction SM37. Enter an asterisk (*) as a wildcard in the mandatory selection criteria fields **Job name** and **User name** as shown in Figure 10.19 ❶. Deselect all job status checkboxes except for **Active** and **Canceled** ❷. Enter a date for analysis and then execute for a list of all failed jobs, plus those currently running. Analyze any error logs found.

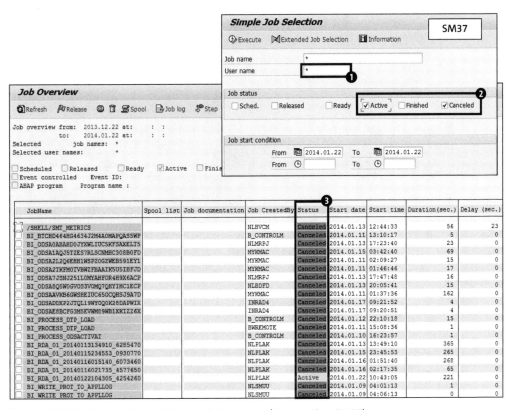

Figure 10.19 Active and Failed Jobs in Job Overview (Transaction SM37)

Database Backup

The DBA Cockpit is a platform-independent tool used to monitor and administer activity in the database. The DBA Cockpit offers a subset of the functionality of database management tools (such as SAP HANA Studio) and can be used to schedule database backups and database system checks. The DBA Cockpit can be accessed via Transaction DBACOCKPIT.

In the DBA Cockpit, the central calendar provides an overview of scheduled database administration actions for all the databases in the SAP system. The actions available differ depending on the database platform. The following tasks are available with the central calendar:

- Manage local system databases in real time
- Manage remote databases of different types and versions, including non-ABAP SAP systems

353

- Manage databases for different versions of an SAP system

- Quickly check whether actions were executed successfully

- Quickly check the number of actions and the actions with the highest status severity for each system

In the production system, check the status of database backups and system checks via the DBA Cockpit by viewing the central calendar (see Figure 10.20). All successful actions will appear in green, and failed actions will appear in red. Take appropriate actions as needed for failed actions.

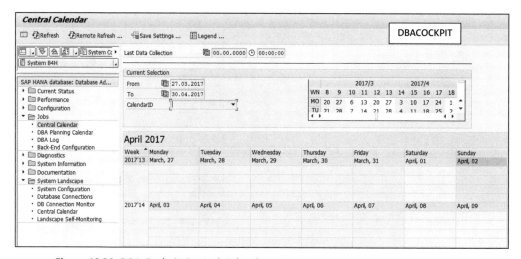

Figure 10.20 DBA Cockpit Central Calendar

Performance Warehouse

Performance Warehouse is only available in SAP Solution Manager systems with solution manager diagnostics (SMD) enabled.

In Performance Warehouse, all relevant performance indicators collected by the DBA Cockpit are stored in an SAP BusinessObjects Business Intelligence (BI) system. This SAP BusinessObjects BI system is used by the SMD backend of an SAP Solution Manager system. SMD also uses SAP BusinessObjects BI to store workload data for SAP applications. To configure the extraction of data into the SMD of SAP BusinessObjects BI, use the SMD Setup Wizard.

Based on this architecture, DBA Cockpit uses SAP BusinessObjects BI technology to provide reports for performance analysis, which you can customize according to your needs. All data collected has a time dimension, so you can analyze the database performance for any point in time or over a specified time frame.

Almost all reports are displayed as charts so you can visualize KPIs. A detailed table view is also available. To navigate within these reports, you can use the SAP Business-Objects BI drill-down feature. Exceptions to performance thresholds are highlighted based on predefined thresholds so that you can immediately identify performance issues.

10.1.5   Automate Daily Tasks

Many of these daily tasks can and should be automated using alerts available in SAP Solution Manager, in which effective measurement and reporting is the basis for a well-integrated system optimization process. There are four core elements of this process:

1. Proactive real-time monitoring
2. Reactive handling of critical events
3. Lower mean time to problem resolution
4. Optimized excellence of technical operations

Manual monitoring is a highly effort-intensive approach that usually requires expert involvement. Analysis and statistical tools are used to capture measurement points and evaluate them on an experience basis. Appropriate actions are then applied to counteract critical events. Automating monitoring processes involves defining and measuring KPIs and comparing and evaluating these with predefined threshold values.

The quality of the automated monitoring concept largely depends on the selected KPIs and the definition of relevant threshold values. With fully automated monitoring, suitable countermeasures are initiated as soon as threshold values are exceeded. Incidents can also be reported to IT service desks.

The appropriate degree of automation depends on the effort and benefits involved. Manual expert monitoring is advisable to verify automated monitoring. If an adequate definition hasn't been made for certain KPIs and their threshold values, then you should adjust the monitoring concept; otherwise, alerts will either be ignored or never raised.

10.2   Daily Load Monitoring

The days of batch processing at night are a distant reality for most twenty-first-century SAP BW/4HANA installations. In most systems, data loads are running around the clock, because users are global, up-to-date information is critical, or volumes are so large that loads can't be restricted to nighttime operational windows.

As a result, data load monitoring has become a critically important responsibility. In some systems, third-party tools are used to monitor process chains, but in many, no external tools are used and monitoring is conducted within the Data Warehousing Workbench, in which a host of monitors are available to help determine the current operational status, identify data load and SAP BW/4HANA object issues, and facilitate resolution.

In this section, we'll cover the following daily data load monitoring tasks:

- Monitoring SAP BW/4HANA Computing Center Management System (CCMS) alerts
- Monitoring process chains

This list is not meant to be comprehensive by any means; each system or implementation may have specific and unique data load monitoring requirements. However, these monitoring tasks represent the minimal list of tasks that should be performed to ensure data is loading successfully into your system. Let's start by monitoring alerts raised in the CCMS.

10.2.1   Monitor SAP BW/4HANA Computing Center Management System Alerts

The CCMS has an alert monitor to help operate SAP BW/4HANA systems. The CCMS BI Monitor contains a selection of SAP BW/4HANA-relevant monitoring trees for process chains and Transaction RSRV consistency checks. These alerts can be used to provide an overview of related issues in the system.

The monitoring trees in the BI Monitor come standard with the following alerts, as shown in Figure 10.21:

- **Process chains**
  This alert contains all process chains executed in the system since it was last started or, if recently restarted, for up to seven days before the last restart.

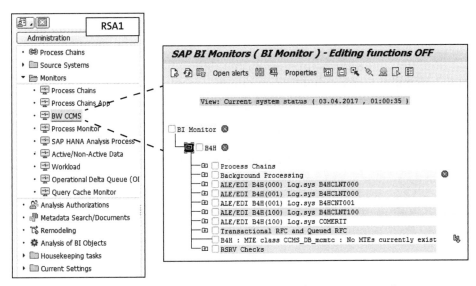

Figure 10.21 BW Computing Center Management System (Transaction RSA1)

Note

After a system is restarted, the monitor will contain the last seven days of PC logs before the restart. This setting can be configured by changing the transfer parameter for method execution DAYS_TO_KEEP_LOGS in method definition RSPC_CCMS_STARTUP. Go to the method definition, run Transaction RZ21, and select menu item **Methods • Definitions**. Once you set the parameter to OFF, process chains won't be monitored in CCMS.

- **Background processing**
  This alert agent runs every hour and monitors all the batch jobs in the system.

Note

The frequency of this agent can be configured by changing the periodicity of batch job SAP_CCMS_MONI_BATCH_DP. By default, it's scheduled to run hourly, but it can be set to run as frequently as every 10 minutes in Transaction SM37.

- **RSRV checks**
  This alert displays the messages for the consistency checks that have been executed

in the analysis and repair environment (Transaction RSRV). The consistency checks must be scheduled manually.

10.2.2   Monitor Process Chains

Although CCMS provides an overview of all process chain runs, from a daily data load monitoring perspective it's most important to monitor only the last execution of each chain. There's a process chains monitor in the Data Warehousing Workbench, under **Administration**. This monitor provides only the current status for each process chain in the system, as shown in Figure 10.22.

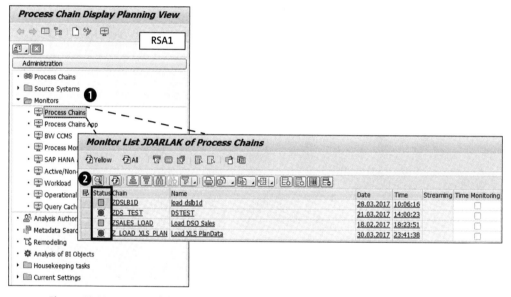

Figure 10.22 Process Chain Monitor in Data Warehouse Workbench (Transaction RSA1)

The process chain monitor can also be accessed directly via Transaction RSPCM. Each active process chain in the system will be listed here with a green, yellow, red, or gray status; gray means the chain has never been executed. If the status is yellow, the chain is currently running. The transaction doesn't distinguish between meta chains and local chains, so all chains will be displayed here.

Filtering the result list by chains with a specific status can be accomplished as shown in Figure 10.23. This can help narrow the focus to find only errors if there are too many chains in the list with another status.

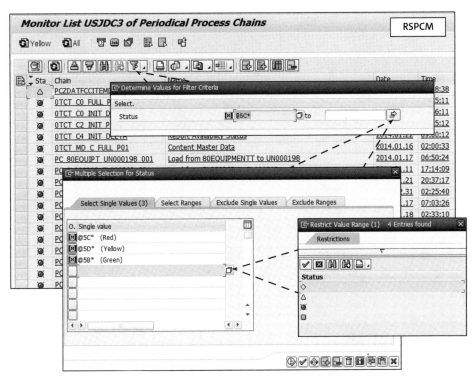

Figure 10.23 Filtering Process Chain Monitor Based on Status (Transaction RSPCM)

10.3   Weekly, Monthly, Quarterly, and Annual Tasks

In this chapter, we've covered many administration tasks that should be executed daily or with another routine frequency. However, this is just the tip of the iceberg; there are many more tasks that should be executed at a less frequent rate, such as weekly, monthly, quarterly, and annually. These tasks are covered in an SAP PRESS book published by some of the same authors as this book, titled *SAP BW: Administration and Performance Optimization*. Many of these tasks are not specific to SAP BW/4HANA but are applicable to all SAP BW systems, regardless of version.

The following tasks are covered in *SAP BW: Administration and Performance Optimization*:

- Weekly tasks:
  - Review SAP EarlyWatch Alert
  - Cleanup requests and changelogs

- Cleanup application logs
- Execute SAP BW housekeeping task list
- Execute other housekeeping task lists
- Execute RSRV consistency checks
- Monitor BI statistics
- Monitor cache usage

- Monthly tasks:
  - Schedule system restart
  - Change portal settings
  - Check SAP notes
  - Act on EarlyWatch Alerts
  - Execute RSRV cleanup tasks
  - Forecast storage capacity
  - Conduct file system housekeeping
  - Archive/near-line data
  - Monitor data load statistics

- Quarterly tasks:
  - Manage users and licenses
  - Test system refresh
  - Maintain hardware
  - Update SAP kernel
  - Apply database updates and parameters
  - Patch operating system
  - Validate system parameters
  - Review open transport requests
  - Execute row-store reorganization
  - Delete obsolete queries and reports
  - Delete obsolete data flows
  - Review configuration settings

- Annual tasks:
  - Upgrade SAP BW/4HANA
  - Apply support packs

- Test high availability and disaster recovery
- Assess system risks
- Review data flows
- Review external performance and optimization

10.4   Summary

In this chapter, we covered many routine or daily administration tasks that should be performed by SAP Basis, SAP BW/4HANA technical, and/or data load monitoring sub-teams within the support organization. We also provided a list of additional weekly, monthly, quarterly, and annual tasks. We recommend adopting a maintenance schedule that enables your support teams to engage in proactive monitoring and resolution of issues before they impact users. Taking care of problems before they become problems will undoubtedly earn your team credibility with your organization's management. In the next chapter, we'll review security—specifically, authentication and access management.

Chapter 11
Security

Securing access to functionality and business information is of high importance in most data warehouses. In this chapter, we'll discuss the security capabilities, roles, and authorizations used in SAP BW/4HANA to help keep your organization's information safe.

SAP BW/4HANA uses the user administration and authentication mechanisms from the Application Server for ABAP (AS ABAP), which is a role-based security framework. The standard ABAP security functions have been enhanced with customizable SAP BW/4HANA analysis authorizations to enable flexible security that can be designed to match the organizational structure in any company easily.

This chapter discusses the most important security concepts: authentication and authorizations within an SAP BW/4HANA system. We'll start by providing an overview of the authentication methods supported by SAP BW/4HANA in Section 11.1, followed by a deep dive into the authorization concept in SAP BW/4HANA (Section 11.2). We'll then review the standard authorization objects provided by SAP (Section 11.3), followed by a discussion of how to define and set up analysis authorizations (Section 11.4). Roles, which tie authorizations together and are used to assign both functionality and data access to end users, will be covered in Section 11.5. The process of assigning roles and other user administration activities will be covered in Section 11.6. Finally, we'll conclude the chapter with a brief discussion of troubleshooting authorization problems (Section 11.7).

11.1 Authentication and Single Sign-On

The authentication process makes it possible to check a user's identity before granting that user access to SAP BW/4HANA or to data in SAP BW/4HANA. Both AS ABAP and the SAP HANA database support various authentication mechanisms, as we'll discuss in the following sections.

11.1.1   Application Server for ABAP Authentication

SAP BW/4HANA generally requires a user ID and password for logon, but it also supports Secure Network Communications (SNC) and SAP logon tickets. To make single sign-on (SSO) available for several systems, users can obtain an SAP logon ticket after logging on to the SAP system. The ticket can then be submitted to other systems (SAP or external systems) as an authentication token. The user doesn't need to enter a user ID or password for authentication and can access the system directly after the system has checked the logon ticket.

As an alternative to user authentication with user IDs and passwords, users with Internet applications via the Internet Transaction Server (ITS) can provide X.509 client certificates. User authentication then takes place on the web server using the Secure Sockets Layer (SSL) protocol without transferring any passwords. User authorizations are valid in accordance with the authorization concept in the SAP system.

> **Note**
>
> SAP BW/4HANA uses the authentication and SSO mechanisms provided by SAP NetWeaver. The security recommendations and guidelines for user administration and authentication described in the Security Guide for SAP NetWeaver therefore also apply to SAP BW/4HANA.

11.1.2   SAP HANA Authentication

SAP HANA Studio supports both standard authentication and SSO using either SAML or Kerberos authentication. Developers working in the Eclipse-based modeling tools will always need access to SAP HANA Studio to work with BW projects to access metadata objects from the backend system (SAP BW/4HANA).

A *BW project* represents a real system connection on the frontend client. Therefore, it requires an authorized user in order to access the backend system. With the standard authentication method, the user enters a user name and password to log on to the backend system.

> **Warning**
>
> Standard authentication with explicit specification of a user name and password means that the user data entered on the frontend client is loaded as plain text into the memory of the local host. A password saved locally is a potential security breach, as it could be extracted from memory by third parties.

> **Tip**
>
> Activating SNC for the selected system connection is mandatory for security reasons.
>
> We recommend using SSO as well. When used with SNC, SSO also meets the security requirements for working with large-scale BW projects. With SSO, the user doesn't need to enter a user name and password and can simply access the system as soon as the logon ticket has been checked.

11.2   Authorization in Application Server for ABAP

SAP NetWeaver authorization is mainly built on the AS ABAP authorization objects. An *authorization object* contains one or more authorization fields that provide access to relevant functions, object values, or activities related to the authorization object. For example, the authorization object for InfoAreas will have an authorization field for assigning InfoArea values and another field for assigning activities such as display or edit. Each authorization object provides access to an object, function, or other component of the SAP BW/4HANA system. Authorization objects are then assigned to users via roles and profiles (see Section 11.5).

AS ABAP authorizations can be used to protect most functions, objects, or values in the system. When you perform an action, an authorization check compares the field values of all relevant authorization objects assigned to the user with the value set needed to execute the action. A user is authorized to perform an action only if the authorization check is successful for every field in an authorization object or authorization. For example, if someone has access to execute a query based on the query name but doesn't have access to the InfoArea where the InfoProvider is located, he can't execute the query. This facilitates implementation of complex user authorization checks. It's important to note that it's possible to grant access, but it's not possible to explicitly deny access. To put it another way, a user doesn't have access unless the user is granted access.

> **Note**
>
> The SAP BW/4HANA web-based reporting requires users to be set up in the Application Server for Java (AS Java) system to allow them to execute reports. However, unless other AS Java functionality is used, the setup is very limited.

The AS Java authorization concept uses ACLs to control access to individual objects in the Java system and roles to assign activities to users. We recommend that you use the standard portal role Business Explorer to define the initial set of authorizations needed in AS Java for end users.

A more detailed discussion of Java is outside the scope of this chapter, which focuses on AS ABAP authorizations only.

The SAP NetWeaver authorizations are structured into authorization object classes. A class can have one or more authorization objects, and each authorization object can have one or more authorizations, as illustrated in Figure 11.1.

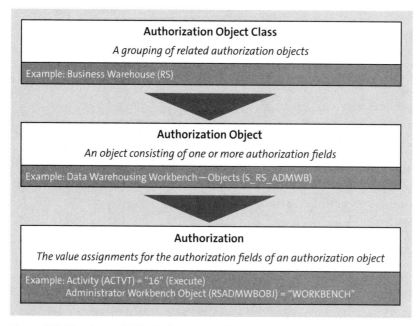

Figure 11.1 Structure of SAP BW/4HANA Authorizations

All SAP BW/4HANA authorizations are included in authorization object class RS. Authorization objects like the one in Figure 11.2 can be displayed in Transaction SU21, which also includes all other standard authorizations available in the system.

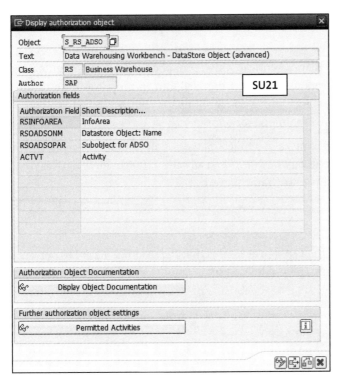

Figure 11.2 Example of Authorization Object

It isn't enough to grant access to the authorization objects in class RS; SAP BW/4HANA also makes use of a lot of standard SAP functionality for system communication, system settings, and maintenance, which will be covered more in Section 11.5, where we'll look at the content of the standard roles provided by SAP.

In the following subsections, we'll cover the authorization fields and activity fields of authorization objects in more detail.

11.2.1   Authorization Fields

Authorization field values control the values for which a user has access. Each authorization object can have one or more authorization fields. Authorization fields can be maintained with the following values:

1. Specific values
2. Patterns in which the asterisk character (*) is a wildcard

3. Ranges of specific values or patterns

4. Full access using * only

In some high-security or business-critical systems, explicit value assignments may be warranted to ensure users aren't overauthorized, but in most cases we recommend using patterns based on naming conventions for technical SAP BW/4HANA objects, which minimizes the maintenance effort.

For example, consider prefixing the technical names of all sales InfoProviders with the pattern SAL*. Then, access can be granted to all sales InfoProviders by assigning the authorization field access to the same pattern.

11.2.2   Activity Fields

The activity field controls the types of activities that the user has access to perform for the authorization object. The predefined set of activities in SAP BW/4HANA can be found in table TACT. Table 11.1 lists the most commonly used activity fields in SAP BW/4HANA.

Activity	Description
01	Create or generate
02	Change
03	Display
06	Delete
07	Activate or generate
16	Execute
22	Enter, include, or assign

Table 11.1 Common Activities in Authorization Objects in SAP BW/4HANA

Developers and administrators should have access to all activities in the development system. The following activities shouldn't be assigned to users in the test and production systems; these activities will force objects to be transported through the system landscape:

- 01: Create or generate
- 02: Change
- 06: Delete

For objects that can't or shouldn't be transported through the system landscape, such as queries, web templates, and reports created directly in production, we recommend maintaining a separate namespace to eliminate the risk of assigning users access to change or delete objects promoted to production via the transport connection.

Now that we've covered the authorization concept, let's review the standard authorization objects provided by SAP. These objects are required to grant access to all SAP BW/4HANA functionality.

11.3   Standard Authorization Objects

SAP BW/4HANA comes delivered with a set of standard authorization objects that control access to general SAP functionality, SAP HANA functionality, SAP BW/4HANA administration, and SAP BW/4HANA reporting objects. These objects can be divided into two types:

1. Developer and administrator authorizations
2. Reporting authorizations

We'll discuss each in more detail in the following subsections.

11.3.1   Developer and Administrator Authorizations

Standard SAP BW/4HANA developer and administrator authorizations are available to limit access to creating and maintaining nonreporting objects in the system.

The SAP BW/4HANA standard authorization objects that control access to the administrator workbench and other administrator functionality are listed in Table 11.2.

Authorization Object	Description
BO_CA_CES	Content administration: BOE system definition
BO_CA_JOB	Content administration: Operations on content-related jobs

Table 11.2 Administration Authorization Objects

369

Authorization Object	Description
BO_CA_RPT	Content administration: Operations on reports
RSANAUMMEN	Authorization for adv. analytics UMM entity
RSHAAP	Authorization for SAP HANA analysis process
RSHAOT	Authorization for SAP HANA analysis element type
RSBPC_ID	Grant user access to an SAP BPC environment
S_ADT_RES	Authorization object for ADT resource access
	Authorization field URI must have value /sap/bw/modeling/*
	Placeholder * is used for URI subfolders
S_RSEC	Infrastructure for analysis authorizations
S_RS_ADMWB	Data Warehousing Workbench—objects
S_RS_ADSO	Data Warehousing Workbench—Advanced DSO
S_RS_ALVL	Planning: Aggregation level
S_RS_B4H	Authorizations for executing programs RS_B4HANA_CHECK_ENABLE and RS_B4HANA_WHITELIST_MAINTAIN
S_RS_CPRO	CompositeProvider (local and ad hoc)
S_RS_CTT	Data Warehousing Workbench—currency translation type
S_RS_DMOD	Data Warehousing Workbench—data flow
S_RS_DS	Data Warehousing Workbench—DataSource
S_RS_DTP	Data Warehousing Workbench—DTP
S_RS_HCPR	Central CompositeProvider
S_RS_HIER	Data Warehousing Workbench—hierarchy
S_RS_HIST	Authorizations for TLOGO object history
S_RS_IOBJA	Data Warehousing Workbench—InfoObject (InfoArea)
S_RS_IOMAD	Data Warehousing Workbench—maintain master data

Table 11.2 Administration Authorization Objects (Cont.)

Authorization Object	Description
S_RS_ISNEW	Data Warehousing Workbench—InfoSource
S_RS_LOPDO	LOPD: Customizing authorizations
S_RS_ODSP_H	ODP: Extraction from SAP HANA
S_RS_ODSV	Data Warehousing Workbench—Open ODS view
S_RS_OHDST	Data Warehousing Workbench—Open hub destination
S_RS_PC	Data Warehousing Workbench—process chains
S_RS_PLENQ	Lock settings
S_RS_PLSE	Planning function
S_RS_PLSQ	Planning sequence
S_RS_PLST	Planning function type
S_RS_RSFC	Authorization for SAP demo content
S_RS_RSTT	Authorization object for RS trace tool
S_RS_SDATA	Authorization check for SAP BW scenario transfer tool
S_RS_THJT	Data Warehousing Workbench—key date derivation type
S_RS_TR	Data Warehousing Workbench—transformation
S_RS_TRCS	Data Warehousing Workbench—InfoSource (InfoArea)
S_RS_UOM	Data Warehousing Workbench—quantity conversion type
S_RS_WSPAC	SAP BW workspace

Table 11.2 Administration Authorization Objects (Cont.)

These authorization objects must be maintained and assigned to developers and administrators to grant them access to develop and administer the system.

Reporting end users require access to a lot of the administrator authorization objects for activities 03 (display), 16 (execute), and 22 (enter, include, and assign) to be able to access the data in the system when executing queries.

11

11.3.2   Reporting Authorizations

Standard SAP BW/4HANA authorization objects are available to limit access to reporting components such as queries, reports, and dashboards.

Table 11.3 lists reporting-related authorization objects.

Authorization Object	Description
S_RS_AO	Analysis Office: Authority object
S_RS_AUTH	BI analysis authorizations in role
S_RS_BEXTX	Business Explorer—BEx texts (maintenance)
S_RS_BITM	Business Explorer—BEx reusable web items (SAP NetWeaver 7.0+)
S_RS_BTMP	Business Explorer—BEx web templates (NW 7.0+)
S_RS_COMP	Business Explorer—components
S_RS_COMP1	Business Explorer—components: Enhancements to the owner
S_RS_EREL	Business Explorer—enterprise report reusable elements
S_RS_ERPT	Business Explorer—enterprise reports
S_RS_FOLD	Business Explorer—folder view on/off
S_RS_PARAM	Business Explorer—variants in variable screen
S_RS_TOOLS	Business Explorer—individual tools
S_RS_XCLS	Frontend integration—Xcelsius visualization
S_RS_ZEN	Design Studio: Authority object
S_RS_ZEN_T	Design Studio: URIs accessible through HTTP tunnel via RFC

Table 11.3 Reporting Authorization Objects

Developers and administrators also require access to these authorization objects to be able to execute queries and reports in the system and to troubleshoot problems reported by end users.

11.3.3 SAP HANA Authorizations

For certain functions in SAP BW/4HANA, you also need authorizations in SAP HANA. In the following sections, we'll discuss the most relevant functions and their corresponding authorizations.

Generating SAP HANA Views

When creating objects in SAP BW/4HANA, you can generate SAP HANA views with the same structures during activation. This supports scenarios in which data modeled in SAP BW/4HANA is merged with data modeled in SAP HANA via SAP HANA tools (also referred to as mixed scenarios).

To be able to access SAP HANA views generated from SAP BW/4HANA, you need certain authorizations in SAP HANA and in SAP BW/4HANA. Various authorizations are provided for the administration of these objects.

Searching for Objects in SAP HANA

To perform searches with SAP HANA, the technical user requires certain system repository authorizations on the _SYS_REPO schema in SAP HANA. For security reasons, we recommend giving authorizations only for the tables required, not for the entire schema. To do this, use the following command:

```
GRANT SELECT ON sap<sid>.<table> TO _ sys_repo WITH GRANT OPTION;
```

Here, `<sid>` represents the system ID of the SAP BW/4HANA system. Information about what to place in `<table>` is provided in Table 11.4.

Table Name	Table Name	Table Name
RSBOHDEST	RSDST	RSOSEGR
RSBOHDESTT	RSDTIM	RSOSEGRLOC
RSDAREA	RSDUNI	RSOSEGRT
RSDAREAT	RSFBP	RSPLS_ALVL
RSDBCHATRXXL	RSFBPFIELD	RSPLS_ALVLT
RSDCHA	RSFBPSEMANTICS	RSQISET
RSDCHABAS	RSFBPT	RSRREPDIR

Table 11.4 Relevant SAP BW/4HANA Tables for Searching in SAP HANA

Table Name	Table Name	Table Name
RSDCUBE	RSKSFIELDNEW	RSTRAN
RSDFDMOD	RSKSNEW	RSTRANT
RSDFDMODT	RSKSNEWT	RSWSPLREF
RSDHAMAP	RSLPO	RSZCOMPIC
RSDHAMAPT	RSLTIP	RSZCOMPDIR
RSDIOBC	RSLTIPT	RSZELTDIR
RSDIOBCIOBJ	RSLTIPXREF	RSZELTTXT
RSDIOBJ	RSOADSO	RSZELTXREF
RSDIOBJCMP	RSOADSOLOC	RSZGLOBV
RSDIOBJT	RSOADSOT	RSZRANGE
RSDKYF	RSOHCPR	RSZWOBJTXT
RSDODSO	RSOHCPRT	RSZWVIEW
RSDS	RSOOBJXREF	TADIR

Table 11.4 Relevant SAP BW/4HANA Tables for Searching in SAP HANA (Cont.)

To be able to work with SAP HANA analysis processes, you need certain authorizations in SAP HANA and in SAP BW/4HANA. In the following subsections, we'll cover the additional authorizations and privileges you will need to work with NLS, SDA, and the Eclipse-based modeling tools.

Near-Line Storage with SAP IQ

For NLS with SAP IQ, you need the following authorization in SAP HANA:

- System privilege: CREATE REMOTE SOURCE

If the remote source isn't created with the SAP<SID> user but with a different database user instead, then this database user must assign the corresponding object authorizations to the SAP<SID> user:

- Object privilege: CREATE VIRTUAL TABLE on VIRTUAL_TABLES (SYS)
- Object privilege: DROP on VIRTUAL_TABLES (SYS)

Authorizations for SAP HANA Smart Data Access

If you use SDA, remote data is accessed from the system with the database user used to connect the system to the SAP HANA database. When you created a remote source in SAP HANA, you specified a user for the connection to the source database. SAP HANA passes SQL statements to this user. Make sure that this user has sufficient authorizations in the relevant schemas and tables in the source database.

Authorizations for Modeling with the Eclipse-Based Modeling Tools

When working with SAP BW/4HANA modeling tools, you can only see or open objects for which you have at least display authorization. The same checks are performed for actions on objects in the modeling tools as for actions in the backend system or in the query. We therefore recommend the following role template for users who work with the modeling tools: S_RS_RDEMO.

If the authorization object has a subobject field defined for an object type (TLOGO), the user needs to have authorization *, or at least Definition, to see the object in the Project Explorer tree. In particular, modelers need authorizations that are specified in authorization objects S_RS_HCPR, S_RS_ODSV, and S_ADT_RES, as shown in Table 11.2.

In the modeling tools, a BW project represents a user-specific view of the SAP BW/4HANA metadata objects of the backend systems (SAP BW/4HANA).

Like all projects in Eclipse, BW projects also have a local representation of their data on the frontend and are managed in a workspace. If you have a BW project, there will therefore be local copies of the SAP BW/4HANA metadata objects on the frontend. This means that it's possible to access metadata located outside the SAP repository at the local file system level.

> **Warning**
> SAP BW/4HANA metadata objects can be found by third parties.

To protect local project resources, we recommend creating workspace folders to store project resources locally, which will prevent third parties from accessing the resources. Use existing security measures available at the OS level.

> **Note**
> Files stored under Windows in the personal substructure of a user can only be accessed by that user or by local administrators.

> **Tip**
>
> We especially recommend using the default workspace that was created when your IDE was installed.

11.4   Analysis Authorizations

SAP BW/4HANA analysis authorizations control access to business information. In this section, we'll walk you through the basics: creating an InfoObject for analysis authorizations, defining analysis authorizations, and generating analysis authorizations.

11.4.1   Creating an InfoObject for Analysis Authorizations

Analysis authorizations are created based on the InfoObjects in SAP BW/4HANA for which your organization requires separate information access. Usually, these are organizational or geographical InfoObjects with primarily static values, such as company code, profit center, country or region, or groupings such as accounts groups, customer groups, or material groups.

To avoid complex authorizations, you should use specific InfoObjects for analysis authorizations. It's possible to define analysis authorizations on all types of InfoObjects, but you shouldn't use InfoObjects that have fast-changing values, such as order numbers, customer numbers, and material numbers. Doing so leads to massive maintenance effort to ensure that authorizations are updated frequently.

Note that analysis authorizations aren't delivered by SAP as standard objects. You must define which InfoObjects must be checked for authorizations before analysis authorizations can be defined for them. To do this, you have to create a specific security-relevant InfoObject and assign it as an attribute updated with the same values as the original InfoObject.

Consider, for example, a scenario in which the standard object for company code, OCOMP_CODE, is used in several InfoProviders. If you specify OCOMP_CODE itself as authorization-relevant, then every InfoProvider in which it's used will become authorization-relevant, and all will need to be maintained in one or more analysis authorizations.

As an alternative, create a new InfoObject, ZSECCOMP, that's an authorization-relevant navigational attribute of 0COMP_CODE. In the transformation that loads 0COMP_CODE, map the value of 0COMP_CODE to ZSECCOMP so that they'll have the same values. You'll only have to maintain analysis authorizations for the InfoProvider when you selectively enable the navigational attribute 0COMP_CODE__ZSECCOMP. This limits the maintenance required and reduces the security burden.

Analysis authorizations are created and maintained in Transaction RSECADMIN. This transaction also provides functionality to generate analysis authorizations and assign them to end users. We recommend that you limit access to this transaction and related authorization object S_RSEC to security and system administrators only.

> **Note**
>
> Some business content InfoObjects are delivered with the authorization flag set, but it can be switched off if you don't need authorization checks on these objects. Switching this flag off keeps you from having to define analysis authorizations for these objects.

11.4.2   Defining Analysis Authorizations

Go to Transaction RSECADMIN • **Individual maintenance** to define a new analysis authorization. For this example, we'll create an analysis authorization for company code 1000.

The following three special characteristics must always be included in the analysis authorization:

- 0TCAACTVT (**Activity in Analysis Authorizations**)
- 0TCAIPROV (**Authorizations for InfoProvider**)
- 0TCAVALID (**Validity of an Authorization**)

These are required to provide access to InfoProviders, so the system shows an authorization error if they're absent. They are assigned access to display all data without a validity date by default.

Once you've added these three InfoObjects, you can add the additional InfoObjects you've configured as authorization-relevant, as shown in Figure 11.3.

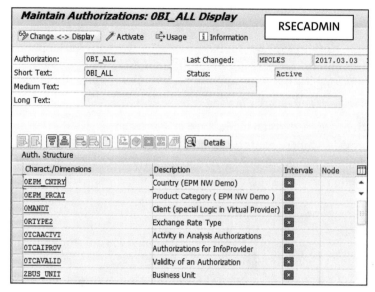

Figure 11.3 Example of Analysis Authorization

You can click the icon in the **Intervals** column to maintain the authorized values for your characteristic. You can also define user exit variables to provide authorizations based on dynamic authorizations determined at runtime in ABAP.

Another option is to assign access based on hierarchy nodes. This is especially useful when hierarchies are already defined for the InfoObject and the definition of the hierarchy can be used for access to business information.

You can restrict access to specific key figures via InfoObject OTCAKYFNM. Don't set this InfoObject as authorization-relevant unless it's required to restrict access to key figures. The key figure InfoObject names should be maintained as authorized values, so you should set specific naming conventions for these key figures to allow for easy maintenance.

11.4.3   Automatically Generating Analysis Authorizations

A standard analysis authorization, OBIALL, is generated automatically in the system for all authorization-relevant InfoObjects. This is assigned to the SAP_ALL profile by default to ensure that SAP_ALL has full access in the system. This analysis authorization shouldn't be maintained manually.

It's also possible to automatically generate analysis authorizations in Transaction RSECADMIN based on uploaded data (see Figure 11.4).

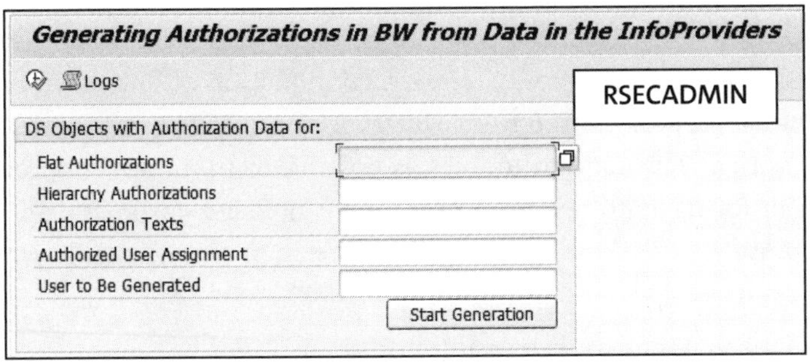

Figure 11.4 Generation Program for Analysis Authorizations

DSOs for generating authorizations have the same structure as authorizations. SAP provides the following five template DSOs:

- 0TCA_DS01: Authorization data (values)
- 0TCA_DS02: Authorization data (hierarchies)
- 0TCA_DS03: Description texts for authorizations
- 0TCA_DS04: Assignment of authorizations to users
- 0TCA_DS05: Generation of users for authorizations

The actual data used in the generated authorizations is found in the 0TCA_DS01 and 0TCA_DS02 template DSOs.

> **Warning**
>
> The program deletes all generated analysis authorizations as a first step and then regenerates them. Therefore, schedule the generation for a time when users aren't logged on to the system to avoid users experiencing authorization errors.

> **Tip**
>
> You can create virtual analysis authorizations using the RSEC_VIRTUAL_AUTH_BADI BADI. These virtual analysis authorizations aren't created and checked until runtime, which means that not only can authorizations be created flexibly, but they can even be read from other systems at runtime. For more information, see the BADI documentation in the SAP BW/4HANA system.

11.5 Roles

SAP BW/4HANA uses SAP NetWeaver role-based authorizations. All users are defined with one or more roles assigned.

It's possible to combine roles into *composite roles*—a combination of one or more roles—for easier maintenance of users and roles. However, you should define a role-based security model with as few composite roles as possible to minimize support costs and make it easier for users to request access. You can create both basic and composite roles via Transaction PFCG, which is used for role maintenance, as shown in Figure 11.5.

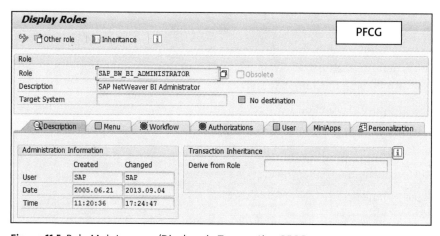

Figure 11.5 Role Maintenance/Display via Transaction PFCG

Analysis authorizations are assigned to roles using authorization object S_RS_AUTH with the assigned value of the defined analysis authorization.

> **Note**
>
> The combined authorizations for the roles assigned to a user are evaluated when authorization checks are executed.

In this section, we'll cover the different role types in SAP BW/4HANA for administrators and end users. We'll conclude with a discussion of the most useful role templates provided by SAP.

11.5.1 Administrator Roles

Administrator roles are required to support the SAP BW/4HANA system. These roles are normally granted to members of the support organization and vary by system in the landscape.

Table 11.5 shows the roles that are regarded as best practices in an SAP BW/4HANA system landscape.

Development System	Test System	Production System
Developer	Production developer	Production developer
Development support	Production support	Production support
Change and transport manager	Change and transport manager	Change and transport manager
SAP Basis support—development	SAP Basis support—production	SAP Basis support—production

Table 11.5 Recommended Administrator Roles by System in Landscape

SAP does provide some template roles that can be used as a starting point for defining support roles, but these roles have extensive access to SAP Basis administration tasks. Therefore, you should modify them to reduce the risk of giving too many people access to change system settings.

11.5.2 End User Roles

There are three general types of end users in an SAP BW system, as follows:

1. **Authors and analysts**
   Authors and analysts require advanced analysis functionality and the ability to perform special data analysis. To accomplish their tasks, they need useful, manageable reporting and analysis tools.

2. **Executives and knowledge workers**
   Executives and knowledge workers require personalized, context-related information provided in an intuitive UI. They generally work with predefined navigation paths but sometimes need to perform deeper data analysis.

3. **Information consumers**

   Information consumers require specific information (snapshots of specific data sets) to be able to perform their operative tasks.

End users' roles should be defined to give access to reporting functionality and reports. We recommend that you limit the number of roles created in the system as much as possible to make maintenance easier and avoid confusion when end users request access to reports.

You should decide on end user roles based on three dimensions, as follows:

1. Business process

2. Business function

3. Business role

Each of these could lead to a different number of technical roles to be defined in the system. Try to choose the method that best suits your organizational setup. An additional dimension for end user roles is access to business information. This access is controlled via analysis authorizations.

We recommend that you assign analysis authorizations via roles if there are fewer than one hundred roles to be maintained. If there are more than one hundred roles, you should maintain access via user assignment in Transaction RSECADMIN by generating the analysis authorizations, as described in Section 11.4.3.

In addition to the end user roles that allow for executing the reports, you can also have a role for super users that allows such users to create ad hoc queries and reports directly in production. This role should allow users to create the objects with a specific name prefix and be limited to that exact prefix. It shouldn't provide access to create global, calculated, and restricted key figures and structures.

11.5.3   Role Templates

SAP delivers a set of standard role templates. The templates for SAP BW/4HANA user roles start with S_RS_R (except for the roles for SAP Business Planning and Consolidations (SAP BPC), which start with S_RS_PL). The templates for SAP BW/4HANA workspace user roles start with S_RS_T.

Use the template roles when creating new roles to quickly add all the authorizations from the template into the profile for the new role.

Table 11.6 describes the most useful role templates and the tasks they facilitate.

Technical Name of Template	Description	Tasks
S_RS_RDEAD	SAP BW/4HANA role: SAP BW administrator (development system)	■ Maintaining the source system and uploading metadata ■ Executing queries for statistics InfoCubes ■ Maintaining aggregates ■ Maintaining analysis authorizations ■ Scheduling broadcast settings ■ Maintaining currency and quantity conversion types, as well as key date derivation types
S_RS_ROPAD	SAP BW/4HANA role: SAP BW administrator (productive system)	■ Maintaining the connection to the source system and executing queries for statistics InfoCubes
S_RS_RDEMO	SAP BW/4HANA role: Modeler (development system)	■ Defining InfoObjects, InfoProviders, transformation rules, DTPs, and process chains ■ Scheduling broadcast settings ■ Maintaining currency and quantity conversion types, as well as key date derivation types
S_RS_ROPOP	SAP BW/4HANA role: Operator (productive system)	■ Uploading data from the source system ■ Executing DTPs ■ Monitoring processes
S_RS_RREDE	SAP BW/4HANA role: Reporting developer (development system)	■ Designing queries, reports, and web applications ■ Maintaining analysis authorizations and their assignments to roles ■ Scheduling broadcast settings ■ Maintaining currency and quantity conversion types, as well as key date derivation types
S_RS_RREPU	SAP BW/4HANA role: Reporting user	■ Executing queries in SAP BEx analyzer or on the web

Table 11.6 Role Templates Delivered in SAP BW/4HANA

Technical Name of Template	Description	Tasks
S_RS_PL_PLANMOD_D	SAP BW/4HANA role: Planning modeler (development system)	<ul><li>Defining aggregation levels</li><li>Defining data slices and characteristic relationships</li><li>Defining planning functions, planning sequences, and planning function types</li><li>Defining queries and web applications</li></ul>
S_RS_PL_ADMIN	SAP BW/4HANA role: Planning administrator	<ul><li>Defining data slices</li><li>Executing planning functions and planning sequences</li></ul>
S_RS_PL_PLANNER	SAP BW/4HANA role: Planner	<ul><li>Displaying plan data in queries and web applications</li><li>Manually entering data in queries that are ready for input</li><li>Executing planning functions and planning sequences</li></ul>
S_RS_TWSPA	SAP BW/4HANA workspace administrator	<ul><li>Creating SAP BW/4HANA workspaces, defining their properties, making central data available in them, and managing them</li></ul>
S_RS_TWSPD	SAP BW/4HANA workspace designer	<ul><li>Loading personal data into a workspace and then creating CompositeProviders</li></ul>
S_RS_TWSPQ	SAP BW/4HANA workspace query user	<ul><li>Executing queries on CompositeProviders</li></ul>

Table 11.6 Role Templates Delivered in SAP BW/4HANA (Cont.)

A full list of role templates can be accessed in Transaction PFCG via the menu option **Utilities • Templates**, as shown in Figure 11.6. It's also possible to define new templates from this same screen.

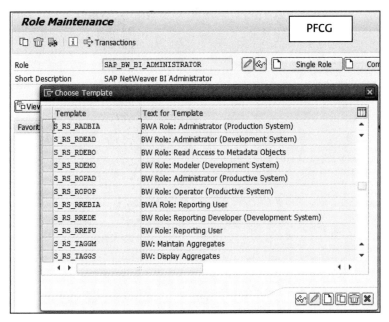

Figure 11.6 Role Templates in the System

Using template roles provides a quick start for defining the roles required in the SAP BW/4HANA system. Of course, you can expect some modification to authorizations from the standard templates when defining the roles that will be assigned to the users in the system via user administration.

11.6   User Administration

User administration includes tasks such as defining users and assigning analysis authorizations to users. We'll cover these tasks ahead, and then we'll conclude the section with a brief discussion of some additional tools that can help with user administration.

11.6.1   Defining Users

Users are defined and maintained in AS ABAP in Transaction SU01 (see Figure 11.7). This transaction should be assigned to security administrators; other administrators and developers should have access to the display-only transaction, Transaction SU01D.

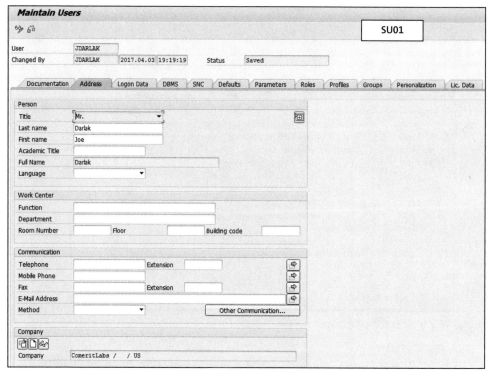

Figure 11.7 Transaction SU01 User Maintenance Screen

Transaction SU01 provides access to the following main tasks:

- Create users
- Maintain users
- Display users
- Delete users
- Copy users
- Lock and unlock users
- Change passwords for users

> **Tip**
>
> Users are maintained with basic information, such as name and address. We recommend that you always maintain email addresses, which are used for information broadcasting functionality.

Logon information maintained includes the user group, which can be used to limit maintenance access to specific users.

When roles are assigned in the **Role** tab, corresponding profiles are automatically added to the **Profile** tab.

> **Note**
>
> Users in AS Java can be read from the AS ABAP user store. This is the recommended approach for SAP BW/4HANA because the users must be present in AS ABAP to enable query executions.

11.6.2   Assigning Analysis Authorizations to Users

You can assign analysis authorizations to users via roles or directly in Transaction RSECADMIN. Recall from Section 11.4 that you should choose a method based on the number of roles that the authorization requires and the company's general authorization strategy. Most companies prefer using role-based assignment because it's aligned with the rest of the SAP systems in the landscape. Let's explore both methods.

Assigning Analysis Authorizations to Roles

Analysis authorizations are assigned to roles using the authorization object S_RS_ AUTH. You can see the analysis authorization OBI_ALL assigned to a role in Figure 11.8.

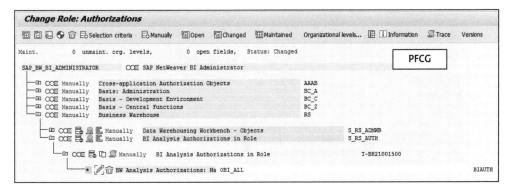

Figure 11.8 Analysis Authorization Assigned to Role

Be sure to put a clear naming convention in place for analysis authorizations to enable maintenance via ranges or patterns. Once an analysis authorization is assigned to a role, it's applied to all users that the role is assigned to in user administration.

Assigning Analysis Authorizations to Users in Transaction RSECADMIN

Assigning analysis authorizations directly to users is an SAP BW/4HANA-specific functionality; it doesn't provide the same reporting capabilities as using roles. You can make assignments in Transaction RSECADMIN in the **User** tab, as shown in Figure 11.9, either individually ❶ or via **Mass Assignment** ❷.

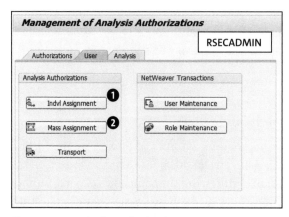

Figure 11.9 Analysis Authorization User Assignment Options

When selecting individual maintenance options, you can select a specific user and maintain the assigned analysis authorizations. It's also possible to see which analysis authorizations are assigned via the **Role-based** subtab under the **Roles** tab (see Figure 11.10).

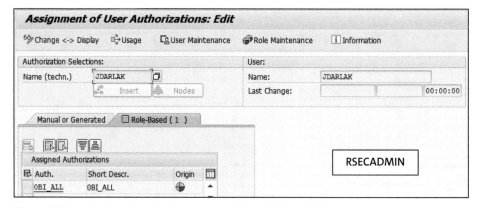

Figure 11.10 Analysis Authorization Assigned via Individual Maintenance

The mass maintenance option shown in Figure 11.11 provides two radio button op-tions to assign analysis authorizations to users: **Authorizations** and **User**.

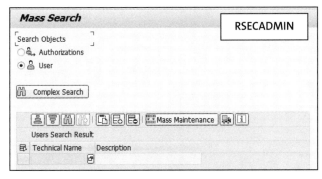

Figure 11.11 Mass Maintenance Search Options

The **Complex Search** button provides various options to select users for mass mainte-nance. Once the users or authorizations have been selected, it's possible to maintain them all in one action and add additional users with the same authorization. You can also change the authorized values, which then update the analysis authorization when it's saved and activated.

11.6.3   User Administration Tools

Some tools exist to assist you with user administration. Next, we'll briefly introduce the User Information System and SAP Access Control.

User Information System

The User Information System in Transaction SUIM, shown in Figure 11.12, provides detailed analysis capabilities for all aspects of the AS ABAP user roles and authoriza-tions.

In addition to the standard User Information System, additional reporting capability provided in Transaction RSECADMIN displays users assigned to specific analysis authorizations. This report is possible via the **Mass Assignment** button in the **User** tab.

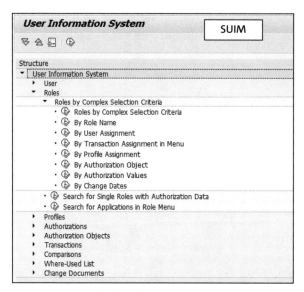

Figure 11.12 Detailed Analysis of Users and Authorizations via Transaction SUIM

SAP Access Control

SAP Access Control is a recommended tool to manage access and maintenance for many SAP and non-SAP systems in a landscape. SAP Access Control provides an enterprise-wide role and user management platform that streamlines user audits and analysis of segregation of duties.

In addition, SAP Governance, Risk, and Compliance (SAP GRC) provides capabilities to manage super administrator activities via privileged user IDs and subsequently report on usage and on tasks performed.

User administration is a never-ending task in an SAP BW/4HANA system, and it causes the most incidents for end users, such as when they're missing access or have other types of authorization problems. We'll cover how to troubleshoot authorizations problems in the next section.

11.7   Troubleshooting Authorization Problems

The most common authorization problems identified when administrating an SAP BW/4HANA system relate to missing authorizations.

There are three types of problems:

1. Missing authorizations for standard authorization objects

2. Missing authorizations for analysis authorizations

3. Missing Java portal authorizations

The last of these, SAP NetWeaver AS Java authorization errors, aren't common in SAP BW/4HANA, so we won't discuss them at length in this section. If they do occur, the result is normally a clear message stating which object the user doesn't have access to. It's then possible to assign access to the object via the user management engine (UME).

Let's look more closely at the other two types of errors.

11.7.1   Standard Authorization Errors

When executing tasks via SAP GUI, you can always get details for authorization errors by executing Transaction SU53, which is shown in Figure 11.13. Several items are displayed here, including the check authorization and the roles and authorizations assigned to the user. This makes it easy to analyze whether the error is caused by a missing role or a missing authorization in an existing role.

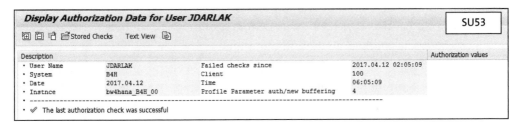

Figure 11.13 Transaction SU53, Last Authorization Check Success or Failure

You can also use Transaction ST01 (Standard Authorization Trace) to analyze errors related to standard authorization objects, as shown in Figure 11.14. This is especially helpful when errors occur in reporting and their sources aren't obvious based on the error messages.

Make sure that you set the type of trace ❶ and a general filter ❷ before activating the trace to avoid tracing for all users active in the system. To do this, click the **General Filters** button and then set the user that should be traced, as shown in Figure 11.14.

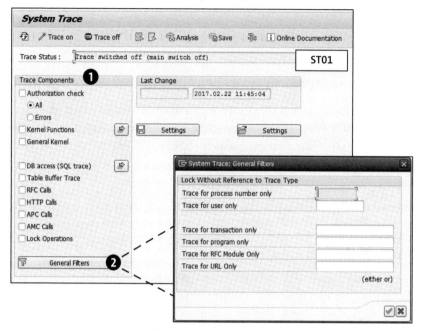

Figure 11.14 Transaction ST01, Standard Authorization Trace

Once this is set, click the **Trace On** button and execute the tasks that caused the authorization errors. Once the tasks are completed, remember to switch off the trace; otherwise, it continues to trace the user activity.

Once the trace has been recorded, it can be analyzed via the **Analysis** button. To find the trace, limit the selection by the user that was traced and the date and time that the trace was recorded.

The trace report should be read as follows:

- RC = 0: Authorization check successful
- RC <> 0: Authorization check failed

Based on the result from either Transaction SU53 or Transaction ST01, you can assign the missing authorizations or roles related to the authorization error message.

11.7.2   Analysis Authorization Errors

SAP BW/4HANA analysis authorization errors can be analyzed using the analysis log in Transaction RSECADMIN. The log provides a detailed breakdown of the analysis authorizations checked during the query execution, including the checked values.

As shown in Figure 11.15, there are two ways to analyze authorization errors: either by executing a query as another user or by configuring the log recording for a user and then asking the user to execute the query while recording is on.

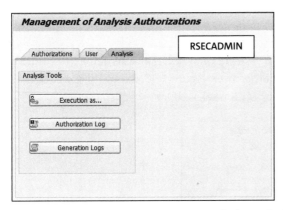

Figure 11.15 Transaction RSECADMIN, Analysis Log Options

Both options result in a detailed authorization log, which can become quite hard to read if you perform too many authorizations or navigations. We recommend that you use bookmarks in either Transaction RSRT or the SAP BEx tools to create the shortest possible log.

The authorization log has three sections:

1. Header: Contains basic information for the execution
2. InfoProvider check: Contains the access check for the InfoProvider
3. Authorization checks: Contains the main checks for the analysis authorizations

These are separated into subnumbers based on the checks required by the structures in the query definition. The number of subnumbers depends on the complexity of the query executed; hundreds of subnumbers are possible.

> **Note**
>
> You can see that the log may display an unsuccessful partial check in the first iteration steps but that the check as a whole is successful. The important result is the one delivered after the last step. However, if a subselection isn't authorized, the system displays the following lines:

- **All Authorizations Tested**
- **Message EYE 007: You Do Not Have Sufficient Authorization** (in yellow)
- **No Sufficient Authorization for This Sub Selection (SUBNR)** (in yellow)

Let's consider the two options for analyzing authorization errors.

Execute as Other User

Executing as a different user allows a security or system administrator to execute a query with the authorizations of another user. Figure 11.16 shows the execution as another user, **JESPER**, and the **With Log** option selected.

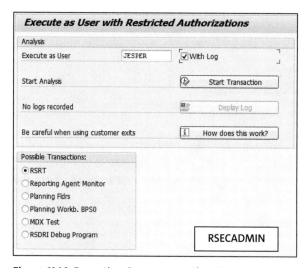

Figure 11.16 Executing Query as Another User

If you execute as another user with a log recording activated, you can analyze it for errors.

The default way to execute the query is via Transaction RSRT (Query Monitor), which allows for selecting a query or a bookmark, as shown in Figure 11.17.

Tip

Use the function module RSEC_GET_USERNAME to avoid problems with authorization user exit variables when executing them as another user from Transaction RSEC-ADMIN.

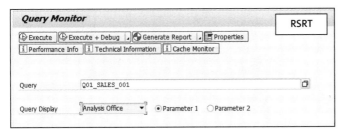

Figure 11.17 Executing Query in Transaction RSRT

The functionality for executing the authorization check as another user can be secured via authorization object S_RSEC by setting the value for authorization field **ACTVT** equal to 16 and the value for authorization field **RSECADMOBJ** equal to RSUDO. We recommend that you assign this functionality only to security administrators.

Configure Authorization Log

The other primary option for troubleshooting authorization errors is to activate an authorization log recording for a specific user to enable troubleshooting of authorization errors. To do, enter Transaction RSECADMIN and go to **Analysis tab • Authorization log**.

Once the user has been activated, recording logs are generated for all actions performed by that user, as shown in Figure 11.18. Therefore, remember to deactivate the recording immediately once the required log has been generated.

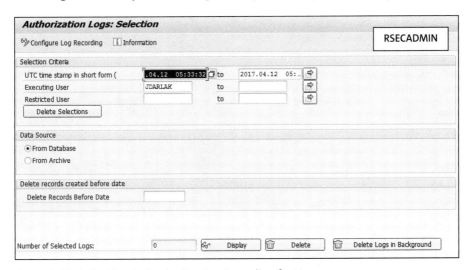

Figure 11.18 Activating Authorization Log Recording for User

SAP BW/4HANA provides advanced functionality to define and manage users and access to functionality and business information. The security definition must be a part of the initial system design to ensure that it's incorporated into the solution, thus avoiding costly rework down the road.

11.8 Summary

In this chapter, we covered the most important security concepts for an SAP BW/4HANA system. We provided an overview of the authentication methods supported by SAP BW/4HANA and then covered the authorization concept in SAP BW/4HANA in detail. We reviewed standard authorization objects, analysis authorizations, and roles. We covered how to perform user provisioning, role assignments, and administration before wrapping up with a brief discussion of troubleshooting authorization problems. In the next chapter, we'll look ahead to the roadmap for SAP BW/4HANA.

Chapter 12

The Future of SAP BW/4HANA

SAP BW/4HANA is a new data warehouse solution offered by SAP with its own dedicated product vision and development path. In this chapter, we'll explore the current state of the SAP BW/4HANA roadmap, its major design principals, and expected innovations.

This chapter will dive into the roadmap and related documentation released so far by SAP for the SAP BW/4HANA application. We'll focus on describing simplifications and enhancements currently offered by SAP BW/4HANA and what to expect in the near future. The information presented in this chapter may be used to steer current development efforts and avoid potential obsolescence and rework down the road.

We'll begin with a look at the roadmap from SAP BW to SAP BW/4HANA before moving on to the four design principles driving development for SAP BW/4HANA: openness, simplicity, modern interfaces, and high performance. We'll use these principles to guide us through the current and expected innovations in SAP BW/4HANA.

12.1   SAP BW to SAP BW/4HANA Roadmap

A brief recap of how SAP arrived at SAP BW/4HANA may be of interest before we look forward at things to come. The path towards SAP BW/4HANA started when SAP BW was first enhanced to run on the SAP HANA database, which happened in SAP BW 7.3 SP 5. The primary goal at the time was to allow SAP BW to run on SAP HANA and therefore enjoy the increased performance offered by the in-memory, columnar database. The term *powered by SAP HANA*, a reference to the increased performance gained, was coined at that time.

For SAP BW versions 7.4 and 7.5, SAP dedicated time and effort to releasing new SAP HANA-flavored modeling objects and system features. SAP also focused on migrating several SAP BW processes from the application layer to the SAP HANA database to increase performance even further. This effort to push to the database, illustrated in

Figure 12.1 and found in many SAP documents, was the new mantra and well under way.

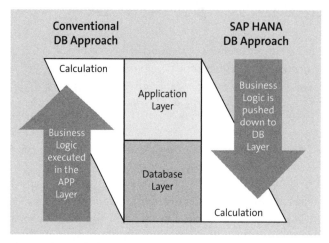

Figure 12.1 Push down Logic to Database

With SAP BW 7.5 SP 4 came an add-on named *SAP BW 7.5 edition for SAP HANA*. This add-on represented an important milestone: SAP officially performed a code split for the SAP BW application. From then on, there were two independent product paths, one for SAP BW and one for SAP BW/4HANA.

The SAP BW 7.5 edition for SAP HANA add-on was the fork in the road. This add-on offers many transfer tools to allow the SAP BW application to become SAP BW/4HANA ready. In other words, the transfer tools are there to assist in converting classic objects into their corresponding SAP BW/4HANA objects. This means converting InfoCubes and DSOs into Advanced DSOs, and MultiProviders into CompositeProviders, just to name a few.

The journey to SAP BW/4HANA ends when the SAP BW system is switched to SAP BW/4HANA with the assistance of Software Update Manager. Of course, this is only applicable for existing SAP customers with years of development requiring conversion, a scenario known as a *brownfield implementation*. In the case of a new or *greenfield implementation*, no conversion is required. A fresh installation of SAP BW/4HANA would precede the development of new data flows based solely on SAP HANA modeling objects. Figure 12.2 illustrates the SAP BW and SAP BW/4HANA product paths.

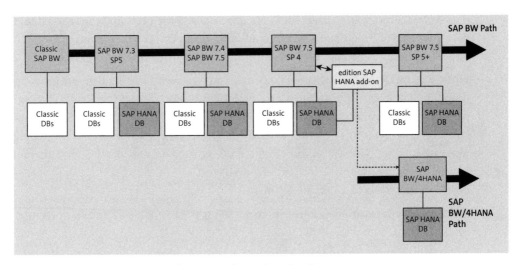

Figure 12.2 SAP BW and SAP BW/4HANA Independent Roadmaps

With two parallel roadmaps, will SAP dedicate the same level of effort and time to both? According to SAP: "SAP BW 7.5 Powered by and Edition for SAP HANA will still be supported release options, however, SAP BW/4HANA will receive the majority of the new innovation being developed moving forward."

Additional information about the future of SAP BW can be found in the PAM, which shows the following maintenance end dates:

- SAP BW 7.0: Maintenance ends on December 31, 2017
- SAP BW 7.3: Maintenance ends on December 31, 2020
- SAP BW 7.4: Maintenance ends on December 31, 2020
- SAP BW 7.5: Maintenance ends on December 31, 2022

We can conclude that SAP BW will remain, at least for now. However, don't expect cool new features for it! SAP's development efforts will be dedicated to the new product path represented by SAP BW/4HANA. Following SAP's lead, we'll also now focus on the SAP BW/4HANA road ahead and things to come.

12.2 Openness

In the context of a data warehousing application, openness refers to flexibility with respect to inbound and outbound flows of data. From an inbound perspective, openness is directly associated with data provisioning methods and the span of connectivity with different sources. From an outbound perspective, openness refers to how easily data can be made available for consumption by different frontend tools.

Why is openness crucial these days? Let's start answering this question from an inbound perspective. Data sources are no longer restricted to a specified format or originate from systems on-premise. Relevant data can reside in the cloud or in data lakes, be of structured or unstructured natures, and be provisioned via a streamed, replicated, or extracted method. This variety of data types, formats, and flavors requires several different data access methods that only a truly open application can cater for. This is the case for SAP BW/4HANA.

SAP BW/4HANA introduces four source system types to enable a flexible, open integration with data sources:

- Operational Data Provisioning (ODP)
- SAP HANA source system
- Big data source system
- File source system

12.2.1   Operational Data Provisioning Source System Type

The ODP source system type is the data provisioning method used by SAP BW/4HANA for the SAP backend system. This means that ODP-enabled SAP DataSources can be consumed easily by SAP BW/4HANA. SAP is increasing the number of ODP-enabled DataSources as a replacement for the classic delta queue-based DataSources. The current list of ODP-enabled SAP DataSources can be found in SAP Note 2232584 (Release of SAP Extractors for Operational Data Provisioning).

12.2.2   SAP HANA Source System Type

The SAP HANA source system type is the data provisioning method that leverages SAP HANA enterprise information management (EIM)—and specifically the SAP HANA smart data integration (SDI) component. SDI includes several different source system adapters, resulting in a flexible and powerful data integration mechanism.

SAP HANA, Hive, third-party RDBMSs, SOAP, Facebook, and Twitter are just a few of the adapter types available via SDI. The SAP HANA source system type also enables optimized loading data processes and caters for scenarios from typical data extraction to direct access for data virtualization and real-time replication.

12.2.3 Big Data Source System Type

The big data source system type is a new option offered with SAP BW/4HANA that enables integration with Hadoop data lakes via the Spark SQL adapter. By making use of Open ODS views and the Spark SQL adapter, it's possible to access and stage data lake contents with SAP BW/4HANA. Further innovation is already planned for this source system type. This includes SAP HANA analysis process, based on Hadoop, as well as automation of data flows between data lakes and SAP BW/4HANA.

12.2.4 File Source System Type

The file source system type enables the traditional data provisioning method of uploading content via file-based DataSources.

The four source system types are collectively referred to by SAP as *simplified data integration* offered by SAP BW/4HANA. In comparison with previous versions of SAP BW applications, SAP BW/4HANA offers more data integration options via fewer source system types (hence *simplified*). Figure 12.3 illustrates this simplification.

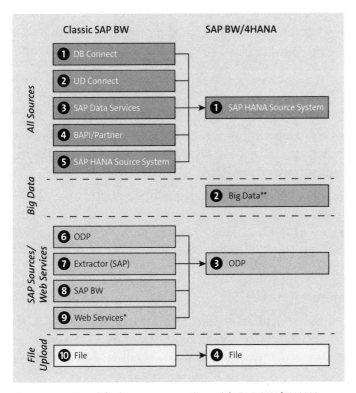

Figure 12.3 Simplified Data Integration with SAP BW/4HANA

Now that we've discussed openness from a data inbound perspective, let's shift to a data outbound perspective. The level of outbound openness of an application is directly related to how easily it can provide data for consumption by different frontend tools. This is especially relevant now that options for analytical and visualization tools are numerous and being created at an impressive pace, including open-source options. An application restricted to proprietary frontend tools can be considered an obstacle more than an enabler.

SAP BW/4HANA allows for automatic generation of SAP HANA views based on queries or any of its modeling objects (CompositeProviders, Advanced DSOs, or Open ODS views). This means that the data modeled in SAP BW/4HANA, including the calculation logic defined in queries, can be exposed to the SAP HANA database and consumed via SQL-based access. By doing so, SAP BW/4HANA enables flexible combinations of SAP BW models and SAP HANA native data sets. Further modeling activities can be performed with the deployment of logic applied via subsequent SAP HANA native models, known as SAP HANA views. The final models can be accessed easily via SQL-access-enabled frontend tools.

Looking at the road map for SAP BW/4HANA, openness will continue to be a driving principle. We expect to see tighter integration with Hadoop, an increased number of SDI sources, and enablement of further ODP DataSources for SAP backend systems.

12.3   Simplicity

In an SAP BW/4HANA context, *simplicity* refers to how processes and procedures can be performed with fewer steps, resulting in increased maintenance agility and development flexibility and reduced cost of ownership.

EDW processes simplified with SAP BW/4HANA are pertinent for data integration, modeling activities, data flow design, data lifecycle management, and business content. This simplification is even more noticeable when comparing how the same processes are performed in other EDW solutions, including previous versions of SAP BW.

12.3.1   Simplicity in Data Integration

Data integration and openness simplification was discussed in Section 12.2, and Figure 12.3 showed a reduction from 10 source types available in previous versions of SAP BW to four source types in SAP BW/4HANA, as well as an added data integration option (i.e., big data).

12.3.2 Simplicity in Modeling Activities

In terms of modeling activities, less is more. As discussed in Chapter 5, *modeling simplification* refers to enabling the same level of modeling activities with a reduced number of modeling objects. The SAP BW/4HANA modeling objects—CompositeProviders, Advanced DSOs, and Open ODS views—provide the same capabilities as the larger number of modeling objects in previous releases of SAP BW.

Table 12.1 shows seven modeling objects present in SAP BW releases and the corresponding four modeling objects that provide similar features in SAP BW/4HANA.

SAP BW Object	SAP BW/4HANA Object
InfoObjects	InfoObjects
DSOs	Advanced DSOs
InfoCubes	
Hybrid Providers	
PSAs	
InfoSets	Composite Providers
MultiProviders	
Virtual Cubes	Open ODS views

Table 12.1 SAP BW/4HANA Modeling Simplification

12.3.3 Simplicity in Data Flow Maintenance

Simplification regarding data flow maintenance is centered on providing functionality for different levels of data integration. For a data warehousing application, *functionality* refers to the reporting and analytics capabilities for a specific data set. *Integration* is how embedded in data models the data should be prior to being functionally available for reporting and analytics.

Prior releases of SAP BW required tight data integration before any reporting functionality was feasible. Inbound data fields needed to be mapped to existing InfoObjects and modeled into InfoProviders before being made available to queries. In other words, prior releases of SAP BW required data integration prior to functionality.

SAP BW/4HANA, on the other hand, allows for functionality with or without data integration. Data providers can be built using InfoObjects or fields. Queries can run against any layer of the data warehouse, from source-like data layers in the case of virtualization enabled via Open ODS views without association with InfoObjects, to tightly integrated, InfoObject-based data marts. This level of data flow flexibility and simplification provided by SAP BW/4HANA is especially important with respect to typical big data analytical demands. It adds agility to tasks such as prototyping or ad hoc reporting, without the burden of extensive development of SAP BW/4HANA-specific elements such as InfoObjects and mappings.

12.3.4   Simplicity in Data Lifecycle Management

Data lifecycle management is another area simplified with SAP BW/4HANA. Available features include, for example, partition-based data temperature management, which enables easy segregation of data content to be moved from hot to warm storage and from warm to cold storage.

With SAP applications powered by SAP HANA, such as SAP BW/4HANA, data is loaded into memory for rapid access first and then replicated to disk for durability. However, this process can be tweaked to better manage data per its relevance and promote a more effective allocation of SAP HANA memory resources. This is the basis for a multitemperature data strategy, discussed in detail in Chapter 9, under which data is classified as *hot*, *warm*, or *cold* based on factors such as frequency of data change or access speed requirements, as illustrated in Figure 12.4.

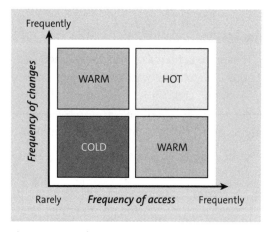

Figure 12.4 Multitemperature Data Strategy

Hot data is usually very volatile, is more recent in nature, and has high relevance for reporting. Such content is the ideal candidate to be kept in memory. Warm data is not as recent and is of a more static nature, but still carries some level of reporting relevance, especially with respect to trend analysis. Warm data may be kept close, but not necessarily in memory for fast access without compromising SAP HANA memory consumption. It stays in memory while required for reporting, then is dropped from memory and only kept in disk.

Cold data is of low relevance, such as static content and data of a historical nature. It's not frequently accessed but still needs to be stored due to regulations or for very specific reporting needs. Cold data is frequently stored within NLS solutions, thus freeing resources from the SAP HANA database but remaining reachable by queries.

SAP BW/4HANA simplifies the implementation of a robust data management strategy via features such as multitemperature data partitions and time-slice-based archiving.

The data stored in the SAP HANA database is considered hot by default, which means it will reside in memory and be replicated to disk for durability. SAP BW/4HANA allows data partitions at the Advanced DSO level to be classified as hot or warm data. Data residing in a partition classified as warm will be stored only in disk and brought to memory on demand as requested. As soon as its use is deemed complete, it will be dropped from memory. Memory resources can be dedicated to the hot, highly relevant data and for better management and to avoid constraints.

Another interesting feature available in SAP BW/4HANA relates to migrating data from SAP HANA to NLS (see Chapter 9 for more information). This option is applicable to scenarios in which cold data can't be archived offline or purged because it must remain accessible and reportable. By leveraging the openness/connectivity characteristics of SAP BW/4HANA, the integration of SAP HANA with Hadoop or SAP IQ can be implemented easily.

Data slices for NLS can be selected based on time and migrated to the NLS platform via the built-in data lifecycle management mechanism of SAP BW/4HANA, which includes data movements, checks, and validation prior to any data deletion in SAP HANA. The same mechanism also enables data to be reimported back from NLS into SAP HANA if required.

Future data lifecycle management developments planned for mid-2017 in SAP BW/4HANA focus on automation of its processes. This refers to the automation of data movement from hot to warm and warm to cold according to the configuration of Advanced DSO partitions and NLS time slices.

12.3.5   Simplicity in Business Content

SAP BW and SAP BW/4HANA business content is a set of preconfigured data models covering selected business operations and industry sectors. It includes elements ranging from basic InfoObjects to complete data flows comprised of transformations and InfoProviders.

A complete new business content package has been developed for SAP BW/4HANA following the new guidelines of LSA++ architecture and use of the new SAP BW/4HANA modeling objects. With this content, SAP has simplified the data flows delivered out of the box.

Per SAP documentation, as of April 2017, the areas in Table 12.2 are covered by SAP BW/4HANA business content.

Business Content Area	Features
Sales and Distribution	Leverage advanced business content objects for analytics in the areas of sales overview, conditions, and delivery service.
Materials Management	Leverage advanced business content objects for analytics in the areas of purchase overview, purchase accounting, invoice verification, contract management, service level, and inventory management.
Financial Management and Controlling	Leverage advanced business content objects for analytics in the areas of finance (accounts receivable, accounts payable, fixed asset accounting, contract accounting, and general ledger) and controlling (profit center accounting, cost center accounting, overhead cost orders, and overhead projects).
Master Data Governance	Leverage advanced business content objects for analytics in the area of master data governance.
Utilities	Leverage advanced business content objects for analytics in the areas of master data, sales statistics, and energy data management.

Table 12.2 SAP BW/4HANA Business Content

SAP is actively developing more business content for SAP BW/4HANA. Refer to the following SAP Notes for the latest updates:

- SAP Note 2395613 (SAP BW/4HANA Content—Additional Information on Delivered InfoObjects)

- SAP Note 2395579 (SAP BW/4HANA Content—Additional Information on Delivered Variables)

- SAP Note 2397520 (SAP BW/4HANA Content—Additional Information on Delivered Business Content)

- SAP Note 2400585 (Collective Note: SAP BW/4HANA Content [BW4CONT & BW4-CONTB])

The SAP BW/4HANA business content is delivered in two packages: the Basis package and the Content package. The Basis package contains InfoObjects and variables, and the Content package is comprised of data flows. The data flows from the Content package include transformations and InfoProviders built with the elements provided with the Basis package. This means that there's a dependency from the Content package on the installation of the Basis package, but not the other way around.

Clients can use business content in the following fashions:

- DataSources only: Source system DataSources are replicated into SAP BW/4HANA. InfoObjects and data flows are custom developed.

- DataSources plus Basis package: Source system DataSources are replicated into SAP BW/4HANA, making use of delivered InfoObjects for mapping. Data flows are custom developed.

- DataSources plus Basis package + Content package: Source system DataSources are replicated into SAP BW/4HANA, making use of delivered InfoObjects, transformations, and data flows.

- DataSources plus Basis package plus Content package as template: Source system DataSources are replicated into SAP BW/4HANA. Custom-developed data flows make use of delivered InfoObjects and use delivered transformations and data flows as reference.

12.4   User Interfaces

SAP BW/4HANA still relies on SAP GUI for some typical data warehouse administrative tasks, but the complete replacement of remaining SAP GUI screens with the new Eclipse-based UI is part of the SAP BW/4HANA roadmap. SAP is actively working to develop and deploy new Eclipse-based interfaces to eliminate the need for SAP GUI in SAP BW/4HANA.

This replacement is already underway with modeling activities, which can only be performed via the BW modeling perspective in SAP HANA Studio. Modeling capabilities were removed entirely from SAP GUI (Transaction RSA1, Administrator Workbench).

12.4.1   Data Flow Modeler

Another interesting modern interface being rolled out with SAP BW/4HANA is the data flow modeler. Those familiar with prior releases of SAP BW may initially consider it a replacement for the data flow visualization feature of Transaction RSA1 (see Figure 12.5).

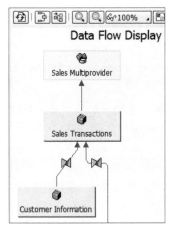

Figure 12.5 Data Flow Visualization Feature in Prior Releases of SAP BW via Transaction RSA1

However, that isn't really the case. The data flow modeler shouldn't be viewed merely as a visualization tool. The word modeler implies the ability to create or modify data flows, and that's exactly what the data flow modeler interface allows by acting as a modeling aid tool and by providing an interactive data flow blueprint. Figure 12.6 shows a data flow accessed via the data flow modeler interface of the BW modeling perspective in SAP HANA Studio.

It's possible to drag and drop existing SAP BW/4HANA providers to the data flow modeler interface and establish transformations among them or between the provider and data sources. The transformations are represented as lines within the data flow. Right-click any modeling object for configuration options such as transformation maintenance, DTP generation, removal of links, and others (see Figure 12.7).

Figure 12.6 Data Flow Modeler Interface in SAP HANA Studio

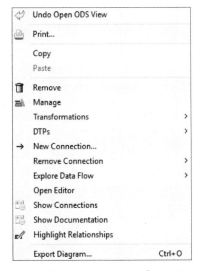

Figure 12.7 Data Flow Configuration Options Available via Context Menu

Transformation maintenance and DTP definition, however, still rely on the SAP GUI interface embedded in Eclipse. When requesting such options from the context menu, the corresponding SAP GUI interface is emulated. Figure 12.8 shows the transformation maintenance via the SAP GUI interface. By mid-2017, SAP plans to deploy Eclipse-based transformation modeling, replacing the current embedded SAP GUI approach.

Figure 12.8 SAP GUI in SAP HANA Studio for Certain Functionalities

As a blueprint modeling tool, the data flow modeler interface also has a palette section containing a list of SAP BW/4HANA object types that can be created in conjunction with the data flow design. These object types are required for designing a data flow when a new object is needed, but the object needed isn't yet available in SAP BW/4HANA.

Dragging an object type from the palette into the data flow initiates the creation of a new modeling object. Figure 12.9 shows the creation of a new Open ODS view being triggered after dragging the corresponding object type from the palette into the data flow blueprint.

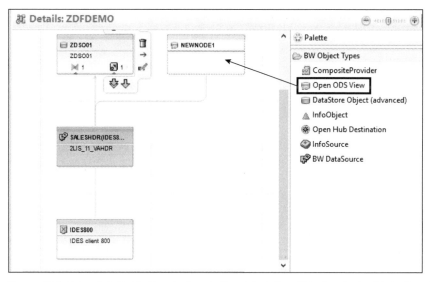

Figure 12.9 Using Palette Options to Create New Modeling Object as Part of Data Flow Design

At this stage, the new Open ODS view is simply a shell without any definition. By double-clicking the new object, you can access its configuration screens to define its fields and properties and complete its activation.

12.4.2 Process Chain Monitor

Modeling activities aren't the only focus of SAP's modern interface development. Another area being modernized in SAP BW/4HANA covers operations—more specifically, process chain monitoring. In prior versions of SAP BW, process chain monitoring relied on Transaction RSPCM (Process Chain Monitor).

The refreshed interface is SAPUI5-based and reuses settings of the backend process chain monitor, which means that process chain monitoring in SAP BW/4HANA is not just web-friendly, but also mobile-friendly in an app.

The currently released SAP BW/4HANA roadmap indicates a future development in system monitoring: the introduction of machine learning for prediction in data warehousing administration. However, a time frame for the release of this feature isn't yet available.

12.4.3 Business User Interface

SAP BW/4HANA doesn't support SAP BEx, the frontend of choice of prior releases of SAP BW. The frontend tools of choice for SAP BW/4HANA are SAP BusinessObjects Analysis for Microsoft Office, SAP Lumira Designer, and SAP BusinessObjects Cloud. SAP BW/4HANA also supports third-party tools based on SQL, MDX, and OData.

This doesn't mean that queries originally developed in SAP BEx will cease to work in SAP BW/4HANA. These queries will continue to operate, but any query maintenance will be performed in the BW modeling perspective of SAP HANA Studio.

12.5 High Performance

Since launching SAP HANA, SAP has been fully committed to pushing down application-related operations and calculations to the database. This push-down concept is at the core of SAP BW/4HANA. Main OLAP, planning, and application functions are already being executed at the database level.

The currently released SAP BW/4HANA roadmap indicates the following push-down deliverables in the near future:

- Q2 2017:
  - Data load management: Enabling of parallel load of master data
  - OLAP functions: Exception aggregation, including currency and unit conversion
- Q4 2017 and beyond:
  - OLAP functions: Top-N/Bottom-N analysis, used during sorting at query level
  - OLAP functions: Stock coverage, used on inventory prediction analysis
  - OLAP functions: Current member variables, making use of replacement path operators.

12.6   Future Innovations

The current state of planning, which may be changed by SAP at any time, suggests some exciting new features, ranging from further openness to tighter integration to cloud offerings and availability of machine learning and predictive capabilities.

The SAP BW/4HANA vision aligns with the needs of modern data warehouse solutions that are no longer restricted to the boundaries of a corporation or specific types of data. A modern data warehouse solution should be data-driven. It should enable the establishment of common semantics and standardized data models regardless of data nature, transfer method, or origin. The resulting solution should be a consolidated information hub, in which integrated data can be seamlessly harmonized under logical models and made available for decision-making processes. Note that we didn't mention required data persistency; the focus is on the logical integration of data sources instead of extraction and data storing per se. This new concept for a data warehouse solution is therefore referred to as the evolution to a *logical data warehouse model*.

The logical data warehouse concept is driving future innovations in SAP BW/4HANA. SAP's goal is to provide features to support major data trends encompassing the expansion of big data lakes, Internet of Things (IoT), cloud-based solutions, machine learning, and predictive analysis.

In terms of integration with big data scenarios, the current SAP BW/4HANA roadmap indicates tighter coupling of processes with big data lakes. Features to be made available in 2018 and beyond include automation of complex big data flows with SAP BW/4HANA and SAP BW/4HANA analysis process with Spark/Hadoop-based execution.

In terms of IoT, SAP BW/4HANA's new features will cater for enhancements of SAP HANA EIM, introducing delta and real-time streaming support for SAP HANA native tables as early as Q4 2017.

The product vision aims for innovations in 2019 and beyond, including machine learning-enabled features and integration with cloud offerings. In terms of machine-learning features, these should include self-monitoring capabilities such as system health prediction and artificial intelligence-based data warehouse administration. As for cloud offerings, the SAP BW/4HANA roadmap points to further seamless integration with SAP SuccessFactors, SAP Ariba, and SAP Hybris.

12.7   Future Migration Options

For current SAP BW clients considering a migration to SAP BW/4HANA, SAP is working to offer an automated conversion program, also known as a *transfer tool*, to make the transition as seamless as possible.

These programs are being made available with the SAP BW, edition for SAP HANA add-on, which requires SAP BW powered by SAP HANA 7.5 SP 04. Depending on the version of your SAP BW application, the first step on the road to SAP BW/4HANA may be to upgrade to SAP BW 7.5 SP 4 or higher.

The transfer tool's goal is to enable the generation of SAP HANA-optimized objects from classic SAP BW objects and to prepare your SAP BW system for SAP BW/4HANA. It takes into consideration dependent objects of specific data flows and convert them all into corresponding SAP HANA-optimized versions. This means that MultiProviders are converted to CompositeProviders, classic InfoCubes and DSOs are converted into Advanced DSOs, and so on.

The main components of the transfer tool are as follows:

- Transaction RSB4HTRF
- Program RS_B4HANA_CHECK_ENABLE
- Program RS_DELETE_D_VERSION_FOR_TLOGO
- Program RS_DELETE_TLOGO
- Program RSO_CONVERT_IPRO_TO_HCPR

These programs and the transaction code can be used as key words for searching within SAP Notes to obtain the latest updates and fixes related to the transfer tool.

The conversion effort can start after installing the SAP BW, edition for SAP HANA add-on in your upgraded SAP BW application. The first step is to run program RS_B4HANA_CHECK_ENABLE and set the compatibility mode status to **On**. After this step, classical SAP BW objects still can be used, but new classical SAP BW objects can no longer be created.

The next steps include the generation of SAP HANA-optimized objects based on the existing classical SAP BW objects. For this process, the transfer tool uses program RSO_CONVERT_IPRO_TO_HCPR. This step is available in two ways: simulation mode and save mode. The simulation mode is used for pre-assessment of potential errors during the conversion. The save mode is used to perform and complete the conversion itself.

The last step involves deleting the original classic objects. The overall objective is to end up with an SAP BW on SAP HANA application containing solely SAP HANA-optimized objects, which is then ready to be switched to SAP BW/4HANA.

12.8   Summary

SAP BW/4HANA is a new product entirely developed for the SAP HANA in-memory database. It preserves the core functionality of SAP BW while drastically reducing the number of data objects and amount of related maintenance. SAP BW/4HANA follows a roadmap independent from the anyDB or powered by SAP HANA versions of SAP BW. In fact, SAP has indicated that it will be focusing on developing new features for SAP BW/4HANA going forward, while moving other SAP BW applications into support mode. This chapter described the innovations currently available with the launch of SAP BW/4HANA and those planned next in its roadmap.

The Authors

Jesper Christensen, a senior partner at COMERIT, Inc., was part of the SAP BW regional implementation group at SAP that initially rolled out SAP BW. He is an internationally recognized subject matter expert in business intelligence, a contributing author to international BI journals, and a frequent speaker at SAP and BI-related conferences. His leadership at COMERIT helped Tetra Pak win the Gartner Award of BI Excellence in 2009. Jesper has helped many global companies migrate their SAP BW system to SAP HANA including optimizing the systems for migration to SAP BW/4HANA.

Joe Darlak, associate partner at COMERIT, Inc., has been successfully implementing SAP BW for clients since 1998, including multiple large-scale, full life-cycle global rollouts. He has significant experience increasing the capacity, reliability, and performance of SAP BusinessObjects BI systems, defining and implementing processes and controls to stabilize service and mitigate risk, and improving the competency and skill sets of implementation and client service teams. Recently, he has architected one of the largest SAP BW migrations to SAP HANA on record and has been instrumental in defining best practices for SAP HANA at Fortune Global 100 clients.

Riley Harrington is a senior SAP Basis associate with COMERIT, Inc. He is the system administrator for COMERIT's infrastructure, in support of remote development, testing, and training services. Riley is experienced in migrations, installations, upgrades and troubleshooting of SAP HANA, SAP BW, SAP ERP, SAP Solution Manager, SAP BusinessObjects, Tableau Server and VMware. He is a veteran of the U.S. Navy's submarine force and received a bachelor of science in management information systems from the University of North Carolina at Charlotte.

Li Kong is BI expert working for COMERIT. He is certified SAP BW consultant with more than 14 years of experience with global BI implementations. He has lead BI teams to implement SAP HANA, SAP BW, and SAP BusinessObjects BI solutions and has successfully migrated SAP BW to SAP BW on SAP HANA. He has worked with the architecture and implementation of SAP BusinessObjects BI, SAP HANA development, and big data

Marcos Poles is a senior SAP business intelligence and analytics solution architect and the author of a number of articles published in international BI journals. His expertise is in SAP BW, SAP BusinessObjects BI, and SAP HANA. Marcos started his SAP career in 1996, became SAP Academy instructor in 1998, and subsequently successfully managed and delivered multiple large-scale solutions for global corporations in Americas and Europe covering major business processes such as order-to-cash, supply chain management, financial accounting and controlling, customer activity repository, and demand signal management.

Christian Savelli is a senior information engineer and business intelligence solution architect with multiple SAP certifications and several published articles in international BI journals. He holds SAP certifications covering SAP HANA, SAP BW, and SAP ERP applications. Chris also has expertise in managing all aspects of the information creation process, and utilizing SAP's BI technologies to satisfy strategic, analytical, and reporting needs. During the last two decades, Chris Savelli has managed, led and delivered several, large-scale BI initiatives for companies across the globe, including the Americas, Europe, and Pacific regions.

Index

- Explore your SAP BW on SAP HANA implementation options

- Get step-by-step instructions for migration, including pre- and post-steps

- Learn how SAP HANA changes data modeling, reporting, and administration for an SAP BW system

Merz, Hügens, Blum

Implementing SAP BW on SAP HANA

If you're making the leap to SAP BW on SAP HANA, this book is your indispensable companion. Thanks to detailed pre-migration and post-migration steps, as well as a complete guide to the actual migration process, it's never been easier to HANA-ify your SAP BW system. Once your migration is complete, learn everything you need to know about data modeling, reporting, and administration. Are you ready for the next generation of SAP BW?

467 pages, pub. 04/2015
E-Book: $69.99 | **Print:** $79.95 | **Bundle:** $89.99

www.sap-press.com/3609

- Learn how SAP S/4HANA enables digital transformation

- Explore innovative financials and logistics functionality

- Understand the technical foundation underlying SAP S/4HANA advances

Baumgartl, Chaadaev, Choi, Dudgeon, Lahiri, Meijerink, Worsley-Tonks, Bardhan

SAP S/4HANA

An Introduction

Looking to make the jump to SAP S/4HANA? Learn what SAP S/4HANA offers, from the Universal Journal in SAP S/4HANA Finance to supply chain management in SAP S/4HANA Materials Management and Operations. Understand your deployment options—on-premise, cloud, and hybrid—and explore SAP Activate's implementation approach. Get an overview of how SAP HANA architecture supports digital transformation, and see what tools can help extend your SAP S/4HANA functionality!

449 pages, pub. 11/2016
E-Book: $59.99 | **Print:** $69.95 | **Bundle:** $79.99

www.sap-press.com/4153

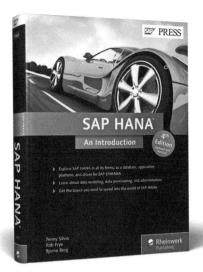

- Explore SAP HANA in all its forms: as database, as application platform, as driver for SAP S/4HANA

- Learn about data modeling, data provisioning, and administration

- Get the basics you need to speed into the world of SAP HANA

Silvia, Frye, Berg

SAP HANA

An Introduction

What does SAP HANA mean for you? This book is your introduction to all the essentials, from implementation options to the basics of data modeling and administration. With cutting-edge coverage of SAP HANA smart data access, SAP HANA Vora, and more, this bestseller has everything you need to take your first steps with SAP HANA.

549 pages, 4th edition, pub. 10/2016
E-Book: $59.99 | **Print:** $69.95 | **Bundle:** $79.99

www.sap-press.com/4160

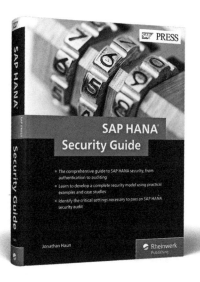

- The comprehensive guide to SAP HANA security, from authentication to auditing

- Learn to develop a complete security model using practical examples and case studies

- Identify the critical settings necessary to pass an SAP HANA security audit

Jonathan Haun

SAP HANA Security Guide

How do you protect and defend your SAP HANA database and application development platform? This comprehensive guide details your options, including privileges, encryption, and more. Learn how to secure database objects, provision and maintain user accounts, and develop and assign roles. Then take an in-depth look at authentication and certificate management before seeing how to enable auditing and security tracing. Up to date for SAP HANA 2.0!

541 pages, pub. 05/2017
E-Book: $69.99 | **Print:** $79.95 | **Bundle:** $89.99

www.sap-press.com/4227

Interested in reading more?

Please visit our website for all new book
and e-book releases from SAP PRESS.

www.sap-press.com